D0850163

WITHDRAWAL

German-American Folklore

AMERICAN
FOLKLORE
SERIES

German-American Folklore

Compiled and edited by
Mac E. Barrick

THIS VOLUME IS A PART OF
The American Folklore Series
W.K. McNeil, General Editor

August House / Little Rock
PUBLISHERS

Printed in the United States of America

10 9 8 7 6 5 4 3 2 1

LIBRARY OF CONGRESS CATALOGING-IN-PUBLICATION DATA

Barrick, Mac E.
German-American folklore.

(American folklore series)
Bibliography: p. 253
1. German Americans—Folklore.   I. Title.   II. Series.
GR111.G47B37   1987   398.2'08931073   87-14449
ISBN 0-87483-036-2
ISBN 0-87483-037-0 (pbk.)

First Edition, 1987

Cover design by Communication Graphics
Cover photograph courtesy Library of Congress
Musical notation by Jan Barger
Production artwork by Ira Hocut
Typography by Arrow Connection, Pollock Pines, CA
Design direction by Ted Parkhurst

This book is printed on archival-quality paper which meets the
guidelines for peformance and durability of the Committee on
Production Guidelines for Book Longevity of the Council on
Library Resources.

AUGUST HOUSE, INC.   PUBLISHERS   LITTLE ROCK

Contents

MAC E. BARRICK, a native of Pennsylvania, teaches in the Modern Languages Department at Shippensburg University at Shippensburg, Pennsylvania. He specializes in the fields of folklore and Spanish, and has published in numerous folklore publications such as *Keystone Folklore Quarterly, Mid-American Folklore,* and the *Journal of American Folklore.*

W. K. McNEIL is the folklorist at the Ozark Folk Center. He holds a Ph.D. in Folklore from Indiana University. The author of many studies in American folklore and editor of two anthologies, McNeil is general editor of the American Folklore Series.

Acknowledgments

A work of this type owes much to the help of many people. William T. Parsons generously made available the materials in the Alfred L. Shoemaker Folk Cultural File and in the Pennsylvania German Collection at Ursinus College. Archivists like Margaret S. Mims of the Wayne State University Folklore Archive, Pat McLaughlin of the Randall V. Mills Archive of Northwest Folklore and Barbara Truesdell of the Indiana University Folklore Archives willingly provided copies of material in their files. F. E. Abernethy, Robert D. Bethke, Simon J. Bronner, Roland Dickison, Gilbert J. Jordan, K. Edward Lay, and Howard W. Marshall graciously sent copies of items in their collections. Hans Meurer, Henry Warkentin, Harold Weigel, and other colleagues patiently listened to interminable questions about linguistic and cultural matters and not only answered them but often provided items from their own experience which are included below. And lastly, special thanks are due to the students whose curiosity and desire for good grades furnished the texts that make up this collection. To all of these and to any others inadvertently omitted, *Danke.*

M.E.B.

Introduction

A brief perusal of the titles of folklore publications will probably leave one with the impression that the most important German-American population in the United States is that in Pennsylvania. There are, of course, many people who would agree with such an assessment, and it is undeniable that the number of articles and books dealing with the oral tradition of non-Pennsylvania German-Americans is miniscule when compared to those dealing with Pennsylvania Dutch lore.[1] One of the reasons for the imbalance of publications is that there has been greater organization for this kind of work in Pennsylvania than elsewhere. At least two different organizations, the Pennsylvania German Society and the Pennsylvania Folklife Society, have been active in publishing folk cultural materials of the Pennsylvania Germans. From 1935 until 1966, when it merged with the Pennsylvania German Society, the Pennsylvania German Folklore Society also contributed several volumes on folk culture. No other state can boast of anything near this degree of support for the scholarly study of its German-American population. Even so, some of the earliest work in German-American folklore did not deal primarily with German traditions in the Keystone State; indeed, one of the first collectors ranged widely over many states in recording material.

Karl Knortz (1841–1918) was a native of Prussia who migrated to this country in 1863 and, during the next 55 years, wrote numerous books and articles on folklore, literature, education, and German-American relations. His 1905 volume *Zur Amerikanischer Volkskunde* (On American Folklore) may well be the first book devoted to the entire spectrum of American folklore, and his *Nachklänge Germanischen Glaubens und*

Brauche in Amerika: Ein Beitrag zur Volkskunde (Survivals of German Beliefs and Customs in America: A Contribution to Folklore) (1903) is one of the best early works on ethnic folklore. Knortz was an avid field worker who collected materials for his numerous books during the many years he spent as a secondary school teacher and minister in Michigan, Wisconsin, Ohio, Indiana, New York, and Pennsylvania.[2] Yet, despite the breadth of his interests and the significance of his writings, Knortz's work is virtually unknown to twentieth-century scholars. The reasons for this current obscurity are easy to ascertain. With one exception all of his books were written in German and most of them were published in Germany.[3] Although on the title page of his *Zur Amerikanischer Volkskunde* Knortz proudly listed himself as a member of the American Folklore Society, he seems to have always remained closer to his German colleagues than to American folklorists.[4] One of his goals was to make American literature better known and appreciated in his homeland, but he was also interested in fostering ethnic pride among his fellow German-Americans, as he indicates in the foreword to his *Die Deutschen Volkslieder und Märchen* (German Folksongs and Fairy Tales) (1889): "Nachstehende Vorträge sind aus dem Bestreben, bei den Deutsch-Amerikanern den Sinn für die Literatur ihres alten Vaterlands zu erwecken und zu kräftigen, hervorgegangen und werden hiermit auf den Wunsch zahlreicher Zuhörer der Oeffentlichkeit übergeben." (The following report is an attempt to awaken and strengthen in German-Americans an awareness of the literature of their homeland; by making this volume it is left up to the desire of the numerous readers of this publication to go further.)[5]

There is one other possibility, besides those already mentioned, that explains why Knortz's work is generally unknown today, namely the folklore theory to which he subscribed. His work was infused with what is now known as solar mythology, a name that refers to the idea that folk narratives originated in a pre-scientific era as poetic fantasies in which forces of nature were represented as living beings. In the course of time through a process called "disease of language" the original meanings of these tales were lost and they gradually became accepted as factual. Thus, when people saw or experienced different natural phenomena they were reminded of its corresponding story. When the sun was surrounded by clouds a story of a dress given by Helios to Medea was recalled, and when a drought dried up streams and destroyed crops it was a reminder of Tantalus, who roasted his own children. Some solar mythologists went to such extravagant lengths in pressing their arguments that they created a strong tide of opposition against their main thesis and it soon became passé. Indeed, Knortz was the last American folklorist adhering to this theory, although it had its advocates on a popular level after his demise. To say that solar mythology is now viewed with scorn is to state the situation mildly, for its proponents have been labeled builders of a school of thought "so fantastic that the modern reader who ventures to examine it begins to doubt his own sanity."[6] Too often when a person's theories are discarded so are many of his data, even though the value of the latter is not necessarily that of the former. Such seems to be the lot of Karl Knortz, for his extensive collections now sit idle and undisturbed on library shelves.

No other early students of German-American folklore were as prolific as Knortz and none ranged so broadly over as many genres and regions of German America. Typically, the traditional lore of this ethnic group was mentioned in passing in a work whose focus was on a number of cultural groups within a single state. This situation is the case, for example, in Mary Alicia Owen's "Social Customs and Usages in Missouri During the Last Century," where a discussion of folk traditions of several European immigrant groups includes a brief account of German-American Christmas customs.[7] Also representative is the work of William G. Bek, a historian whose interest in folklore was confined to the study of German survivals within the borders of Missouri. His essay "Survival of Old Marriage Customs Among the Low Germans of West Missouri" is also typical of turn-of-the-century studies in its emphasis on the unusual rather than the commonplace.[8] A belief that "Germanness" was rapidly dying out was a major impetus for many studies, of which the best recent example is Charles van Ravenswaay's *The Arts and Architecture of German Settlements in Missouri: A Survey of a Vanishing Culture* (1977). In recent decades the work of Owen, Bek, and similar scholars in Missouri has been improved upon by Adolf Schroeder, a retired German professor at the University of Missouri. A native of Germany, Schroeder first came to Missouri in the 1940s and, after spending several years in Ohio, returned to the Show Me State in 1964. From that time he has worked on several aspects of German-American folklore, contributing most in the areas of customs and place-naming.

The folklore of Texas Germans has, like that of their Missouri countrymen, been the subject of a number of publications, some of the most important coming from a single family. Gilbert J. Jordan, for over thirty years a professor of German at Southern Methodist University in Dallas, has produced two books of interest to folklorists. The first of these, *Yesterday in the Texas Hill Country* (1979), is a nostalgic account of Texas German life, while *German Texana: A Bilingual Collection of Traditional*

Materials (1980) is a traditional collection. His son, Terry G. Jordan, has also contributed several worthwhile publications on folk architecture from the standpoint of a cultural geographer. His book *German Seed in Texas Soil* (1966) is among the better studies of German-American folklife. The volume is a consideration of the extent to which German immigrants influenced agricultural life in the areas of Texas where they settled and the degree to which they, in turn, were affected by the culture and physical environment of Texas. Jordan traces the agricultural backgrounds of the Germans and of the Anglo-Americans among whom they settled and then proceeds to describe and analyze the degree of assimilation as seen by the changing farming practices of the immigrants and their descendants. Jordan's subsequent works, *Texas Log Buildings* (1978) and *Texas Graveyards* (1982), only tangentially deal with German-Americans, although the lengthiest chapter in the latter book is devoted to German graveyards in Texas—seen as "the most thoroughly Teutonic places left in the state."[9] The photo-filled volume is an interesting survey of infrequently studied materials.

While the folklore of Missouri and Texas Germans has been treated at some length, traditions of German-Americans in several other states have been less often considered. Nevertheless, there are some worthwhile works that deserve mention. One of these is Walter Robbins's 1969 Ph.D. dissertation at the University of North Carolina, "The German-American Custom of Wishing In and Shooting In the New Year," which was excerpted for an article in the volume *American Folklife* (1976). Not surprisingly, he found that the custom as practiced in North Carolina indicated strong parallels with the tradition as it existed in Europe. Other than this specific custom the only extensive scholarly attention given to North Carolina German folklore has concerned religious music, specifically that of the Moravians. An M.A. thesis at the University of Iowa in 1935 was the first lengthy work in this area, followed by an M.A. thesis in 1953 and a Ph.D. dissertation in 1958 by Donald M. McCorkle.[10]

John Fred Strang's unpublished 1929 M.A. thesis at the University of Nebraska, "Remainders of Superstitions Among German-Americans," is a rambling, dated work but, unfortunately, one of the few studies of Nebraska German lore. There are some scattered references to German-American traditions from that state in such works as Roger L. Welsch's *A Treasury of Nebraska Pioneer Folklore* (1967) and Everett Dick's *The Sod-House Frontier 1854–1890* (1954). The situation is even worse in Kansas, where the only printed examples of German-American folklore are occasional notes such as S. J. Sackett's "German Proverbs From Around Fort

Hays, Kansas," a list of 21 proverbs with translations.[11] The folklore of Wisconsin Germans is somewhat better documented, owing to a number of publications that have appeared in the years since World War II. Noteworthy among these is Walter M. Dundore's *The Saga of the Pennsylvania Germans in Wisconsin*, written in 1948 and published by the Pennsylvania German Folklore Society in 1954. Although largely devoted to politics, economics, and similar matters, the book does include a section on "Folklore and Social Custom."[12] Also valuable is Harry Swain and Cotton Mather's cultural-geographic study, *St. Croix Border Country* (1968), which contains much information on the folklife of Germans and other European ethnic groups in the state. Richard H. Zeitlin's *Germans in Wisconsin* (1977) is a useful folklife survey amply illustrated with excellent photographs. Worthy of mention also is the Spring 1982 edition of *Midwestern Journal of Language and Folklore*, a special issue devoted to Wisconsin folklore, containing one article that deals with German-American traditions. There is also an excellent study by Philip V. Bohlman titled "Music in the Culture of German-Americans in North-Central Wisconsin," which was an M.A. thesis in ethnomusicology submitted at the University of Illinois in 1979.

Some works dealing with German-American lore have not focused on state boundaries or even on folklore. Books such as John A. Hostetler's *Amish Society* (1963) and *Hutterite Society* (1974) are anthropological studies that contain historical data as well as considerable information about beliefs and customs. Hostetler was born and raised Amish, so he has the advantage of knowing the Amish as an insider, a fact that gives his publications greater insight and authority than would otherwise be possible. Nicely adding to Hostetler's work on the Amish is a Ph.D. dissertation by Rupert Kar Hohmann which treats "The Church Music of the Old Order Amish of the United States." Hohmann supplements the previous studies of Amish music by describing the history and providing stylistic analyses of hymns and other tunes taken from literary sources and records.[13]

There have also been several studies of log cabins that are relevant to the present discussion, the publications of Henry Glassie and Terry Jordan being especially pertinent. Specifically, these scholars have debated the extent of Germanic influences on the construction of log buildings. In a number of articles and an M.A. thesis, among other places, Glassie contended that barns, fences, and outbuildings in the southern United States were mostly of Pennsylvania German or German derivation.[14] Jordan at first leaned towards the same interpretation but has recently opted for a thesis that American log building styles are a synthesis of several European styles.[15]

When turning from other German-Americans to the Pennsylvania Dutch one goes from near poverty to sudden wealth, at least as far as publications of folklore are concerned. The late Richard Dorson said that German Pennsylvania is the most fully collected of all American regions.[16] Whenever oral traditions and German-Americans are mentioned, usually only those in Pennsylvania are considered. Thus, in a recent book on German culture in America the only article devoted to folklore is an essay on Pennsylvania German folksongs.[17] On a popular level aspects of the traditions of this cultural group have periodically found nationwide appeal. For example, folk speech, or what was presumed to be folk speech, served as the unifying element in Irving Gordon's "Mama From the Train," a nostalgic song about a Pennsylvania Dutch lady who spoke in "bits of broken English" that became one of the big popular hits of 1956.[18] In short, the folk culture of these German-Americans has achieved a level of awareness in American society that has been accorded few other traditional groups, and the reasons for this situation are manifold. Already noted is the strong organizational support for publicizing folk traditions, but the considerable ethnic pride that led to the establishment of such organizations is another. The existence of a clergy actively involved in collecting folklore is still another, and among many other possibilities, the desire to correct erroneous stereotypical views of the Pennsylvania Dutch through the use of folklore should not be dismissed. This was part of the impetus behind the publications of one of the first authors to collect Pennsylvania German folklore intentionally.

Walter James Hoffman (1846–1899) was a native of Weidasville, Pennsylvania, who entered the study of folklore after leaving behind a medical career. From 1879 to 1895 he was associated with the Bureau of American Ethnology in Washington, D.C., and produced sixteen publications dealing with American Indian folklore. During this same time he also published six articles on Pennsylvania German traditions, three in the *Journal of American Folklore,* two in the *Proceedings of the American Philosophical Society,* and one in *Science.*[19] His own German ancestry gave his consideration of these matters special significance, and he was aware of his unique position. He noted that some writers have occasionally presented "accounts of the customs and superstitions of this people; but as the writers were generally not of the people . . . the accuracy of such descriptions may reasonably be questioned."[20] He then proceeded to discourse at length about customs, beliefs, foodways, house types, folk medical practices, witchcraft, ghost legends, folktales, and proverbs, amply illustrating his comments with numerous examples of the various traditions. Hoffman took his material from several sources, including oral tradition, printed matter, his own memory, and even such seemingly unlikely places as legal reports; the resulting compilations in the *Journal of American Folklore* touch on most of the genres of folklore. Considering his first profession it is hardly surprising that folk medicine was one of his major interests, one that he discussed briefly in the second *Journal of American Folklore* article, a note in *Science,* and at greater length in an essay in the *Proceedings of the American Philosophical Society.* [21] Folk speech, discussed in the first *Journal of American Folklore* paper and in an extensive work in the *Proceedings of the American Philosophical Society,* was the second most appealing aspect of Pennsylvania German folklore for Hoffman. [22] All of this material was presented from a survivalistic, evolutionary viewpoint then in vogue: Most traditions were merely relics left over from an earlier time and flourished only in the more rustic areas among those occupying a low rung on the evolutionary ladder, those that had been denied the benefits of education and the opportunity to mingle in cultured society. [23]

Shortly after Hoffman's first articles appeared, the Pennsylvania German Society was founded. Established April 15, 1891, the organization issues a yearly book devoted to cultural and folk materials, a series that includes some of the most important published collections of Pennsylvania German folklore. For a number of years this was the only association regularly issuing volumes on the traditions of these people. Then in 1935 the Pennsylvania German Folklore Society was established, largely due to the efforts of John Baer Stoudt (1878–1944), one of the many Pennsylvania German clergymen active in collecting and publishing folklore. In 1936 this new organization began issuing an annual volume of miscellaneous papers. Despite its name and the fact that it was founded in an era when folklore meant just oral traditions, during its life this society was concerned with the totality of Pennsylvania German life. Some representative titles indicate the scope of the various issues. One of the early volumes was *Lewis Miller, Pennsylvania German Folk Artist* (1939), which was followed by *The Folk Culture of the Pennsylvania Germans: Its Value in Modern Education* (1940). Later volumes included *Pennsylvania German Historical and Art Collections in Various Museums* (1943) and *The Pennsylvania German Versammlinge* (Societies) (1944), and still other individual numbers deal with Pennsylvania German wills, tombstones, and *Fraktur,* a type of illuminated manuscript produced primarily in the eighteenth and nineteenth centuries.

In 1966 the two societies were merged under the name of the older

Pennsylvania German Society. The annual volumes still appear, recent issues dealing with such varied matter as photographs of rural life in Pennsylvania, folk art, and Pennsylvania German hand towels. Headquartered at Birdsboro, the society also publishes a journal, *Der Regeboge* (The Rainbow), which is edited by Fred Weiser. Although it includes much material of folkloric interest it is rarely consulted by folklorists outside Pennsylvania and most are probably not even aware of its existence.

A third organization devoted to publishing Pennsylvania German folk cultural materials was established in 1949 as the Pennsylvania Dutch Folklore Center but since 1956 has been known as the Pennsylvania Folklife Society. Since 1953 it has sponsored a highly successful week-long folk festival at Kutztown and in 1961 established a museum near Lancaster. Although the society has published some books it is known more for its journal, which started in 1949 as a weekly titled *The Pennsylvania Dutchman.* In 1954 it became a monthly and three years later, in 1957, acquired a new name, *Pennsylvania Folklife.* Since the mid-1960s it has been a quarterly, but throughout the 37 years of its existence its contents and format have remained fairly consistent; amply illustrated articles by amateurs and academics alike are found in its pages. A sampling of a couple of issues will illustrate the scope. The Spring 1975 number contained papers dealing with material culture, German script, games, economics among Old Order Mennonites, architecture, astronomy, and astrology. The Summer 1976 issue included essays on folk medicine, anthracite mining, Fraktur, and an immigrant's inventory. While designed to appeal mostly to a non-academic audience, *Pennsylvania Folklife* has certainly not neglected scholars. The contributions are generally well-written and include much useful information. Periodically, useful reference tools such as bibliographies appear.[24] To aid amateur collectors, longtime editor Don Yoder ran a series of folk-cultural questionnaires that dealt with such topics as home reading matter, broadsides and printed ephemera, the rural marketing system, and home remedies.[25]

In addition to the organizations already mentioned, a couple of others active in promoting Pennsylvania German folk culture should be noted. The Pennsylvania Dutch Folk Culture Center at Lenhartsville is noteworthy for its Russel Baver Memorial Library, a collection particularly rich in Pennsylvania German materials. The primary purpose of the Folk Heritage Institute at Glenville is to promote festivals and craft shows, one of the most visible forums for Pennsylvania German folk artists and craftsmen. Also worthy of mention are the various projects associated with Historic Schaefferstown. These include the Alexander Schaeffer Farm Museum, an annual folk festival, and the Thomas R. Brendle Museum, a major collection of furnishings, tools, and photographs dealing with the history of Pennsylvania German settlement in that area. Historic Schaefferstown also publishes the *Historic Schaefferstown Record,* edited by C. Richard Beam, who is one of the more active scholars of the Pennsylvania German language. He has recently received a grant to revise and expand *Lambert's Pennsylvania German Dictionary,* which was originally published in 1924. This volume is still regarded as the best reference work in the field. The same grant will also fund publication of two or three volumes of Pennsylvania Dutch folklore edited from material collected by Thomas R. Brendle.

Publications on Pennsylvania German folklore are so numerous that it would be impossible to list all the titles in the space allowed here. Therefore, in the following pages only a representative sampling will be presented. Because the authors of most of these publications adopt a genre approach it seems wise to break the following discussion down into genre categories.

For many Americans folklore means ballads and folktales, perhaps in part because these genres have been better publicized than most others. Even so, except for Anglo-Americans, collections of either genre have not been numerous. Among those collecting Pennsylvania German folklore, folktales—by which are meant traditional fictional prose narratives told solely for entertainment—have received relatively little attention. There have been numerous articles that have periodically appeared, but only one entire volume has been devoted to folktales. This book, Thomas R. Brendle and William S. Troxell's *Pennsylvania German Folktales* (1944) was the fiftieth volume of the Pennsylvania German Society. Although it is largely devoted to folktales, the total contents are more accurately described in the subtitle *Legends, Once-Upon-a-Time Stories, Maxims, and Sayings Spoken in the Dialect Popularly Known as Pennsylvania Dutch.* A collection rather than a theoretical work, the 238 pages provide a good sampling of the folk narratives found in German Pennsylvania. Nevertheless, it is hardly the final word on the subject, especially since it gives the most popular type of folktale—the joke— short shrift.

When it comes to other forms of folk narrative, specifically legends, Brendle and Troxell's book is also worthy of mention, especially since it is also one of the most extensive published collections of legendry from this region. A number of valuable essays on legends have appeared primarily in *Pennsylvania Folklife,* but to date no volume devoted solely to the topic has been issued. George Korson's *Pennsylvania Songs and Legends* (1949) is the nearest approximation to such a book but, as the title indicates, it deals with more than German-American material. It does contain an article by Henry W. Shoemaker on "Central Pennsylvania Legends" that includes some Pennsylvania Dutch items. Anyone using this article should be aware that Shoemaker's reputation has fallen in recent years; much of his work is now discredited. Often "inventive" rather than scholarly, his writings should be relied on cautiously. He should not be confused with the careful collector Alfred Shoemaker, one of the founders of the Pennsylvania Dutch Folklore Center and Pennsylvania Folklife Society, whose archives are now at Ursinus College. Even so, not all of Henry W. Shoemaker's work is valueless and some of the items in this article seem to ring true. Another important published source is Korson's *Black Rock: Mining Folklore of the Pennsylvania Dutch* (1960), although the book has been strongly criticized for a number of reasons.[26] Only one of the twenty chapters deals exclusively with legends but some of the others include relevant material. Equally valuable is an article by Don Yoder, "The Saint's Legend in the Pennsylvania German Folk-Culture," that was presented at a 1969 conference on American folk legend held at UCLA. This essay considers the saint in folk medicine and magic, transplanted European saints' legends, and native analogues, illustrating points with several examples drawn from oral tradition and printed sources. Yoder concludes that students of legendry must take into account the stratification system of the culture that produced and used legends. He rightly insists that historical, cross-genre, and cross-media studies are needed as well as investigations of shifts and trends in the concept of sainthood in the United States.[27]

Historical studies such as Yoder called for have rarely been attempted in American folklore in general and even less so with Pennsylvania German legends. Korson's atte..tion to Philip Ginder, presumed discoverer of anthracite coal in Pennsylvania, is one exception.[28] Mac E. Barrick has also contributed two valuable essays to the slim store of historical studies dealing with Pennsylvania German legendry. His essay on David Lewis (1788–1820), a thief and according to tradition a Robin Hood, is an exemplary work (though Lewis himself was Scotch-Irish, legends about him are preserved among the Pennsylvania Germans). Also recommended is his article on the barber's ghost, the latter paper providing not only a historical account of a legend but a useful discussion of the relationship between folktale and legend.[29] Despite these examples and a few others that could be cited, the number of historical studies of Pennsylvania German legendry is not appreciably larger than it was in 1971 when Yoder's paper was published.

When it comes to customs there is a considerable body of literature, which is probably not too surprising since the uniqueness of the culture is frequently emphasized and customs are seen as one of the chief distinctive features of Pennsylvania German culture. Many of these works are aimed for a popular audience or tourist trade rather than scholars. This is certainly true of such titles as Ammon M. Aurand's *America's Greatest Indoor Sport* (1930), a small booklet on bundling, and *Little Known Facts About the Amish and the Mennonites* (1938), and even such more pretentious volumes as Edwin V. Mitchell's *It's an Old Pennsylvania Custom* (1946). But there are a number of more systematic works, several of them issued by the Pennsylvania German Folklore Society. In one of their earliest publications C. E. Beckel provided a lengthy account of *Early Marriage Customs of the Moravian Congregation in Bethlehem, Pennsylvania* (1938) and a later number considered Christmas lore and customs from the perspective of five authors. Edwin Miller Fogel, primarily known for a proverb volume and a collection of beliefs, discussed Pennsylvania German customs in general, while R. E. Myers and G. E. Nitssche examined the Christmas *putz* or *crêche* (literally adornment or decoration), a type of Christmas tree decoration believed to have been introduced to the United States by Moravians around Bethlehem, Pennsylvania. The publication was completed with a selection of Christmas poetry and an account of early Christmases in Bethlehem, Pennsylvania. This issue is one of the few extensive works on American Christmas traditions done from a folklore viewpoint.

A number of articles on Pennsylvania German customs appear in the pages of *Pennsylvania Folklife* and *Der Regeboge* and in such volumes as Phebe Gibbons's *The Plain People*, a 1960s reprint of a work originally issued in 1872 under the title *"Pennsylvania Dutch" and Other Essays*. Generally, the items in *Pennsylvania Folklife* include comparative data but often those in *Der Regeboge* do not. Gibbons's essays were written with a popular audience in mind and in a day when comparative references in writings on the customs of non-aborigines was relatively uncommon. She, and most later writers, focused on "unusual" customs that they thought set the Pennsylvania Germans apart from other people, thereby ignoring those traditional practices that they hold in common with other cultural groups.

Beliefs and superstitions—the latter a more inclusive term including belief, behavior, experiences, and often sayings or rhymes—have been especially appealing to the Pennsylvania German collectors. Most significant of the early collections is Edwin Miller Fogel's *Beliefs and Super-stitions of the Pennsylvania Germans* (1915), which was originally sub-mitted as a Ph.D. dissertation in Germanics at the University of Pennsylvania.[30] More than 2,000 beliefs are presented in a systematic manner, the German dialect original given first, followed by an English translation and a list of counties in which the belief is known, as well as some comparative data and German texts. Although like most American collectors of the time Fogel concentrated primarily on the lore rather than the folk, his comparative approach is praiseworthy and more detailed than was usual at the time. His impressive field collecting, carried out in the fourteen "more distinctive Pennsylvania German counties," and his focus on rural rather than urban items was in the mainstream of work in American folklore.[31] Even today, over seven decades after its publication, Fogel's massive collection of beliefs and superstitions remains valuable even though flawed, its chief short-comings being the lack of comment on specific informants, collecting situations, or fieldwork techniques.

One aspect of Pennsylvania German tradition that has attracted con-siderable attention is the practice of decorating barns with symbols popularly called "hex signs." Actually these might be considered folk art because they are used by many persons in a purely decorative sense, but at one time traditional belief also played a strong part in their existence. Generally consisting of some kind of star within a circular disk, the signs have been discussed at varying degrees of length by almost everyone who has written in any detail on Pennsylvania Dutch folklore. Much of the literature has asked the same question Louis J. Heizmann pondered—"Are Barn Signs Hex Marks?"—some concluding they are and others reaching the opposite view.[32] On the other hand relatively little attention has been given to the origin of such symbols, a matter that did concern August C. Mahr, a German professor at Ohio State Univer-sity. In a 1945 essay titled "Origin and Significance of Pennsylvania Dutch Barn Symbols" he used barn typology and historical records of immigration in tracing the barn symbols to Switzerland, specifically the Canton of Bern.[33] Mahr's conclusion is logical but not necessarily acceptable to most others who have written about "hex signs."

Also falling in the area of belief and superstition is the practice of folk medicine, which has also received much attention from Pennsyl-vania German scholars. Significant articles have been published by Don Yoder and John Hostetler,[34] but the largest work on this subject is *Folk Medicine of the Pennsylvania Germans* (1935), co-authored by the prolific Thomas R. Brendle and Claude W. Unger. Brendle and Unger confine their attention to non-occult cures, however, whereas most recent writers have dealt with the *powwow* or occult folk beliefs and practices.[35] Because the word *powwow* is Algonquin it is sometimes assumed that powwowing as practiced among the Pennsylvania Germans is largely derived from the American Indian. That assumption is erroneous. Instead it owes much to European traditions and in turn influenced other American folk traditions such as that of the Negro.

Perhaps no aspect of Pennsylvania German lore has attracted so much attention as folk speech. Since the 1872 publication of S. S. Haldemann's *Pennsylvania-Dutch* a flood of articles and booklets on this subject has appeared. Many of these publications are intended for the tourist trade, their main thrust suggested by the title of one pamphlet, *Quaint Idioms and Expressions of the Pennsylvania Germans* (1939).[36] More on the scholarly side are such studies as John W. Frey's *The German Dialect of Eastern York County, Pennsylvania* (1941).[37] Rev. J. M. Hark's *Ein Handfull Färsh* (1900), a 31-page booklet of "experiments in Pennsylvania-German verse" that includes "an Introduction on the Capability of the Pennsylvania-German for Poetic Expression," is representative of a number of works devoted to folk speech.[38] Their sheer volume indicates that many agreed with Hark that the language was indeed quite capable of poetic expression.

While much has been written about folk speech in general, relatively little has been done with proverbs. Hoffman's *Journal of American Folklore* articles was one of the first published collections but the largest such work is Edwin Miller Fogel's *Proverbs of the Pennsylvania Germans* (1929). Fogel considers the proverb "the very bone and sinew of the dialect" and discusses the "surprisingly prominent role" it occupies in Pennsylvania German speech.[39] Among the topics he covers is the matter of origins, specifically determining by the use of parallels whether the adages are of English or German derivation. He concludes that the majority are German, one tenth British, and another tenth both German and British, while the rest are of indeterminate origin. Fogel used the same format as in his book on beliefs and superstitions. The dialect text is given first, followed by an English translation, then parallel sayings in *Hochdeutsch* (high German) and English. Also, like the earlier volume, this Fogel publication has not been superseded.

Works on Pennsylvania German folk art—by which term is meant products that are created largely for decorative or recreational impulses but which may also serve other functions—are numerous. Many of these are of a semi-scholarly nature and most focus on rural items. One of the most interesting and unusual is Henry C. Mercer's *The Bible in Iron* (1914), which is more accurately described in the subtitle *or, the Pictured Stoves and Stoveplates of the Pennsylvania Germans*. Mercer, a bachelor of considerable means, began a lifetime project of study and collecting in the 1880s, ultimately assembling an enormous collection that was to become the museum and headquarters of the Bucks County Historical Society in Doylestown. In 1897 he also produced the first major work on Fraktur, an article published in the *Proceedings of the American Philosophical Society* that for forty years was to be the best article in print on the topic.[40] This was supplemented by Henry S. Borneman's *Pennsylvania German Illuminated Manuscripts* (1937) and by Donald A. Shelley's *The Fraktur-Writings or Illuminated Manuscripts of the Pennsylvania Germans* (1958–1959). All three publications are still worthwhile reading, not only because they consider Fraktur as an art of intrinsic interest and provide summaries of the work done prior to their time, but also because they outline the research yet to be done on one of the most frequently studied examples of folk art. In recent years, Fred Weiser, editor of *Der Regeboge,* has become the recognized authority on Pennsylvania German Fraktur.

Beginning roughly at the same time as Mercer was Dr. Edwin Atlee Barber, whose specialty was pottery. His major work is *Tulip Ware of the Pennsylvania-German Potters* (1903), which is still one of the most important works on this particular topic, valuable for its examples and illustrations as well as for its discussion of the relationship between German and New World pottery. Another type of highly decorative Pennsylvania German product was the subject of Frederick William Hunter's *Stiegel Glass* (1914), which discussed the enameling and chasing of glass in the style attributed to Henry William Stiegel, a German glassmaker active in the colony of Pennsylvania fom 1750 to 1785.

The 1940s saw a significant number of publications on Pennsylvania Dutch folk art, the three most important being Frances Lichten's *The Folk Art of Rural Pennsylvania* (1946), Henry J. Kauffman's *Pennsylvania Dutch American Folk Art* (1946), and John Joseph Stoudt's *Pennsylvania Folk-Art* (1948). Lichten's book is the most comprehensive and is also representative of much Pennsylvania German folk art scholarship. It deals only with rural, historical art, coming no closer to modern times than the middle of the nineteenth century. Arrangement of artifacts is determined by artistic rather than folkloristic reasons, perhaps because Lichten envisioned collectors as her main audience, and the entire mood is nostalgic rather than analytic. Her later *Folk Art Motifs of Pennsylvania* (1954) is cast in the same mold but is noteworthy for its several illustrations. Stoudt's book is a revised edition of an earlier work,

Consider the Lilies, How They Grow: An Interpretation of the Symbolism of Pennsylvania German Art (1937), and, like that publication, advances the thesis that folk art does not represent the natural world but instead is an attempt to depict the transcendent world. The 1948 volume is distinctive for its large number of illustrations, as are two subsequent titles, *Early Pennsylvania Arts and Crafts* (1964) and *Sunbonnets and Shoofly Pies* (1973). Kauffman's book is the shortest of the three mentioned at the beginning of this paragraph but is useful for its brief but generally thorough, well-written discussions of various art products.

After the 1950s the number of volumes on Pennsylvania German folk art slowed down but, of course, did not stop. One author active since then deserves mention. Earl F. Robacker (1904–1985) was a Pennsylvania native who spent much of his career as a high school teacher in White Plains, New York. His heart, however, was always in German Pennsylvania. In order to be able to read old Pennsylvania Dutch manuscript writing he spent six years learning German. Beginning in the early 1930s he and his wife Ada amassed one of the larger private collections of folk art and antiques; these materials served as the basis for several books and articles. His lengthier works, such as *Pennsylvania Dutch Stuff* (1944) and *Arts of the Pennsylvania Dutch* (1965), are in the same mold as Lichten's work. As a readable, nostalgic view of the arts and crafts of a special group in a bygone era they are useful, but they are certainly not the sort of presentation professional folklorists would prefer.

Pennsylvania German folk art specialists have generally produced descriptive rather then theoretical works and have rarely been concerned with current folklore techniques of presentation or analysis. Their historical emphasis has given the impression that folk art passed out of existence decades ago—a view that few folklorists would agree with. On the other hand, the massive body of publications is not lacking in merit and has insured that the historical aspects of Pennsylvania German folk art are known in greater detail than is the case for most American cultural groups.

Many of the items considered folk art are also examples of what is called material culture—homemade fences, cabins, barns, and other constructions whose building techniques are passed on traditionally. Much of the work on Pennsylvania German material culture has centered on determinations of origins. Considerable space has been devoted to the source of certain types of log cabin construction techniques once common to German Pennsylvania. V-notching particularly has received a lot of discussion. In 1927 Henry Mercer suggested that such notching came to Pennsylvania from Sweden.[41] More than three decades later Henry Glassie and Fred Kniffen disputed Mercer's conclusion, arguing instead that it was introduced to the Keystone State in the 1730s by the Schwenkfelders, a small group of German pietists.[42] More recently Terry G. Jordan has supported Mercer's original conclusion, unlike Glassie and Kniffen or, for that matter, Mercer, basing his conclusion on extensive fieldwork in Europe.[43] To some, controversies such as this may seem pointless or unimportant, but they are not valueless. By determining such matters one can fill in not only some otherwise missing links in regional history but also aid in finding the source of other cultural influences. Whatever its merits, it is the sort of question one might expect to be debated in a relatively new area of intellectual inquiry like material culture studies.

Not all work in material culture, of course, is concerned with determining origins. Some, such as Charles H. Dornbusch's *Pennsylvania German Barns* (1958), consist solely of classifications. Going beyond this level are several titles in a new series, American Material Culture and Folklife, edited by Simon J. Bronner. Two titles deal with Pennsylvania German topics, Joseph Glass's *The Pennsylvania Culture Region: A View from the Barn* (1986) and Beauveau Borie, IV's *Farming and Folk Society: Threshing among the Pennsylvania Germans* (1986). The latter is particularly interesting and goes far beyond mere classification. Borie's aims are fourfold and include the obvious one of providing a complete account of Pennsylvania German threshing techniques. He also researched migration patterns of eighteenth- and nineteenth-century European immigrants in order to map Pennsylvania settlement patterns. Flails are classified according to the methods of fastening club to handle, this typology being an attempt to establish connections with European prototypes. Such determinations could then, it is hoped, be used in tracing settlement patterns by studying the distribution of a single item of material culture. Finally, Borie hoped to map dialect differences in flail terminology as a contribution to the development of an eventual linguistic atlas of the state. He was not completely successful in achieving these goals. It soon became apparent that compiling a dictionary of terms for flailing was impossible, because the technique disappeared several generations ago and much of the lore and language involved with it has also been forgotten. Even so, Borie's slender volume provides much useful data gleaned from extensive fieldwork and also admirably demonstrates some of the problems and benefits involved in doing research on historical material culture.

Pennsylvania German specialists have been more active than most other fieldworkers in taking down folk traditions, so it is somewhat surprising to find that they have done relatively little with folksongs, perhaps the most thoroughly mined vein of American folklore in general. The first work in Pennsylvania dates only back to the early 1930s and resulted largely from the interest aroused by the Pennsylvania Folk Festival, held at Allentown in 1935 and at Bucknell University in 1936 and 1937. Directed by George Korson, who had done significant fieldwork in mining folksong, festival performances indicated that the commonly held opinion that Pennsylvania German tradition was singularly lacking in folksongs might be erroneous. Two prolific scholars, Thomas R. Brendle and William S. Troxell, set out to see if they could find the traditional songs, and during the course of several summers prior to World War II took down over two hundred numbers. Their collection consisted of songs from Germany or Switzerland, those indigenous to Pennsylvania, translations of English and American songs, and variants of English and American items. A selection of 28 of these songs appeared in *Pennsylvania Songs and Legends* (1949), the texts printed in German dialect with English translations and melodic transcriptions. Brendle and Troxell provide names of singers and dates of collection but nothing more about their informants. Much of their commentary on individual entries deals with song histories, these remarks often being speculative. More recently, Albert Buffington has presented further riches of the type Brendle and Troxell found in his *Pennsylvania German Secular Songs* (1974).

Despite the efforts of Brendle and Troxell, aided in large part because the bulk of material was not published, throughout the 1940s the general view of the Pennsylvania Dutch was that they had no folksongs. A more accurate picture emerged after the publication of Walter E. Boyer, Albert F. Buffington, and Don Yoder's *Songs Along the Mahantongo: Pennsylvania Dutch Folksongs* (1951), a collection of 62 songs taken down in the 1940s. The three editors offered much greater detail for their collection than did Brendle and Troxell. They begin their book with a fifteen-page essay on the folksong tradition in the Mahantongo Valley and preface each song with fairly extensive comments about the history and function of each song. In addition they provide biographical data on singers and discuss some of the individual collecting sessions, capping this information with comparative data. Unlike Brendle and Troxell, and most other American folksong collectors, they did not rely exclusively on elderly informants but recorded material from various age groups, including children. Each song text appears in dialect then in rhymed English translations with melody transcriptions. Although completed over thirty years ago, *Songs Along the Mahantongo* still holds up remarkably well as a scholarly presentation of folksongs.

Another aspect of Pennsylvania German folksong is admirably treated in Don Yoder's *Pennsylvania Spirituals* (1961), a study based on 150 song texts collected in German Pennsylvania. In ten well-crafted chapters, Yoder treats the histories, sources, and themes of the spirituals, which he considers the only living folksongs found among Germans in the state. He argues persuasively that Pennsylvania was a seedbed of folk hymns and they are the last surviving form of German language hymnody in use among Pennsylvania Dutch groups. Not only is this book one of the only extended studies of Pennsylvania German folk hymnody, it is also one of the few lengthy works on American traditional hymns.

In several respects the history of German-American folklore studies parallels that of American folklore scholarship in general. Overall, the work has been generically and geographically spotty, with some groups, notably the Pennsylvania Germans, receiving vastly more coverage than others. Until relatively recently most of the work was done by enthusiastic amateurs, a term that is not used here in a pejorative sense. The efforts of these non-professionals were absolutely essential, for only in the last four decades has it been possible to receive extensive professional training in American folklore. It is easy enough to find fault with a majority of the work in German-American folklore, as it is with any body of scholarship that has been conducted mostly informally. But it seems best not to concentrate on the flaws but, rather, to be grateful that the material bequeathed by these researchers has often been far better than we might have expected.

W. K. McNeil
Ozark Folk Center

Notes

[1]The terms Pennsylvania German and Pennsylvania Dutch are used interchangeably in this introduction.

[2]His most important works in folklore include *Folklore: Amerikanische Kinderreime* (Folklore: American Nursery Rhymes) (1896); *Streifzüge auf dem Gebiete Amerikanischer Volkskunde* (Explorations of American Folklore) (1902); *Nachklänge Germanischen Glaubens und Brauchs in Amerika: Ein Beitrag zur Volkskunde* (1903); and *Zur Amerikanischer Volkskunde* (1905). Most of these books relied heavily on material collected by Knortz.

[3]Some of his brief pamphlets were in English, but the only lengthy work not in German was *Representative German Poems, Ballad and Lyrical* (1885)—not a folklore collection.

[4]Many of his works were designed primarily for German rather than American readers and he was frequently complaining about an anti-German bias on the part of Americans. His last book, published shortly before his death, was on this topic. For whatever reason, Knortz was generally overlooked by late nineteenth- and early twentieth-century American folklorists, and although he was a prodigious publisher, his name appears only rarely in the footnotes of contemporary American scholars. This neglect continued to the present to such an extent that Alan Dundes could write in 1964 that "few students of folklore are aware of the works of Karl Knortz" (Alan Dundes, "Robert Lee J. Vance: American Folklore Surveyor of the 1890's," *Western Folklore* 23 [January–March, 1964]: 27).

[5]Karl Knortz, *Die Deutschen Volkslieder und Märchen* (Zurich: J. Schabelitz, 1889), iii.

[6]Stith Thompson, *The Folktale* (New York: Holt, Rinehart and Winston, 1946), 371.

[7]Owen's article originally appeared in the *Missouri Historical Review* 15 (1920): 176–90.

[8]Bek's article originally appeared in the *Journal of American Folklore* 21 (1908): 60–67.

[9]Terry G. Jordan, *Texas Graveyards: A Cultural Legacy* (Austin: University of Texas Press, 1982), 122.

[10]The Iowa study was James A. Keen, "Some Musical Aspects of the Moravian Church, including the Easter Service at Winston-Salem, North Carolina," the 1953 thesis is "An Introduction to the Musical Culture of the North Carolina Moravians in the Eighteenth Century," and the 1958 dissertation is "Moravian Music in Salem: A German-American Heritage."

[11]S. J. Sackett's note appeared in *Western Folklore* 18 (1959): 99.

[12]Dundore's study appeared in volume 19 of the Pennsylvania German Folklore Society publication, 37–166.

[13]Hohmann's dissertation was submitted at Northwestern University in 1959.

[14]These works include "The Smaller Outbuildings of the Southern Mountains," *Mountain Life and Work* 40 (Spring 1964): 21–25; "The Old Barns of Appalachia," *Mountain Life and Work* 40 (Summer 1965): 21–30; "The Pennsylvania Barn in the South," *Pennsylvania Folklife* 15 (Winter, 1965–1966): 8–19, and 15 (Summer 1966): 12–25; "The Types of the Southern Mountain Cabin" in Jan Harold Brunvand, *The Study of American Folklore: An Introduction* (New York: W. W. Norton & Company, Inc., 1968), 338–70; and "Southern Mountain Houses: A Study in American Folk Culture," M.A. Thesis, American Folk Culture Program, Copperstown, State University of New York College at Oneonta, 1965.

[15]Terry G. Jordan, "Alpine, Alemannic, and American Log Architecture," *Annals of the Association of American Geographers* 70 (1980): 155–69.

[16]Richard M. Dorson, *Buying the Wind: Regional Folklore in the United States* (Chicago: The University of Chicago Press, 1964), 108.

[17]E. Allen McCormick, *Germans in America: Aspects of German-American Relations in the Nineteenth Century* (New York: Columbia University Press, 1983), 125–44.

[18]The song was most successfully sung by Clara Ann Fowler, professionally known as Patti Page.

[19]The *Journal of American Folklore* articles are "Folk-Lore of the Pennsylvania Germans" (I [1888]: 125–35); "Folk-Lore of the Pennsylvania Germans" (II [1889]: 23–35); and "Folk-Lore of the Pennsylvania Germans, III" (II [1889]: 191–202). The articles that appeared in the *Proceedings of the American Philosophical Society* are "Grammatical Notes and Vocabulary of the Pennsylvania Germans" (xxvi [1889]: 187–285) and "Folk-Medicine of the Pennsylvania Germans" (xxvi [1889]: 329–53). The *Science* article was "Notes on Pennsylvania German Folk-Medicine" (xxi [1893]: 355).

[20]Hoffman, "Folk-Lore of the Pennsylvania Germans I," 128.

[21]See footnote 19 above.

[22]See footnote 19 above.

[23]Hoffman, "Folk-Lore of the Pennsylvania Germans I," 128.

[24]See, for example, William Woys Weaver, "Pennsylvania German Architecture: Bibliography in European Backgrounds," *Pennsylvania Folklife* 24 (Spring 1975): 36–40, and Wendy Leeds, "Fraktur: An Annotated Bibliography," *Pennsylvania Folklife* 25 (Summer 1976): 35–46.

[25]Yoder provided a new questionnaire with almost every issue; the topics mentioned here are taken from a random sampling.

[26]For the specific criticisms see Angus K. Gillespie, *Folklorist of the Coal Fields: George Korson's Life and Work* (University Park: Pennsylvania State University Press, 1980); 136–45.

[27]The article appears in Wayland D. Hand, *American Folk Legend: A Symposium* (Berkeley: University of California Press, 1971), 157–83.

[28]The section on Ginder is the first one in the book and is titled "Philip Ginder, Folk Hero." George Korson, *Black Rock: Mining Folklore of the Pennsylvania Dutch* (Baltimore: Johns Hopkins Press, 1960), 1–31.

[29]Mac E. Barrick, "Lewis the Robber in Life and Legend," *Pennsylvania Folklife* 17 (Autumn 1967): 10–13, and " 'The Barber's Ghost': A Legend Becomes a Folktale," *Pennsylvania Folklife* 23 (Summer 1974): 36–42.

[30]The 345-page dissertation was submitted in 1907.

[31]Edwin Miller Fogel, *Beliefs and Superstitions of the Pennsylvania Germans* (Philadelphia: American Germanica Press, 1915), Introduction.

[32]Heizmann's article appeared in the *Historical Review of Berks County* (1946), 11–14. For two differing views on this question see Cornelius Weygandt, *The Red Hills: A Record of Good Days Outdoors and In, With Things Pennsylvania Dutch* (Philadelphia: University of Pennsylvania Press, 1929), 126, and John Joseph Stoudt, *Consider the Lilies, How They Grow: An Interpretation of the Symbolism of Pennsylvania German Art* (Allentown: Pennsylvania German Folklore Society, 1937), 11.

[33]Mahr's article appeared in *The Ohio Archaeological and Historical Quarterly* 54 (1945), 1–32.

[34]The Yoder article is "Hohman and Romanus: Origins and Diffusion of the Pennsylvania German Powwow Manual" and appears in Wayland D. Hand, *American Folk Medicine: A Symposium* (Berkeley: University of California Press, 1976), 235–48. Hostetler's article, "Folk Medicine and Sympathy Healing among the Amish," appears on pp. 249–58 of the same volume.

[35]Some articles on this subject are Betty Snellenburg, "Four Interviews with Powwowers," *Pennsylvania Folklife* 18 (Summer 1969): 40–45; Marcia Westkott, "Powwowing in Berks County," *Pennsylvania Folklife* 19 (Winter 1969–70): 2–9; Robert L. Dluge, Jr., "My Interview with a Powwower," *Pennsylvania Folklife* 21 (Summer 1972): 39–42; and, of course, the article by Yoder cited in footnote 34 above.

[36]The booklet was written by Ammon Monroe Aurand, Jr., and was published by the Aurand Press, Harrisburg, Pennsylvania.

[37]This study was published by the University of Illinois, Urbana.

[38]Hark's booklet was volume 10 of the *Proceedings and Addresses* of the Pennsylvania-German Society.

[39]Edwin Miller Fogel, *Proverbs of the Pennsylvania Germans* (Allentown: Pennsylvania German Society, 1929), 1.

[40]The article is "The Survival of the Mediaeval Art of Illuminative Writing Among Pennsylvania Germans," *Proceedings of the American Philosophical Society* 36 (1897): 424–33.

[41]Henry C. Mercer, "The Origin of Log Houses in the United States," *Old-Time New England* 18 (July 1927): 17, and 18 (October 1927): 52, 55, 57. The same paper appeared in *Papers, Bucks County Historical Society* 5 (1926): 568–83.

[42]Henry H. Glassie, "The Appalachian Log Cabin," *Mountain Life and Work* 39 (Winter 1963): 10; Fred Kniffen and Glassie, "Building in Wood in the Eastern United States: A Time-Place Perspective," *Geographical Review* 56 (1966): 40–66, see p. 59.

[43]Terry G. Jordan, Matti Kaups, and Richard M. Lieffort, "New Evidence on the European Origin of Pennsylvanian Notching," *Pennsylvania Folklife* 36 (Autumn 1986): 20–31.

CHAPTER ONE

The Germans in America

Germans began arriving in the New World among the earliest permanent settlers. William Penn, on receiving a charter for his colony in 1681, sought out suitable settlers. He recognized a kindred spirit between his English Quaker friends and certain Anabaptist sects in southern Germany and issued a printed invitation for them to migrate there, pointing out its advantages and the generous terms he offered. Penn traveled to Germany in 1671 and 1677 to extend the invitation personally.

The Palatinate which he visited was the garden spot of Germany, but because of its location it was a constant battleground from Roman times on. When the inhabitants embraced Protestantism during the Reformation, both Protestants and Catholics made the Palatinate a theater of war again. Seeing their lands devastated during the Thirty Years War and again after the death of Elector Philip Wilhelm in 1688, the Palatines, many of whom were pacifists, despairing of the horrors of war, began to seek homes elsewhere, in Holland, England, eastern Europe, and of course, in Penn's new province. Much is made of the belief that most early settlers migrated for religious reasons. The Treaty of Westphalia in 1648 did reaffirm the medieval principle that the ruler of an area could determine its religion, but the economic status of the inhabitants, ravaged as it was by wars, was more logically their motivation for leaving.

Over the next century hundreds of families accepted Penn's invitation, the first arriving in Philadelphia October 6, 1683, establishing a community at nearby Germantown. Subsequent arrivals sought out fertile farmland farther inland, in the rolling hills of south-central Pennsylvania, an area remarkably like the Palatinate from which they came, and a region that is still popularly known as the Pennsylvania Dutch country. The word Dutch is a misnomer of course, resulting from an anglicizing of the Pennsylvania German word *Dietsch* — "German" — which these people call themselves and their language. The language itself is a dialect of Old High German, still spoken in the areas of their origin. Several of the Anabaptist groups, notably the Mennonites and the Amish, still use this dialect in family communication, though they use standard German in their church services and English in dealing with their worldly neighbors.

During the War of the Spanish Succession (1701–1713), the Palatinate was again overrun, and migration to Pennsylvania began in earnest. Fearing that these Germans would become a dominant force, the Pennsylvania Assembly passed laws requiring them to swear allegiance to the British Crown, increasing taxes on newcomers, and threatening disenfranchisement until they learned English.[1] The attitude of the English toward the Germans is epitomized in a letter written by Benjamin Franklin in 1753, characterizing them as "the most stupid of their nation," and expressing the fear that German would soon become the official language of the state.[2] Ironically, there is an apochryphal legend that when the first national House of Representatives met in 1789 to decide, among other matters, the official language of the new nation, a tie vote between German and English was broken by the speaker, Friedrich Augustus Mühlenberg, a Pennsylvania German, who voted in favor of English.[3]

Not all of the Palatine migrants came directly to Pennsylvania. Many fled to England, where their increasing numbers were seen as a threat by British authorities, who soon shipped them off to the New World. One group settled in the Mohawk and Schoharie valleys of New York but, dissatisfied with conditions there, continued their migration southward into the Tulpehocken Valley of Berks County, Pennsylvania.[4] Another group was sent to North Carolina, settling in the coastal areas around New Bern. A more significant number moved to the interior valleys of that state from Pennsylvania, beginning about 1745; Pennsylvania German was still spoken in the Piedmont counties of North Carolina as late as 1830.[5]

Migration from Pennsylvania was responsible for the introduction of Germanic elements into most of the states along the Appalachian Mountains and the Shenandoah Valley. This movement was partly the result of frequent Indian raids on the homes of frontier settlers, culminating in the French and Indian War. However, another reason for the exodus was the relatively high land prices in the settled areas of Pennsylvania, less attractive to German farmers than the more reasonable terms offered by the governors of Maryland and Virginia.[6] Charles, Lord Baltimore, encouraged the development of the western part of Maryland, and many Germans settled around such villages as Monocacy, Frederick, and Hagerstown.[7]

Other Germans left Lancaster County, Pennsylvania, when the fertility of the soil there showed signs of depletion in the mid-nineteenth century. They settled first in Ohio, which still has significant colonies of Amish and Mennonites. Following the band of agricultural fertility across the country, they eventually reached into Illinois, Iowa, Kansas, and Nebraska.[8] Their movement is recapitulated by the travels of another family toward the end of the century. Foster Barrick, born in Perry County, Pennsylvania, recalled how his family moved westward state by state, eventually reaching California:

I was only 1 year old when we left there and went to Northern Ill—near Rockford Illinoise. From there we went to Northwest Kansas. We moved by covered wagon 4 different times in my life. The way things have changed just in the space of one life time would fill a grate big book.[9]

Another significant German migration to America occurred as the result of economic and political crises that affected Europe from 1816 to the 1840s. The economic crisis resulted from the end of the Napoleonic Wars with the subsequent excess of manufacturing capability, a population density that exceeded the productivity of the land, the meteorological catastrophe of 1816, and the resultant famine. Small farmers who held insufficient land to support their families couldn't afford to buy more. But the high price of land enabled them to sell what they had in order to move to America and buy larger farms.[10] Another wave of migrants came in the aftermath of the failed revolution of 1848. These were intellectuals and professionals, in contrast to earlier groups who were primarily farmers, and they tended to remain in urban areas, where they were often treated badly.[11] Large numbers came to settle in Missouri and Wisconsin.

Though the first Germans in Missouri were second-generation Pennsylvanians and North Carolinians who arrived after 1799, the significant migration to that region came in the 1830s and 1840s. Germans eventually became the dominant culture group of the lower Missouri River Valley.[12] Many were attracted by Gottfried Duden's *Bericht über eine*

Reise nach den westlichen Staaten Nordamerica ("Report of a Journey to the Western States of North America"), published in Germany in 1829, which depicted the area as an edenic Rhineland, perhaps the site of a new Germania. Numerous emigration societies were formed to encourage Germans to come to the region. Some came as farmers, but substantial numbers remained in St. Louis, where their liberal political inclinations helped keep Missouri in the Union during the Civil War.[13] The German settlers in Missouri were far from a homogeneous group, coming as they did from different provinces, with different dialects, different religious beliefs, and different interests. Though they tended to settle among other Germanic groups, they formed no pure Germanic communities but rather blended with migrants from other states and countries.[14]

Similarly in Wisconsin, Pennsylvania Germans who had lived for a time in Kentucky, Indiana, Ohio, Tennessee, or Illinois constituted a considerable number of settlers in the southern counties.[15] However, the majority of German settlers were Forty-eighters—political refugees who had arrived with an intention of establishing German republics in the New World. In fact, when Wisconsin was admitted to the Union in 1848, there was an unsuccessful attempt to establish it as a solely German state.[16] Between 1836 and 1850, about forty thousand immigrants, mostly from southern Germany, many of them Catholic, arrived in the state. One immigrant noted as early as 1852 that "German customs and usage reign in Milwaukee."[17] The long-lasting evidence of their influence, here as in St. Louis, was the founding of German breweries, making Milwaukee synonymous with beer production in the United States.[18]

Texas was the only state of the Deep South to undergo significant German settlement. Germans began arriving there before Texas gained its independence, but most came between 1836 and 1845. In 1831 Friedrich Ernst, from Oldenburg, established a farm in what is now Austin County. His enthusiasm expressed in a letter published in Germany attracted many immigrants. As in Missouri there were several attempts to establish "New Germanys" in Texas, but they were too scattered to have much effect.[19] Organized efforts at German colonization in west-central Texas attracted thousands in the 1840s, so that by 1850 fully 20 percent of the population there was German. Immigration, interrupted during the Civil War years, continued into the 1880s, creating a broad area of German development across the south-central part of the state.[20] The Wends who settled the Post Oaks region of Texas represent a curious anomaly. Though they were in fact Serbo-Lusatians from Prussia and Saxony, they abandoned their European folklore since it had little association with the area in which they now lived. Then, through religious fraternalization and intermarriage with neighboring Germans, they adopted the German culture, something they had resisted in the Old World.[21]

German Mennonites from East Prussia, having first migrated to southern Russia, began to arrive in Kansas in the years following the Civil War. Large settlements were established there and in Nebraska between 1876 and 1878.[22] German immigrants were among the earliest settlers in Nebraska, many arriving during the 1850s. Spurred by the Homestead Act of 1862, these arrivals increased considerably in the years after the war. Large numbers came from Russia in 1873, and by 1880 almost seven percent of the state's population of 452,402 was German-born, most of them settling in the agriculturally attractive area of the east. By 1890, the peak of German immigration there had passed.[23]

Iowa also sought immigrants. In 1869, the Iowa General Assembly created a Board of Immigration and put together a brochure to attract them. Germans came in large numbers, some as a result of political crises of the nineteenth century, but many continuing to arrive well into the twentieth century—despite the considerable anti-German sentiment in that state during World War I.[24]

Though there were Germans in Michigan before 1840, large groups of them settling around Detroit and Ann Arbor,[25] the significant influence of the German in that state dates from later migrations, particularly those following the two world wars. Migration in the latter half of the nineteenth century was sporadic, rising during times of war when conscription influenced young men to leave Germany. But there were other factors. Mack Walker discovered an interesting correlation between peak industrial economic growth and high levels of emigration, particularly from the more rural areas of northern and eastern Germany.[26] In the 1890s migration from the more industrialized regions became the dominant tendency, and naturally these people established themselves in the more industrialized areas of the New World. California attracted many of these later immigrants, as did the urban areas of Washington to the north.

Not surprisingly, most twentieth-century migration from Germany occurred in the years immediately preceding and following the two world wars. Many of these people were displaced persons whose way of life had been destroyed along with their homeland. Others were members of professional classes who sought to improve their economic status. A number came as brides of American soldiers. These disparate elements had few unifying similarities, and their dispersement throughout the country has thus far made it difficult to determine their role in the cultural history of the German in America. Their folklore, of course, appears in archives and collections across the country, and numerous examples of it are included in the survey that follows.

A word is necessary regarding the language of the texts below. Standard German is the language of the schools and the official language of state documents and public situations. But most Germans communicate at a different level of linguistic competence, in a variant of one of countless local dialects spoken in the different regions of Germany, broadly divided into Niederdeutsch, Mitteldeutsch, and Oberdeutsch—Low, Middle, and High—according to the geographical area in which they are spoken: lowlands in the north and west, midlands in the central part, and highlands to the south. Naturally the folklore of migrants to America is preserved in the common dialect of the region from which they came. The Palatine migrants who settled in Pennsylvania spoke a variety of High German dialects that eventually coalesced into a single semi-standardized form, borrowing and germanizing words from English for concepts that didn't exist in the dialect. Since Pennsylvania German existed until recently only as a spoken language, controversy developed as to its correct spelling when the need and desire arose to preserve it in print. In fact one recent collector insisted that "spelling varies so much you must spell it the way it sounds." With many of the items in the Alfred H. Shoemaker collection, considerable differences often exist between the text as it was collected in letters or manuscript notes and the version which later appeared in print in Shoemaker's columns in the *Pennsylvania Dutchman* and the *Reading Eagle.*

Insofar as possible, the texts below have been presented as their collectors recorded them. Some diacritical marks have been changed to reflect standard practice. In a few cases collectors lacking umlauts on their typewriters resolved *ä*, *ö*, and *ü* as *ae, oe,* and *ue;* in these cases the umlaut has been restored. Obviously erroneous spellings have been corrected, but no attempt has been made to regularize the arbitrary German system of capitalizing nouns.

CHAPTER TWO

Proverbs

Proverbs are traditional phrases that serve as a form of oral shorthand. Some summarize common experiences and others pose moral solutions to a given problem by alluding to well-known tales or fables. Despite the common assumption often implied by dictionary definitions, not all proverbs contain moral lessons, however. Some are playful phrases used for amusement, such as the retort to *Wie gehts?--Auf zwei Beinen, wie eine Gans* (No. 8 below). Some are based on puns or word plays, as in *Wanns net fur des wann waer* ("If it were not for *if,"* where the conjunction *if* is treated as a noun; compare No. 133).

There are obvious semantic differences between "proverb" (called in German *Sprichwort)* and "apothegm" or "adage" (German *Spruch)*. The proverb is used figuratively and is recognizable by its out-of-context reference. When one speaks of "locking the stable-door after the horse is stolen" (No. 35), for example, no literal stable or horse is implied; a now forgotten tale is called to mind to describe or warn against taking precautions too late. On the other hand, the adage contains no such metaphor but has been used so frequently that it has acquired proverbial currency. There can be no misunderstanding about the meaning of "What you don't know can't hurt you" (No. 135). Its meaning is clear and direct. In the minds of their users, however, there is no functional difference between the two phrases. Both are used to moralize about given situations and to offer advice, either tacitly or openly, and both provide apparent philosophical insight with a minimum of original thought.

German proverbs in America have not been systematically collected or studied. There are useful early collections of Pennsylvania German phrases by W. J. Hoffman ("Folklore of the Pennsylvania-Germans," *Journal of American Folklore* 2 [1889]: 197–202), Abraham Horne ("Proverbs and Sayings of the Pennsylvania-Germans," *Pennsylvania German Society Proceedings* 2 [1892]: 47–54), and Edwin M. Fogel (*Proverbs of the Pennsylvania Germans* [Fogelsville: Americana Germanica Press, 1929]). Marie Gabel has studied "Proverbs of Volga German Settlers in Ellis County" (*Heritage of Kansas* 9.2–3 [1976]: 55–58) and Gilbert J. Jordan has collected and published German proverbs from Texas (*German Texana* [Austin: Eakin Press, 1980], 124–35). But there is little from other areas.

1. *Abend wahrens die Faulen fleissig.*
At night the lazy ones get ambitious.

2. *Der Apfel fällt nicht weit von Stamm.*
The apple does not fall far from the tree trunk.

3. *Wann d'r abbel mol zeitich is fallt 'r runn'r.*
When the apple is ripe it will fall.

4. *Alter schuetzt vor Torheit nicht.*
Age is no guarantee against stupidity.

5. *Arbeit macht das Leben süss.*
Work makes life sweet.

6. *Si hot d'r bakofe geritte.*
She has ridden the bake-oven.

7. *Es wirt immer dafür gesorgt dass die Bäume nicht zu weit in den Himmel wachsen.*
It is always taken care of that the trees don't grow too tall.

8. *Wie geht's? Auf zwei Beinen, wie eine Gans.*
How's it going? On two legs, like a goose.

9. *Neia besem kehra gut.*
New brooms sweep clean.

10. *Es gibt kein Bier auf Hawaii.*
There is no beer in Hawaii.

11. *Alla bis'l helft, hot di alt frâ gsât.*
Every little helps, said the old woman.

12. *Jedes Bohnchen gibt ein Tönchen, jede Erbse einen Knall.*
Every bean gives a tone, and every pea a detonation.

13. *Wont's bry rayert, hut mer ken leffel.*
When it rains pap one is always without a spoon.

14. *Wer en buck schtehlt is ken schof dieb.*
Whoever steals a ram is no sheep thief.

15. *Är nemt der bull bai dä här'ner.*
He takes the bull by the horns.

16. As dumb as Jake Way's bull.

17. *Bussie waiirt ows, kocha dut net.*
Kissing wears out, cooking don't.

18. *Far denka kann em nimmant henka.*
For thinking one cannot be hanged.

19. *Die kleena Dieb hängt mer, die grossa losst mer laafa.*
Small thieves are hung, big ones go free.

20. *Dinn un lang macht n schtang. Kantz un dick macht aw n schtick.*
Thin and long make a rod. Short and fat add up to something too.

21. *Was grevver iss ass dreck, geet selvert aweck.*
What is coarser than dirt goes away of itself.

22. *Une drubel hot m'r nix.*
Nothing without trouble.

23. *Eigenlob stinkt.*
Self-praise stinks.

24. *Ein Esel heysst den anderen Sackträger (Langohr).*
One ass calls the other "Long Ears."

25. *Wann mer der essel nennt, no kummt er gerennt.*
When one names the ass, he comes running in.

26. *Langes Fädchen, faules Mädchen.*
Long thread, lazy maiden.

27. *Wer will seien fein, der muss leiden pein.*
One who wishes to be beautiful must suffer to do so.

28. *Wann du der finger net ins feier schteckscht, dann ferbrennscht en aw net.*
When you don't stick your finger in the fire, you won't get burned.

29. *Ohne Fleiss, kein Preis.*
Nothing has any value unless you work for it.

30. *En fraw ass net hausst, schmeisst mee naus mit em tee-leffel, ass der mann rei-bringt mit da schauffel.*
A wife that does not know how to keep house throws out more with the teaspoon than a man can bring in with a shovel.

31. *Fress oder verek.*
Eat or perish.

32. *Fu'der macht di gail.*
Fodder makes the horse.

33. *Wer gut futtert, gut buttert.*
Who feeds well churns much butter.

34. *Ma gschenkta gaul guckt mar net ins maul.*
Don't look a gift horse in the mouth.

35. *Wan der gaul gshto'la is shlist mer der shtal.*
When the horse is stolen, one locks the stable.

36. *Mit Geduld und Spucke, fangt man eine Mucke.*
With patience and spit, one can catch a mosquito.

37. *Gros gekrisch un wennig woll.*
Great cry and little wool.

38. *Ein gutes Gewissen ist ein sanftes Ruhekissen.*
A good conscience is a soft pillow.

39. *Frisch gewogt is halwer gewunna.*
Well begun is half done.

40. *Glee un schmart iss aw dawert.*
Small and smart is worthwhile too.

41. *Glück und glass, wie leicht bricht das.*
Both good luck and glass are easily broken.

42. *Jeder ist seines Glückes Schmied.*
Everyone is his own luck maker.

43. *Es ist nicht alles Gold, was glänst.*
Not everything is gold that glitters.

44. *Geh mer weck mit Grotte uff em Eis.*
Away with your toads on ice!

45. *Glena grutta hen aw gift.*
Little toads have poison too.

46. *Wer anri gruuva grawbt, fallt selvert nei.*
He who digs a ditch for others falls in it himself.

47. *Eine Hand wäscht die andere.*
One hand washes the other.

48. *En eerlichi hand geet darrich s gansa land.*
An honest hand goes a long way.

49. *Viele Hände machen schnell ein Ende.*
Many hands make quick work.

50. *Vun Hand zu Mund, vun Orsch zu Grund.*
From hand to mouth, from arse to ground.

51. *Harren und hoffen, das hot getroffen.*
Waiting and hoping paid off.

52. *Do is wū der hâs im pef'fer sitst.*
Here is where the hare sits in the pepper.

53. *Wenn alte Häuse brennen, denn brennen sie Lichter ho'.*
When old houses burn, they burn out of control.

54. *Katza hawr sin glei gebascht.*
Short hair is soon combed.

55. *Wer net heert, muss fiela.*
He who will not hear must feel.

56. *Eigener Herd ist Goldes wert.*
Your own stove is worth gold.

57. *Was du heute kannst besorgen das verschiebe nicht auf morgen.*
Whatever you can get finished today, do not push it off until tomorrow.

58. *Hoffen und harren dass macht manchen zum narren.*
Waiting and hoping make fools of some people.

59. *Der höler is so schlecht wie der schtehler.*
The concealer is as bad as the stealer.

60. *Yeder mus sei egne hout zum gerwer drawga.*
Everyone must carry his own hide to the tanner.

61. *Kummscht ivver der hund, so kummscht ivver der schwans.*
If one can get over the dog, he can get over the tail.

62. *Zu viele Hunde sind des Hasen tod.*
Too many dogs are the rabbit's death.

63. *Der Hunger is der bescht Koch.*
Hunger is the best cook.

64. *Est fur der Hunger das kommt.*
Eat for the hunger that comes.

65. *Yunge Hure, alde Beddlerin.*
Young whoremonger, old beadle.

66. *Jung gefreit, hat nie gereut.*
Young marriages have no regrets.

67. *Kaushit naut, kaushit drisch, dat jeft en schene bubbits diech.*
Cowshit wet, cowshit dry, it makes a nice dough.

68. *Jeder kehre vor seiner Tür.*
Everyone sweeps in front of his own door.

69. *Fiel kepp, fiel sinn.*
Many heads, many minds.

70. *Die kinner un die narra schwetza die wawret.*
Children and fools tell the truth.

71. *Gleena kinner, gleena druvvel, groossa kinner, groosser druvvel.*
Small children, small troubles; big children, big troubles.

72. *Kindchen willst du Suppe essen darfst dass blassen nicht vergessen.*
Children who eat soup should not forget to blow on it.

73. The more children, the more Lord's prayers.

74. *Aule en 'ne Reaj aus Klosses Tjeaj.*
All in a row like Klassen's cows.

75. *Kleider machen Leute.*
Clothes make the man.

76. *Dee Kleagste jeft aum easchte.*
The cleverest one gives in first.

77. *Was mer net im kopp hot, muss mer in da fiess havva.*
What one hasn't got in his head, he has to have in his feet.

78. Two heads are better than one, even if one is a cabbage head.

79. *Der Krug geht so lange zum Wasser bis er bricht.*
The jug goes so long to the water until it breaks.

80. *Die hinnerscht kuu macht's fallder tsu.*
The last cow closes the door.

81. *Eine gute Kuh sucht man im Stalle.*
One seeks for a good cow in the stable.

82. *Es kummt net uff die grees aw, sunscht kennt en kuu en haws fange.*
It does not depend on size, otherwise a cow could catch a rabbit.

83. *Man wirt so alt wie eine Kuh und lernt noch immer was dazu.*
One can get as old as a cow and still always learn something new.

84. *Waer's letscht lacht lacht's bescht.*
Who laughs last laughs best.

85. He who holds the ladder is as guilty as he who mounts the wall.

86. *Besser 'n laus im kraut das gâr ken flesh.*
Better a louse in the cabbage than no meat at all.

87. *Ist kein Leit so schlimm wie das dass der Mensch sich selber schaft.*
There is no trouble so bad as that which one creates for oneself.

88. *Lügen haben kurze Beine.*
Lies have short legs.

89. *Luschtig gelebt un selig g'schtorwa, Is 'm Deiwel sei Rechling verdorwa.*
A merry life and a pious death spoil the devil's reckoning.

90. *Mädchen die flöhten und Hühne die krehen muss mann bei zeiten den Halz abdrehen.*
Girls who whistle and hens that crow will in time get their necks broken.

91. *Wann die Maus sat ist, ist der Mehl bitter.*
When the mouse is full, then the meal is bitter.

92. *Messer, Gabel, Sher, und Licht sind fur die kleine Kinder nicht.*
Knives, forks, scissors, and lights are not for little children.

93. *Es ist noch kein Meister vom Himmel gefallen.*
No master has ever fallen from heaven.

94. *Wer's erscht in die Mihl kummt, krigt's erscht gemahla.*
Who first comes to the mill grinds first.

95. *Morgen, morgen nur nicht heute sagen alle Faulen leute.*
Tomorrow, tomorrow, just not today, that's what lazy people say.

96. *Morgenstund hat Gold im Mund.*
The morning has gold in its mouth.

97. *Müssiggang ist aller Laster Anfang.*
Idleness is the root of all evil.

98. *En nar macht tswe.*
One fool makes two.

99. *Zub on deiner egna naws.*
Pull on your own nose.

100. *In der not schmeckt die Wurst auch ohne Brot.*
In bad times you like sausage without bread.

101. *Ochs mol ochs is kelver geblau.*
Ox times ox is calves bawling.

102. Paper is patient.

103. *En paarchen wie Paul und Clarchen.*
A pair like Paul and Clare.

104. *Ist kein Pott so schaf dos un Deckel nie passt.*
There isn't a pot so bent that there isn't a lid to fit it.

105. *En frier morgen raega un en alder weiver-dans waera net lang.*
An early morning shower and an old woman's dance do not last long.

106. *Reden ist silber, Schweigen ist gold.*
Talk is silver, silence is golden.

107. *Ess regnet. Got signet.*
It's raining. God's blessing.

108. *Wenn es nicht regnet denn dröppelt es.*
If it doesn't rain, it sprinkles.

109. *En blindi sau finnt alsemol en eechel.*
A blind pig finds an acorn sometimes.

110. *Sauerkraut un seida-schpeck, sell macht die alta weiver fett.*
Sauerkraut and a side of bacon make the old woman fat.

111. He was born in a sawmill.

112. *En glēn shōf is glai kshō'ra.*
A small sheep is soon shorn.

113. *Geduldige Schafe gehen viel in den Stall.*
Tame sheep can be stabled in great numbers.

114. *Scheisse macht hunger.*
Shit makes hunger.

115. *Wu Schmok is, is ah Feier.*
Where smoke is, there is fire.

116. *Zu schorf schneit net, und zu schpitsich schtecht net.*
Too sharp does not cut, and too pointed does not stick.

117. *Mit schpeck fongt mer die meis.*
With fat, one catches mice.

118. *An Gottes Segen ist alles gelegen.*
Everything depends on God's blessing.

119. *Wer Sorgen hat, der hat Liquor.*
One who has troubles turns to drink.

120. *Besser ein Sperling in der Hand als ein Traube auf dem Dach.*
Better a starling in the hand than a dove on the roof.

121. I threw a stone in your yard as I came by.

122. *Wer sucht der finnt; wer awhalt, der gewinnt.*
Who seeks, finds; who keeps on, wins.

123. *Wann mer satt iss, schmackt aw die supp sauer.*
When one isn't hungry, all soup tastes sour.

124. *Man soll den Tag nicht vor dem Abend loben.*
One should not praise the day before the evening.

125. *Der Teufel huckt unter der Brücke in Paris und heult weil er keine Mode mehr denken kann.*
The devil squats under the bridge in Paris and cries because he cannot think up any more fashions.

126. *Jedes Tierchen, sein Plesierchen.*
Each animal has his own pleasures.

127. *Übung macht den Meister.*
Practice makes the master.

128. *Ein Unglück kommt selten allein.*
A bit of bad luck seldom comes alone.

129. *Wat den eenen sien Uul, is der annern sien Nachtigal.*
One person's owl is another person's nightingale.

130. *Viel fährt mann auf dem Wagen.*
Large amounts have to be carried on a wagon.

131. *Der Vogel der so früh singt, den fängt die Katze.*
The bird that sings too early, the cat catches it.

132. *Wer schteht un lauert an der Wand, Der heert sei eg'ne Schimp un Schand.*
He who stands and listens at the wall, hears his own insult and shame.

133. *Wann daut "Wann" nich wea, wea maunchelei aundasch.*
If it were not for "if," then many things would be different.

134. Still water runs deep.

135. *Was ich nicht weiss macht mich nicht heiss.*
What I don't know won't bother me.

136. *Gut g'wetst is halwer g'meht.*
Well whetted is half mowed.

CHAPTER THREE

Riddles

Riddles are traditional questions worded in such a way as to mislead the person answering. Riddles are mentioned in the earliest writings of the Far East, in the Bible, and in classical mythology. One, the so-called Riddle of the Sphinx—"What walks on four legs in the morning, two in the afternoon, and three in the evening?" with the answer "Man"—is still current in most Western cultures. Their role in medieval tales, where a young man who correctly answers a riddle or a series of riddles wins the hand of the princess in marriage or gains fabulous wealth, may indicate an association with primitive cultures where the riddle is a form of intelligence test leading to kingship or priesthood. In some areas the riddle is still an important element in rites of passage, puberty ceremonies, and wakes.[1]

Traditional riddles, which folklorists often call "true riddles," generally involve a comparison between the unstated answer and another object. The description usually has two parts, one a positive statement, such as "What has four legs," and a contradictory one, "—but can't walk?" with the answer to be guessed by the listener. Sufficient information is given that a person familiar with riddle forms can come up with the solution, "table" or "chair" or whatever other piece of furniture the riddler is willing to accept.

Modern riddles are joking questions and are virtually unsolvable unless one has heard them before. Sigmund Freud called this type of riddle *Scherzfragen*, "'facetious questions' . . . because the joking answers that they call for cannot be guessed in the same way as are the allusions, omissions, etc. of jokes."[2] Many in fact are conundrums based on puns

47

or wordplay, as in the English riddle, "When is a door not a door? When it's ajar." Phonetic puns depend for their humor on the misinterpretation of words that sound alike or words that have double meanings, as in riddles No. 128 through 143, below. Often the similarity is far-fetched (Nos. 89, 90, and 141). Sometimes the pun is based on syntactic differences. The verb *smell* has two meanings, to detect odor and to cause odor (No. 144). The plurals of words often change form, and this is sometimes the basis for wordplay (No. 134). *In* and *out* can signify location or direction, and a small amount of humor results (No. 115). And in some cases (No. 153, for example), a shift in grammatical function from adverbial to objective can be both humorous and painful. In many cases the pun is so deeply rooted in the language that it must be explained, rather than translated, and the humor is lost. Such is the case with the riddles, "Wie konn mer en Ent aus er Gans mache? Wann mer sie esst,"[3] and "Was ist der Unterschit zwischen einer Jungfrau und Persil? Persil bleibt Persil."[4]

As the form of riddles has changed over the years, so has their function. Older folks remember riddles with pleasure: "We used to sit around the stove at night and Mom and Dad would ask us these riddles. We thought that was a lot of fun,"[5] and "Riddles . . . were a part of our childhood store of wit and humor to be used in entertaining our playmates, and now and then an unwary grown-up was also trapped."[6] Today's riddle is more a parody of the old form than a true riddle. With it the child makes fun of the mathematical or factual questions asked by teachers in school. He jokes about the minutely detailed biblical questions asked in catechism class or Sunday school. He confronts the absurdity of the world around him by joking about it ("What's green and flies? Super-pickle"). The tension surrounding such tragic events as the *Challenger* explosion and the Chernobyl nuclear accident is effectively released by parodic questions: "What has feathers and glows? Chicken Kiev."[7]

With these and similar riddles children soon discover that they can embarrass or annoy the grownups around them. One favorite riddle type is the pretended obscene riddle, in which a description is made of a sexual act or of an apparently "dirty" situation (see Nos. 46, 47, 95, and 152, below).

Occasional examples occur of a riddle type known as the Neck Riddle,[8] because the person posing it literally saves his neck. The riddle is part of a narrative in which a prisoner is offered his life or freedom if he can offer a riddle that the king (or judge) cannot answer. He draws on a personal experience whose details are known only to himself, and thus he outwits his opponent. Samson's riddle, "Out of the eater came forth meat, and out of the strong came forth sweetness" (Judges 14:14), is of this nature. John Baer Stoudt cites the classic European example:

Auf Ilo geh ich,
Auf Ilo steh ich,
Auf Ilo bin ich hübsch und frei,
Ratt meine Herren was soll das sein.[9]
(In Ilo I walk, in Ilo I stand, in Ilo I am happy and free —guess, my lord, what can this be?)

The explanation is that the man had a dog named Ilo, and when the dog died, the man had a pair of shoes made from his hide. The following version occurs among the Pennsylvania Germans:

In Ginni gee ich,	In Ginny I walk,
In Ginni schtee ich,	In Ginny I stand,
In Ginni bin ich hibsch un fei.	In Ginny I am handsome and fine.
Wer kann rooda was des mawg sei?	Who can guess what this riddle is?[10]

Not surprisingly, many of the same riddles told among the Pennsylvania Germans are still known in areas to which the Palatines migrated. And some of those riddles are still being told, in English, several generations later by descendants of those migrants who no longer speak German.

The following riddles are arranged roughly according to the classification system established by Archer Taylor in his standard dictionary of English and American riddles, *English Riddles from Oral Tradition,* and in the *Brown Collection of North Carolina Folklore.*[11] German riddles in America have not been widely collected, although there are significant contributions by John Baer Stoudt and Gilbert J. Jordan.[12] In Pennsylvania Alfred Shoemaker collected numerous examples of riddles in the dialect, but the results of his efforts were published only sporadically in the early issues of *The Pennsylvania Dutchman* and in a few newspaper columns.

1. *Was schteet uff eem bee un hot's hatz im kopp? (En graut-kopp.)*
What stands on one leg and has its heart in its head? (A head of cabbage.)

2. *Was hot s hatz im gansa leib? (En bawm.)*
What has its heart in the whole body? (A tree.)

3. *Was wachst uf seim Schwantz? (Rüb.)*
What grows on its own tail? (Turnip.)

4. *Was geet mit sex fies darrich die grick un grickt uscht fiera nass? (En mann uff em gaul am reita.)*
What goes through a creek with six legs and gets only four of them wet? (A man riding a horse.)

5. *Was geet uff'm wasser un watt net nass? (N gans.)*
What goes on water without getting wet? (A goose.)

6. What has four legs and only one foot? (A bed.)

7. *Nas geht un geht, un steht un steht? (En Mühl.)*
What goes and goes, and yet stands and stands? (A mill).

8. What goes around the house and only makes one track? (Wheelbarrow).

9. *Was geet uff der offa un ferbrennt sich net, geet darrich die dier un glemmt sich net, un geet uff der disch un schemmt sich net? (Die sunn.)*

What goes on the stove and doesn't burn itself, what goes through a door without pinching itself, what crawls on the table without being ashamed of itself? (The sun.)

10. *Was geet far da sunn un macht ken schadda? (Der wind.)*
What passes in front of the sun without casting a shadow? (The wind.)

11. What walks on its head? (A shoepeg.)

12. What jumps over the fence and leaves his tail behind? (Needle and thread.)

13. *Was geht ums Haus rum un legt weisse Schnupdücher uf die Fenstere? (Der Reife.)*
What goes around the house and places white handkerchiefs upon the windows? (Jack Frost.)

14. What goes to the well and doesn't drink? (Cowbell.)

15. *Was lawft un brauch ken fiess? (Wasser.)*
What walks (runs) and doesn't have any feet? (Water.)

16. *Was lawft un brauch ken fiess? (En rotznaws.)*
What runs and doesn't need legs? (A snot-nose.)

17. *Was hot awga un kann net seena? (N grummbier.)*
What has eyes and cannot see? (A potato.)

18. What has a mouth and can't talk? (The run [brook].)

19. *Was geet die schteek nuff un reegt sie net aw? (Der schmook.)*
What mounts the stairs without touching them? (Smoke.)

20. *Was geet um's haus rum Dripp Drapp, Dripp Drapp? (Der reega fum dach.)*
What goes around the house and makes "Dripp Drapp, Dripp Drapp"?
(The rain falling from a roof.)

21. *Was schpringt net unna s hot redder im kopp? (Die uur.)*
What won't run unless it's got wheels in its head? (A watch.)

22. *Was schwimmt un guckt net wuu's hie geet, avver guckt wuu's schuun
wawr? (Der grebs; der schwimmt hinnerschich.)*
What swims and doesn't look where it is going, but looks where it was
already? (The crab; it swims backwards.)

23. *Eisa geili, floxa shwentzly,
Da shtarier os geila shpringt
Da kotzer os shwentzly naidt? (En nae-machine.)*

An iron horse, a flaxen tail; the faster the iron horse runs, the shorter the
tiny tail grows. (A sewing machine.)

24. *Es is en Dierli,
Es heest Mariele,
Es hot nein Häut,
Un beist alle Leut. (En Zwievel.)*

There is a little animal, its name is Mariele, it has nine skins, and bites
everybody. (An onion.)

25. *En feld foll braune Schoff, un der Hiltze Jergel schiest danoch. (En Bockoffa foll Brod.)*

A field full of brown sheep, and wooden Jergel shoots at them. (A bakeoven filled with baked bread.)

26. *Es steht im Wald ein Männlein*
Auf einem Bein,
Es hat auf seinem Haupt
Ein schwartz Käpplein klein,
Sagt wer mag das Männlein sein,
Was da steht im Wald allein,
Mit seinem Kleinen
Schwartzen Käppelein.

Little man in the woods on one foot,
Little cap on his head black as soot,
Little man, black cap, down by a tree,
Guess what his name is and come tell me. (Mushroom.)

27. *Hubber-de-bubber-de, unnichem Bank,*
Hubber-de-bubber-de, owwichem Bank,
Siss kenn Mann im ganse Land
Das Hubber-de-bubber-de fange kann. (En Fatz.)

Hubber-de-bubber-de, under the bench,
Hubber-de-bubber-de, over the bench;
There is no man in all the land
Can catch Hubber-de-bubber-de again. (A fart.)

28. *Es kummt en Mann von Mickelbrück,*
Un hot en Gläde von Tausend Stück,
Un hot en Knochig an g'sicht,
Un hot en lederner Bard. (Hahne.)

A fellow comes from Mickelbridge,
And has a suit of a thousand patches,
He has a bony countenance,
And a leather beard. (Rooster.)

29. *En dicki mammi, en grummer dawdi un drei gleena, schpitzicha kinner.*
Was iss es? (En eisa-kessel.)
A fat mother, a crooked father and three little, pointed children. What is
it? (An iron kettle.)

30. What grows with its roots up? (An icicle.)

31. *Was waxt hinnerwatts? (N kie-schwans.)*
What grows backwards? (A cow's tail.)

32. *Was is das? In Weisenberg im Damm, dort wachst en gehli Blum; un wer die*
gehl Blum will havve, der mus gans Weisenberg verschlage? (En oy.)

What is this? At Weisenberg in the dam, there grows a yellow flower; and
whoever wishes to get the yellow flower, must destroy whole Weisenberg. (An egg.)

33. *Ich weiss ein kleines weisses Haus,*
Hat keine Fenster, keine Thore,
Und will der kleine Wirth heraus,
So muss erst die Wand durchbohren. (Ey.)

I know a little white house,
It has no windows and no doors,
And if the little guest wants out,
He must first pierce the wall. (Egg.)

34. *Drauss uff m hivvel schteet n grie haus. In dem griena haus iss n weiss*
haus. In dem weissa haus iss n root haus. Un in dem roota haus sin fiel sch-
watza niggers. (N Wassermeluun.)

Out on the hill stands a green house. In the green house is a white house.
In the white house is a red house. And in the red house are many black
fellows. (A watermelon.)

35. *Ein kleines fessel wool gebunna,*
Un sei leeva noch ken reef drum kumma. (N oi.)
A tiny barrel well bound,
And never had a hoop around. (An egg.)

36. *Rie, Raw, Ribbel,*
Geel iss der tsibbel,
Schwatz iss es loch
Wuu der Rie, Raw, Ribbel drin kocht. (N rieb imma eisa-kessel.)

Yellow is the tip and black is the hole in which "Rie, Raw, Ribbel" is cooking. (A carrot in an iron pot.)

37. *Vier rolle Ronse,*
Vier Kappe danze,
En Knick-knock,
un en Brod-sock. (En man, wage und vier Gäul.)

Four round bellies,
Four caps a-dancing,
A knick-knack,
And a bread sack. (A man, wagon and four horses.)

38. What is high as a house, low as a mouse, green as grass, black as ink, bitter as gall, yet sweet after all? (A walnut.)

39. *Was iss rund an da tswee enner un hooch in da mitt? (Ohio.)*
What is round at both ends and high in the middle? (Ohio.)

40. *Fanna wie en butterfass,*
hinna wie en "berstears" schtock.
Was iss es? (N katz.)

In front like a ball of yarn, in the middle like a churn and at the end like a can. What is it? (A cat.)

41. *Was is fanna fleesch, hinna fleesch un in de mitt hols un eisa? (En mann mit geil am bluua.)*
What is flesh in front and in back and wood and iron in the middle? (A man plowing with horses.)

42. *So dick wie lang,*
So hooch wie breet,
Die drei weega drumm
Iss es gleich beleegt. (N fier-eckichi box.)

As far as long, as high as broad, All three ways around it's made alike. (A square box.)

43. *Loch, loch, alles loch. Heebt un tsiegt doch. Wass iss es? (N kett.)*
Hole, hole, everything a hole, yet it pulls and holds just the same. What is it? (A chain.)

44. *Ick weit en ding, hett veer ecken. Dor kann ein ap den annern seihn.*
I know a thing, has four corners. In it one ape can see another. (Mirror.)

45. *Erst weiss wie Schnee,*
Dann grün wie Klee,
Dann rot wie Blut,
Schmeckt allen Kindern gut. (Eine Kirsche.)

First white as snow, then green as clover, then red as blood, tastes good to all the children. (A cherry.)

46. *Wass dutt mar weech nei un nemmt's hatt raus? (En leeb broot.)*
What is put into something soft and taken out hard? (A loaf of bread.)

47. What goes side by side, arm in arm, and tickles the hole? (A guitar.)

48. I ain't got it, I don't want it, but if I had it, I wouldn't take a million dollars for it. (Bald head.)

49. *Was iss dass, wann's n tsoll tsu kats is un du machscht noch en tsoll ab, dass no lang genunk watt? (En grawb.)*
If it is an inch too short and you add an inch, it will fit. What is it? (A grave.)

50. *Was ist das? Ja mehr du isst, desto mehr hast du?*
What is that? The more you eat, the more you have? (Walnut shells.)

51. *Wer es macht, der sawgt es net. Wer es nemmt, der kennt's net. Wer's kennt, der will's net. Was iss's? (Falsch geld.)*

He who makes it does not reveal it; he who takes it does not recognize it, and he who recognizes it doesn't want it. What is it? (Counterfeit money.)

52. *Was ist des? Der blind hot gaawt er hett's gseena. Der eebeenich hot gsawt er weer em noo gschprunga. Der dumm hot gsawt er wisst's un der nackich hot gsawt er hett's in der bussem gschteckt. (Ei, en lieg.)*

What is the answer? The blind man said he saw it. The one-legged man said he ran after it. The dullard said he knew it and the naked one said he had stuck it in his bosom. (Why, a lie.)

53. *Wie kenna drei oier mit nanner deela un s bleibt noch eens in da schissel leia? (Wann der letscht die schissel mit m oi nemmt.)*

How can three people divide three eggs so that there remains one in the bowl? (If the third takes the bowl with the egg in it.)

54. *Wie fiel grund iss im ma loch en fuus eckich un n fuus dief? (Kenner.)*
How much ground is there in a hole a foot square and a foot deep? (None.)

55. *Was iss des? Es wawr moll en miel mit acht ecka; in yeederm eck wawr en sack un in yeederm sack wawr en katz mit acht yunga. Der miller un sei fraw wawr aw noch drin. Nau wiffel fiess wawra doo drin? (Yuscht fiera. Die katza hen ken fiess; sie hen dappa.)*

What is the answer? There was once a mill with eight corners. In each corner was a bag and in each bag there was a cat with eight young. The miller and his wife were in the mill too. How many feet were there altogether? (Just four. Cats don't have feet; they have paws.)

56. *Wiffel schticker kann mar aus am kucha schneida? (Juscht eens, die annera dutt mar abschneida.)*
How many pieces can one cut out of a cake? (Just one; all the other pieces are cut off the cake.)

57. *Wie weigt fliegt en grapp in der busch? (Halbweegs. Danoo fliegt sie aus m busch.)*
How far does a crow fly in a woods? (Just halfway; after that it's flying out of it.)

58. *Wann neun Vogel uf em Baum hocke un du scheisht drei defon runner, wie viel hocke noch druf? (Keene.)*
If nine birds sit on a tree and one shoots three down, how many remain sitting? (None. [The others fly away.])

59. A duck ahead of two ducks, a duck behind two ducks, a duck between two ducks. How many ducks were there? (Three.)

60. *Wann es beef-fleesch en halva dawler iss in Fildelfi, was sin die fensariggel in Barricks Caunty? (Hols.)*
If beef is half a dollar in Philadelphia, what are fence rails in Berks County? (Wood.)

61. *Welle lichter brenne länger, die von Inschlich oder die von Wachs? (Sie brenne kärtzer net länger.)*
Which candles burn longer, those of tallow or those of wax? (They burn shorter, not longer.)

62. *Wann's en faddel pund pulfer nemmt far ma bull der schwans abschiessa, wie fiel nemmt's far ma biffel die hanner abschiessa? (En biffel hot ken hanner.)*

If it takes a quarter-pound of powder to shoot off the tail of a bull how much does it take to shoot off the horns of a biffel? (A "biffel" is a cow without horns.)

63. *Dei Mutter hot en Kind g'hat, es war net dei Bruder un au net dei Schwester. Wer war's? (Dich selver.)*
Your mother had a child, which was neither your brother nor your sister. Who was it? (Yourself.)

64. *Wer hot geleebt un iss gschtareva un wawr nie net gebawra? (Awdam.)*
Who lived and died and was never born? (Adam.)

65. *Wer wawr gebawra un iss net gschtareva? (Du un noch fiel annera leit.)*
Who was born and never died? (You and a lot of others.)

66. *Wuu hot Noah der eerscht naggel hiegschlagga? (Uff der kopp.)*
Where did Noah hit the first nail? (On its head.)

67. *Wuu wawr Moses wie's licht ausganga iss? (Im dunkla wie mier aw.)*
Where was Moses when the lights went out? (In the dark, the same as the rest of us.)

68. How'd the first grain of buckwheat come across the ocean? (Three-cornered.)

69. *Wie grickt mar der hammer fescht so ass mar sich net uff der dauma gloppt? (Mit da tswee hend am schtiel.)*
How does one take hold of a hammer so that he doesn't hit his finger? (Take hold of the handle with both hands.)

70. *Wie kann mer en hinkel essa eb's gebawra iss? (Wann mer's oi esst.)*
How can one eat a chicken before it is born? (By eating the egg.)

71. *Wie lang schlooft die katz uff em hoi? (Bis es uumed druff geduu werd noo schlooft sie datt druff.)*
How long does a cat sleep on hay? (Until the second crop of hay is put in the barn.)

72. *Wie kann mar da gansa weeg noch da schtatt reida im schatta? (Wann mar als runner geet un lawft wuu's kenner hot.)*
How can one ride to town in the shade? (By getting off and walking where there is no shade.)

73. *Wass iss der unnerschitt gschwischich n budderfass un n hawna? (Es budderfass hot sei fliggel in wennich un der hawna aus wennich.)*

What is the difference between a butter churn and a rooster? (The churn has its wings on the inside and the rooster has his on the outside.)

74. *Far was iss en grass widow wie en hoi-schrecker? (Sie jumpa alla beed an da eerscht chance.)*
Why is a grass widow like a grasshopper? (They both jump at the first chance.)

75. *Wuu her sin sei net wie menscha? (Weil mer sei doot macha muss eb mer sie kuura kann.)*
In what respect are pigs unlike people? (Because one has to kill pigs before one can cure them.)

76. *Wass iss der unnerschitt gschwischa n alter silverner dawler un n neier kuppericher cent? (Nein-un-neintsich cent.)*
What is the difference between an old silver dollar and a new copper cent? (Ninety-nine cents.)

77. *Was iss der unnerschitt tswischa n lawyer un en shubb-karrich rawd? (Den eena muss mar schmutsa tsu greischa macha; den anner muss mar schmutsa tsu greischa schtoppa.)*

What is the difference between a lawyer and the wheel of a wheelbarrow? (One must be greased to get him to make a noise; the other must be greased to keep it from making a noise.)

78. *Was ist der Unterschied zwischen einem Beamten und einem Stück Holz? (Das Stück Holz arbeitet.)*
What is the difference between a state employee and a piece of wood? (The piece of wood works.)

79. What kind of trees are there most of in the woods? (Round ones.)

80. *Was far schtee hot's menscht im wasser? (Nassa.)*
What kind of stones are most frequently found in water? (Wet ones.)

81. *Was kauft mer bei der Yord un weart es aus beim Fuss? (Karabet.)*
What is bought by the yard and worn by the foot? (Carpet.)

82. *Was guckt innevennich wie ausevennich? (En fenschderglaws.)*
(What looks the same on the inside as on the outside? (A windowpane.)

83. *Weller fisch hot die awga s neegscht beinanner? (Der glennscht.)*
Which fish has the eyes closest together? (The smallest.)

84. *Was winscha mier tsu havva, avver brooviera far es loos tsu warra? (En guuter abbedit.)*
What is it we wish to have and at the same time try to get rid of? (A good appetite.)

85. What's older than its mother? (Vinegar.)

86. *Was is fertig un werd täglich emacht? (Es Bett.)*
What is finished and yet is made daily? (The bed.)

87. *Was iss immer hinner-seits? (Der deckel fun ra watsch.)*
What is always behind time? (The lid of a watch.)

88. *Was ist das Weisse in Hühnerscheisse? (Das ist auch Hühnerschiesse.)*
What is the white stuff in chicken shit? (That's chicken shit too.)

89. *Was sin Portugese? (Porchegeese sin Gens die ihre Oier unnich em Porch laegge.)*
What are Portuguese? (Porch-geese are geese that lay their eggs under the porch.)

90. *Waescht was'n Grouch iss? (Sell iss der Blatz wu mer die Machine drin halt.)*
Do you know what a grouch is? (That is the place where one parks the car.)

91. *Was ferennert sei nawma s gschwinscht? (N meedel, wann s heiert.)*
What changes its name faster than any thing else? (A girl, when she gets married.)

92. *Was duht der Hahne wann er uf eem Bee steht? (Es anner nuf heve.)*
What does the rooster do when he stands on one leg? (Holds up the other leg.)

93. *Was kann en Kuh duh ass en Weibsmensch net duh kann? (Im wasser rumbaade bis an de Ditz uns Orsch net nass griegge.)*
What can a cow do that a woman can't? (Walk in water up to her tits and not get her ass wet.)

94. *Was hot n mann in da hossa dass n fraw es bescht gleicht? (Sei backa-buch.)*
What does a man carry in his trousers that a woman likes best of all? (His pocketbook.)

95. *Was haest mer en kind das ken Bibs hot? (En Maedle.)*
What do you call a child that has no penis? (A girl.)

96. *Was iss es bescht watt an ma weibsmensch? (Es letscht.)*
What is the best word that comes from a woman? (The last.)

97. *Was geet's gschwindscht darrich der hund? (Sei nawma; wann'd en sawgscht, schiddelt er schunn der schwans.)*
What passes most quickly through a dog? (Its name; as soon as you say it, the dog wags its tail.)

98. *Was dravelt's schtarrigscht—hitz adder die kelt? (Ei, die hitz. Es kalt kannscht fanga.)*
What travels faster—heat or cold? (Why, heat. One can easily catch cold.)

99. What's blacker than a crow? (Its feathers.)

100. *Was macht heller ass wie ee licht? (Tswee lichter.)*
What is brighter than a light? (Two lights.)

101. *Was iss lenger ass en fensa-riggel? (Tswee fensa-riggel.)*
What is longer than a fence rail? (Two rails.)

102. *Was hot meener feddera ass en gans? (Tswee gens.)*
What has more feathers than a goose? (Two geese.)

103. *Was hots grösst Schnubduch in der Weld? (En Hinkel.)*
What uses the largest handkerchief in the world? (A hen; for it wipes its nose anywhere on the earth.)

104. *Was iss es dummscht schtick fie? (En gans; die bickt sich far tsum scheier-door nei.)*
What is the most stupid of all animals around the barn? (A goose; it bends to get through the barnyard door.)

105. *Was iss's unnaedichscht Ding uffme Ewwer? (Die zwae roi Ditz.)*
What is the most useless thing on a boar? (The two rows of tits.)

106. *Well is es stärkest gedhier in der Welt? (En Schneck.)*
What is the strongest animal on earth? (A snail, because it carries its house on its back.)

107. *Was iss's scharrefscht Ding in der Welt? (En Fatz. Es geht darrich de Hosse wie'n Nodle un macht ken lecher.)*
What is the sharpest thing in the world? (A fart. It goes right through trousers like a needle and leaves no hole.)

108. *Wann jumpt der fux ivver der schtumba? (Wann der bawm ab iss.)*
When does the fox jump over the stump? (When the tree is cut down.)

109. *Wuu halta die hensching s wawrmscht? (Am offa.)*
Where do gloves keep one warmest? (At the stove.)

110. *Far was geet n hinkel ivver die schtrooss? (Far uff die anner seit.)*
Why does a chicken cross the street? (To get over to the other side.)

111. *Fer was hen Hund immer kalde Naes? (So das die anner Hund ihre Orsch net verbrenne wann sie draa rieche.)*
Why does a dog always have a cold nose? (So he doesn't burn the other dog's arse when he smells him.)

112. *Far was schiddelt der hund sei schwans? (Der hund iss schdarriger ass sei schwans, schunscht deet faleicht der schwans der hund schiddla.)*

Why does a dog wag its tail? (The dog is stronger than its tail. If the reverse were true, it would be the tail wagging the dog.)

113. *Warum fressen die weissen Schafe mehr Gras als die schwarzen? (Es gibt mehr weisse Schafe als schwarze.)*
Why do white sheep eat more grass than black ones? (There are more white sheep than black ones.)

114. *Ferwas drickt der hawna die awa tsuu fer greea? (Er wees es ausewennich.)*
Why does a rooster close its eyes while crowing? (He knows it by heart.)

115. *Farwas guckt der schuumacher in die schuu? (Weil er net nei kann. Ei, wann er drin weer, noo kennt er raus gucka.)*
Why does a shoemaker look in a shoe? (Because he isn't in the shoe. If he were in it, he would look out.)

116. *Far was schteet die uur im haus? (Weil s haus net in da uur schtee kann.)*
Why does a clock stand in a house? (Because a house cannot stand in a clock.)

117. When a cat comes into the house, why does she look first to one side and then to the other? (She can't look both ways at once.)

118. *Far was baua die bauera der seischtall gschwischich's haus un die scheier? (Far die sei nei.)*
Why do farmers build their pigsties between the house and the barn? (For the pigs.)

119. Why does the chimney smoke? (Because it can't chew.)

120. *Far was weert der miller en weisser huut? (Far der kopp tsu-decka.)*
Why does a miller wear a white cap or hat? (To cover his head.)

121. *Far was dutt der hawna ivver die wagga-glees schritta? (Weil s tsu weit iss
drum rum tsu gee.)*
Why does a rooster step over a wagon rut? (Because it is too far to go all
the way around.)

122. *Far was geet der fux ivver der barrick? (Weil er net unna darrich gee kann.)*
Why does a fox go over the hill? (Because he can't go underneath.)

123. Do you know why Mennonites won't have intercourse standing up?
(It might lead to dancing and that's a sin.)

124. *Far was schwimmt der fisch im wasser? (Weil er ken bee hot far lawfa.)*
Why does a fish swim in water? (Because it hasn't got legs to walk.)

125. *Far was hen die grotta ken schwens? (Weil sie kenni breicha.)*
Why don't toads have any tails? (Because they don't need any.)

126. *Fer was geht der Bauer in die Mühl? (Weil die Mühl net zum Bauer
kummt.)*
Why does the farmer go to the mill? (Because the mill will not come to the
farmer.)

127. *Far was geet der hund im gringel rum eb er sich hieleegt? (Er guckt; er
meent es deet iem en koppakissa hinna rausfalla, far sich druff leega.)*
Why does a dog walk in a circle before he lies down? (He thinks a pillow
might fall out of his rear end.)

128. Why did the German chorus girl want to be buried under the
Autobahn? (Because everyone wanted to ride on her.)

129. *Far was hen sie m William Penn sei naws dreitsee tsoll lang gemacht?
(Wann sie sie tswelf tsoll lang gemacht hetta, hett er n fuus im gsicht katta.)*

Why did they make William Penn's nose thirteen inches long when they
made his statue? (If they had made it twelve inches long, he would have
had a foot in his face.)

130. *Was farricha awga hot n mensch ass er net seena kann mit? (Greeawga.)*
What kind of "eyes" does one have that he cannot see with? (Corns ["gray eyes"].)

131. *Was fann bawm kann mar net graddla? (N batzel-bawm.)*
What kind of tree can one not climb? (A somersault.)

132. *Was far ebbel waxa net uff am bawm? (Moiebbel.)*
What kind of apples do not grow on a tree? (May apples.)

133. *Was fann eesel kann mer net reida? (En hanneesel adder en kellereesel.)*
What kind of mule can one not ride? (A hornet or a sow bug.)

134. *Wann is n fux n fux? (Wann er lee iss; wann's tswee sin, sin's fix.)*
When is a fox a fox? (When he is alone; when he's plural, he's foxes.)

135. *Was fer haws hut ken shwontz? (Pon Haws.)*
What kind of rabbit has no tail? (Scrapple.)

136. *Was fer'n leeb brillt net? (En leeb broot.)*
What kind of lion doesn't roar? (A loaf of bread.)

137. What kind of milk is it that makes a man pull down his pants and a woman pull up her dress? (Milk of magnesia.)

138. *Wann is die lengscht un die hellscht nacht im yawr? (Uff fawsanacht, die is 24 schtunn lang; dawgs is aw fawsanacht.)*
What is the longest and brightest night of the year? (Fasnacht day [Shrove Tuesday], which is 24 hours long.)

139. Which ring is getting fatter? Goering.

140. *Was farricha soola weera s lengscht? (Fiess-soola.)*
What kind of soles wear the longest? (The soles of one's feet.)

141. *Was farricher Vieh fresst ken Hoi? (Ge-og-ro-vieh.)*
What kind of cattle eat no hay? (Geography.)

142. *Was fern Vogel hot ken Fligel, ken Feddre un ken Schnavel? (Mortervogel.)*
What bird has no wings, no feathers, and no bill? (Hod ["mortar bird"].)

143. *Was fann wascht kammer net essa? (N hans-wascht.)*
What kind of sausage can one not eat? (A clown.)

144. *Was schmackt (riecht) es menscht in ra abbadeek? (Dei naws.)*
What smells the most in a drug store? (One's nose.)

145. *Far was blafft der hund? (Far seim schwans.)*
Why (before what) does the dog bark? (Before his tail.)

146. *Was iss der glennscht huns nawma? (En dippel.)*
What is the smallest or shortest name for a dog? (Dot.)

147. *Welli huns nawma kannscht banna? (Feier un Wasser.)*
What dog names cannot be charmed? (Fire and Water.)

148. *Es war en Mann in unser'm Land,*
Rätschel war sein name,
Er war von Saddlerback gemacht,
Un drei mohl sag ich sei nahme. (War.)

There was a man in our country,
His name was a riddle,
He was made of Saddlerback,
And three times have I repeated his name. (Was.)

149. *Kaiser Karolius hot ein hund,*
Er gibt iem ein nawma mit seim mund.
Wie heest m Kaiser Karolius sei hund? (Wie.)

Kaiser Karolius has a dog,
He gives him a name with his mouth.
What is the dog's name? ("What" is his name.)

150. *Nach dem essen en kau dūbak, un das schtēt in d'r bībel.*
After meals a chew of tobacco, and that stands in the Bible. ("That" is in the Bible.)

151. What do you call that thing under a horse's tail? (His asshole. Any horse's ass knows that.)

152. *Was iss's? Es hot'n wesserich Schlitz, siss rund un hot Haar drum? (Sin die Aage.)*
What is it, it has a watery slit, it's round and has hair around it? (It's the eye.)

153. *Den Monat stechen die Hummler net.*
Bumblebees don't sting this month. (They don't sting the month.)

154. Do you know how many hairs a pig has on his face? (Count them the next time you shave.)

155. *Ich fliehe vor dem Tageslicht,*
Und geh' den Nacht nur aus;
Das Wildpret ist mein Leibgericht,
In Klüsten ist mein Haus.
Liest du auch vor- und rückwärts mich,
Mein Nam' ist unveränderlich. (Uhu.)

I flee from daylight
And go out only at night.
Wild game is my life's food,
In caves is my home.
If you read forward or backward,
My name is unchanged. (Horned owl.)

CHAPTER FOUR

Rhymes

The function of folk rhymes is varied. Many examples of rhymed proverbs and riddles exist, and rhymes often have a narrative function, serving as a moralizing summary of a fable or tale or even as the central element in a story, as in the cante fable. A major role of rhyme is in song, and many extant examples of folk rhymes are nothing more than folksongs recited by those who can't carry (or remember) a tune.

From the comments made by those who remember the rhymes, reciting them was a means of amusing children. Adults held a child on their lap while they manipulated its fingers, nose, chin, or toes to the accompaniment of an appropriate little poem. Sometimes the singsong rhythms of traditional verses were used to lull a child to sleep. Cleverness and parody were necessary with older children who soon learned that they could impress their playmates by reciting these same verses.

One favorite among young children seems to have been the horse-riding rhyme, considering the frequency with which it was recalled. Here the child is placed on the foot of an adult's crossed leg and bounced to the recitation of the rhyme.

Counting-out rhymes had a special role in the folklore of children. They determined who would be the dreaded "It" character in games, a function that has been tracked to early cultures where some such means was used to identify sacrificial victims. The strange words themselves suggest this primitive source, and many of the apparently meaningless words in counting-out rhymes have been traced to mystic origins.

Some tongue-twisters are intended to embarrass a speaker who has difficulty pronouncing certain sounds, often causing him to say, accidentally, of course, naughty or obscene words. A child is told to hold his tongue and say, "Molasses on the table," which comes out, "My ass is on the table." Like tongue-twisters, catches are a form of game in which the experienced reciter leads the novice into saying something embarrassing, such as admitting to eating an old dead crow or looking like a monkey.

Nonsense rhymes have never been adequately studied. Most are recited simply to entertain, but they undoubtedly belie a subconscious social concern with the absurdity of the world around one.

Proverbs and folk rhymes occasionally contain an element of what the Germans call *Ortsneckereien* (banter about places) and the French *blason populaire*. Traditional attitudes toward one's hometown and neighboring areas continue to appear in verse long after their basis for being has disappeared. The Palatine immigrants carried with them jokes and sayings about Swabians from adjoining provinces of Germany, and as immigrants of other nationalities appeared, the same jokes and sayings were adapted to them.

Rhymed epitaphs, among those groups who saw the need to fill the bare expanse of stone with something to give pause to passersby, drew inspiration from hymnbooks or from other tombstones. Significant collections of German epitaphs include Alfred Shoemaker's "German Epitaphs in the Dutch Country" (*Pennsylvania Dutchman* 2.1 [1950]: 2), Leo M. Kaiser's "German Verse in American Cemeteries" (*German American Review* 26 [1960]: 25–28), an examination of several cemeteries in St. Louis, Missouri, and Gilbert Jordan's collections from Texas cemeteries (*German Texana,* 59–76).

Frau Wirtin rhymes are part of the folklore of the recent German immigrant. German university students sing and recite the rhymes in beer halls. Examples occasionally appear in *Kommersbuchen* (student songbooks) or in privately printed collections in Germany and Austria, but their normal means of circulation is oral. There is a similarity of structure and content between these rhymes and the American limerick, and like the limerick, the Wirtin poems are the province of the intellectual classes.

Tickling and Dandling Rhymes

1. The following is recited while touching a baby on the head, forehead, eyes, cheeks, nose, mouth, and chin, and ending by tickling the child under the chin:

Louse-head,
Fore-head,
Eye-winker,
Tom Tinker,
Nose-smeller,
Mouth-eater,
Chin-chopper,
Gully, gully, gully, gully.

2. Knock at child's forehead and say, "Knock at the door." Half close each hand, holding them before the child's eyes and say, "Peep in." Then pulling at child's nose say, "Pull the latch." And then stick index finger in child's open mouth and say, "Walk in."

3. The child is placed across the knees, face down, and asked, "Was witt? Pieki, Fauschti, Flatti, Cutti, Craw?" (What do you want? Pecking [with thumb and forefinger], pounding [with both fists], slapping [with open hands], sawing [across back with both hands], clawing.) The child guesses which of these ticklings is going to be done to him, and if he guesses correctly, he is released.

4. *Es hockt en bobbli uff der wand;*   There is a baby on the wall;
Es hot en gackli in der hand.   There is an egg in its hand.
Es hot es wella brooda,   It wants to fry the egg,
Avver es iss em net grooda.   But doesn't get anywhere.

At this point the reciter quickly says, "XDYD-Fensmeisli," and tickles the child's chin.

5. *Doo hockt die maus*
Un baut n haus.
Doo hockt die mick
Un baut n brick
Doo hockt der floo
Un macht soo, soo.

The mother points to the child's forehead and says, "Here there sits a mouse; it's building a house." Pointing next to the child's nose, she says, "Here there sits a fly; it's building a bridge." And then pointing to the infant's chin, she says, "Here there sits a flea and goes like this." She then tickles the baby's throat.

6. *Tjleena Finja*
Goldrinja
Langhauls
Buttaletja
Lustjetjnetja.

Little finger,
Gold-ringer,
Long-neck,
Butter-licker,
Louse-cracker.

7. *Kleiner Finger,*
Dummer Finger,
Langer Finger,
Laus Knecker,
Haver Stecker.

Little finger,
Dumb finger,
Long finger,
Louse-cracker,
Oats-sticker.

8. a. *Das ist der Daumen,*
Der schüttelt die Pflaumen,
Der sammert sie auf
Der bringt sie nach Haus.
Und diese kleine Schlingel
Isst sie alle auf.

This is the thumb,
This one shakes the plums,
This one gathers them up,
This one brings them home,
And this little rascal
Eats them all up.

b. *Das ist der daumann,*
Der schuttelt die pflaumen,
Der habt sie ap,
Der traet sie heim,
Der isst sie alle auf.

This is the gardener;
He shakes the plums,
He picks them up,
He carries them home,
He eats them all up.

c. *Des is der dauma,*
Der schiddelt die blauma,
Der leest sie uff,
Der drawgt sie heem,
Un der glee schellem
freest sie all deheem.

This one is the thumb;
This one shakes the plum tree;
This one picks them up;
This one carries them home;
And this little rascal
Eats them all up.

9. a. *Backa, backa, kucha,*
Der becker hot geruufa,
Wer will scheena kucha havva,
Der muss havva sivva sacha:
Budder un schmals,
Oier un sals,
Millich un meel
Un saffran macht die kucha geel.

Bake, bake, a cake.
The baker says,
He who wants good cakes
Needs seven ingredients:
Butter and lard,
Eggs and salt,
Milk and flour,
And saffron makes the cake yellow.

b. *Backe, backe, Kuchen,*
Der Backer hat gerufen,
Wer will guten Kuchen backen,
Der muss haben sieben Sachen:
Eier und Schmalz,

Butter und Salz,
Milch und Mehl,
Safran macht den Kuchen gel'.

c. *Backa, backa, oier-kucha,*
Die katz, die will sie aw fersucha.
Bake, bake, some omelets; the cat wants to taste them too.

d. *Backa, backa kuchli,*   Bake, bake a cake,
Mier un dier un kuchli,   A cake for me and you,
Un da annera all menanner   And for all the others together
Dreck, dreck, dreck.   Dirt, dirt, dirt.

10. *Die mammi backt waffla.*
Sie backt sie tsu hatt.
Doo backt sie nuun widder
Un gebt mer net satt.
So backt sie drei dauset
Un gebt mer net satt.
So mach ich mein bundel
Un sawg guut nacht.

Mother makes waffles and bakes them too hard. She makes another batch but doesn't give me enough to satisfy me. She bakes three thousand and it's still not enough to satisfy me, so I pack my bag and say good night.

11. *Mammi, mammi, budder broot,*
Schlack die katz im keller doot.
Mommy, mommy, butter bread,
Kill the cat in the cellar dead.

12. a. *Reita, reita, geili,*   Ride, ride a horsey,
Alla schtund a meili,   Every hour a mile,
Alla meili n wattshaus.   Every mile an inn.
Bring mer n glessli wei raus. Bring me out a glass of wine.
Siess abbel sauer,   Sweet sour-apple,
Hoch uff der mauer   High on the wall
Hockt n bobbli an da wand,   A baby sits on the wall,
Hot n gackli in da hand.   He has an egg in his hand.
Hett's gern gebrooda,   He wants it fried,
(Name) muss es brooda.   (Name) shall fry it.

b. *Reita, reita, geili,*
Alla schtunn e meili.
Alla meili n wattshaus.
Geb mer moll n schmawler raus.
Reitschda ivver der grawva.
Fallscht du nei, so muss ich sawa:
Bumps! Datt leischta drin.

Giddap, little horsey. Every hour a mile. Every mile an inn. Hand me out a drink of whiskey. Should you then fall in the ditch, I'll have to say: "Bang! There you lie."

c. *Reiti, reiti, geili*
Alla schtund en meili.
Mariya wella mar havver drescha,
Noo kann's geili fuuder fressa.

Ride, ride, tiny horse, every hour a mile. Tomorrow we want to thresh oats, then the horse will have something to eat.

d. *Reida, reida, geili,*
Alla schtund a meili.
Es geili schpringt der hivvel nuff,
Es buuveli (meedeli) leest die gnoddla uff.

Ride a horsey, every hour a mile. The horsie runs up the hill and the little boy (or little girl) gathers up the horse droppings.

13. *Hop, hop, hop!*	Hop, hop, hop!
Pferdchen lauf gallop.	The horsey goes gallop.
Über Stock und über Stein,	Over stick and over stone,
Brech dir aber nicht ein Bein.	But don't you break a bone.
Hop, hop, hop!	Hop, hop, hop!
Pferdchen lauf gallop.	The horsey goes gallop.

14. *Hop, hop, Reiterlein,*	Hup, hup, little rider,
wenn die mädchen kleine sein	When the girls are little
reiten sie auf Mutters Schoss;	They ride on mother's lap.
wenn sie grösser werden,	When they grow bigger
reiten sie auf Pferden.	They ride on horses.
Macht das Pferdchen trippel trop,	If the horse makes "tripple trop,"
bumps da fällt das Mädchen alle.	Bump—the girls fall off.

Counting-out Rhymes

15. *Ieni, mieni, hickeri, hen!*
Wann ich widder rummkumm,
Bin ich widder do,
Ich un der Tschann un der Tschimm un der Tschoo.

Ieni, mieni, hickeri, hen!
When I come around again,
I'll be here again,
I and John and Jim and Joe.

16. *Ente dinte minte fass,*
Geh in die schule und lern etwas.
Ente dinte minte fass,
Go to school and learn something.

17. *Ani beni dunke funke*
Rabe Schnabe diebe daube
Kassi nabi oli boli rose
Du liegst raus, Du bist aus.

18. *Enderly, benderly, sickerly, sol,*
Heebsha, deepsha, heller knoll.

19. Indi-mindi, unicorn,
apple siess and briar thorn.
Briar, briar, nimble-lock.
Three geese in the flock.
O-u-t, out.
With a rotten dishcloth out.

20. *Hicker, hacker, hei.*
Der miller hot sei fraw ferlawra.
Es hundel hot sie gfunna.
Die katza schlagga die drumma.
Die meis wescha es haus aus,
Die ratta drawga der dreck naus.
Es hockt en feggeli uff em dach
Un hot such schier-gawr schepp gelacht.
Es kummt en groossi flettermaus
Un pickt em feggeli's lechel raus.

The miller has lost his wife. The dog found her and the cats beat the drum. The mice wash the house and the rats carry out the dirt. On the roof there sits a tiny bird and laughed itself to death. Along comes a bat and picks out the eye of the little bird.

21. *Hicka, hacka, Hollerstock,*	Hick, hack, elderbush,
Wie viel Hanna hat der Bock,	How many horns has the ram,
Ans, zwa, drei;	One, two, three;
Zucker auf der Brei,	Sugar in the pap,
Salz auf der speck,	Salt in the lard,
Hahne geh wek	Rooster go away
Oder ich schlach Dich in der Dreck.	Or I'll knock you in the dirt.
22. *Eens, tswee, drei,*	One, two, three,
Hicker, hacker, hei.	Hicker, hacker, hay.
Tsucker uff'm brei,	Sugar in the pudding,
Sals uff'm schpeck.	Salt in the lard.
Hawna, gee weck,	Rooster, go away,
Du schtinkscht noch hinkel-dreck.	You smell of chicken shit.
23. *Ein, zwei, drei, vier,*	One, two, three, four,
In dem Clavier,	In the piano
Sitzt eine Maus,	Sits a mouse,
Die muss raus.	The mouse must go away.

24. *Eens, tswee, drei adder fier,*
Meedli, wann du dansa witt, dans mit mier,
Fimf, sex, sivva, acht,
Meedli, wann du dansa witt, dansa in da nacht.

One, two, three or four, sweet little girl, if you want to dance, dance with me. Five, six, seven, eight, if you want to dance, dance at night.

25. a. One, two, three,
Granny caught a flea.
Flea died, and Granny cried,
Bye, baby, bye.

b. A, B, C,
Mammy caught a flea.
Flea died and Mammy cried,
A, B, C.

26. *A, B, C,*
Die katz lawft im schnee.
Der schnee geet aweck,
Die katz lawft im dreck.
Der dreck geet aweck.
Die katz lawft in der schtumba.
Der schtumba gracht,
Die katz lacht.

A, B, C,
The cat walks in the snow.
The snow goes away,
The cat walks in the dirt.
The dirt goes away.
The cat walks in the stump.
The stump cracks,
The cat laughs.

27. *Ich und du, Müller's Kuh,*
Müller's Esel, das bist du.
I and you, the miller's cow,
The miller's donkey, that is you.

28. a. *Noodla, noodla, faadem, fingerhuut,*
Schteet em bauer aus em huut.
Kummt die fraw ins hinkel-haus
Un sucht die drei beschta hinkel raus.
Hawna mit da yunga fawna,
Sprech sie aus.
Wer muss raus?
Ich adder du
Adder es Beckers brauni, schwatzi bella kuu?
Un des bischt du.

Needles, needles, thread, thimble; they all stick out of the farmer's hat.
The lady comes into the chicken house and picks out the three best
chickens. Rooster with the young feathers, tell who is out. Me or you, or
Becker's brown, black bell cow? And that is you.

b. *Nodel, Faade, Finger,*
Der Bauer is so gut.
Do geht die Fraa ins Hinkelhaus,
Un sucht die beschte Haahnehinkel raus.
Tick, taeck, tock,
Weller finger muss ab,
Ich odder du?—'S is du!

Needle, thread, finger,
The farmer is so good.
The lady goes into the hen-house
And picks out the best rooster.
Tick, tack, tock,
Which finger must go out,
I or you? It's you.

29. *Der mann will boddle schlagge,*
Wiffel neggel muss or havve?
(Drei.)
Eens, tswee, drei, du bischt frei.

This man wants to hit bottles. How many nails does he need?
(Someone answers, "Three," or any number). One, two, three,
you are free.

30. *Gauli, gauli, bschlagga.*
Wiffel neggel musscht du havva?
Eens, tswee, drei,
Peter kumm rei
Un grick dei drei.
There is a horse to be shod. How many nails are needed? One, two, three,
Peter come on in and get your three.

Tongue Twisters

31. *Miller Michel Moser, mach mer mei Moschmehl, mei Mommie muss mer*
Mosch mit Millich mache.
Miller Michael Moser makes me my mush-meal; my Mommy must make
me mush with milk.

32. *Hinnich Henner's huls-hocker-haus hovvich hoonert hawsa haira hooshta.*
Behind Henry's woodchopper house I heard a hundred rabbits coughing.

33. *We wetta weiver windla wesha wonn wosser wei wairt?*
How many women would wash diapers if water were wine?

34. *Groomy, grawdy, sheppy suppa-schissel.*
Crooked, straight, lopsided soup dish.

35. *Fischers Fritz fischt frische Fische;*
Frische Fische fischt Fischers Fritz.
Fritz Fischer fishes for fresh fish;
Fresh fish fish for Fritz Fischer.

36. Say "Dampfer, Dampfer, Dampfer, Dampfer, Dampfer," rapidly.

37. Say "Meis im eckel" rapidly.

38. Say "Fuftsich bulla, fuftsich kie," real fast.

Catches

39. *Ich sawg dier wawr.*   I tell you the truth,
Dei kopp hot hawr.   Your head is wet.
Ich sawg dier was,   I tell you more,
Dei hand iss nass.   Your hand is wet.

40. A second player is instructed to respond to everything, "Ich aw" (So do I). Then the reciter begins—

Ich gee in der busch.	*(Ich aw.)*
Ich nemm die ax mit.	*(Ich aw.)*
Ich hack n bawm um.	*(Ich aw.)*
Ich schleef n heem.	*(Ich aw.)*
Ich mach n sei-drook raus.	*(Ich aw.)*
Die sei fressa raus.	*(Ich aw.)*

I go into the woods. I take an axe along. I cut down a tree. I drag it home. I make a pig-trough out of it. The pigs eat out of it.

41. The second child is told to respond, "Grawd wie ich" (Just like me).

Ich gee ee drepp nuff.	*(Grawd wie ich.)*
Ich gee tswee dreppa nuff.	*(Grawd wie ich.)*
Ich gee fier dreppa nuff.	*(Grawd wie ich.)*
Ich gee sex dreppa nuff.	*(Grawd wie ich.)*
Ich gee in en schtupp.	*(Grawd wie ich.)*
Ich guck in en schpiggel.	*(Grawd wie ich.)*
Siss en monkey im schpiggel.	*(Grawd wie ich.)*

I go up one step. I go up two steps. I go up four steps. I go up six steps. I go in a room. I look in a mirror. There is a monkey in the mirror.

42. The second player is told to answer "Pig tail" to every question:

What did you comb your hair with this morning?	(Pig tail.)
Who washed your face this morning?	(Pig tail.)
What are you going to have for dinner?	(Pig tail.)

Smart-Aleck Answers

43. What fer?—Cat fur, to make kitten britches.

44. *Was?—*
En alt fass. Dei naws soll der schtopper sei.
Meini iss grawd,
Deini iss grumm,
Deini gate in alla 'ecka rumm!

What? An old barrel. Your nose shall be the stopper. Mine is straight, but yours is crooked and wanders about all over.

45. *Weescht was?—*
Wann's reert, macht's nass;
Wann's schneet, macht's weiss;
Wann's kisselt, macht's eis.

What? When it rains, it gets wet; when it snows, it gets white; when it hails, there is ice.

46. What did you say?—I don't chew my cabbage twice.

47. What's your name?	Window pane.
Where do you live?	Down the lane.
What do you do?	Teach school.
How many scholars?	Twenty-four.
What do they set on?	Little stools.
What do they look like?	Little fools, just like you.

48. What time is it?—Half past a cat's ass, a quarter to his balls.

Ortsneckereien

49. *Ich bin en Schwoob fun Schwoova-land.*
Ich hab fimf finger an yeedera hand.
Essa un drinka kann ich guut
Un schwetza dunn ich wie's mar kummt.

I am a Swabian and hail from Swabia. I have five fingers on each hand. I am good at eating and drinking and I say just what comes in my head.

50. *Wo reiten sie hin, wo kommen sie her?*
Von Sicksen, von Sachsen
wo die schönen Mädchen wachsch.

78

Hätt ich drau gedacht
Hätt ich mir ein schönes Mädchen mitgebracht.

Where do they ride, where do they come from?
From Sicksen, from Sachsen
Where the beautiful girls are found.
If I had thought of it
I would have brought a beautiful girl along.

51. *Ach, Ballin, du aaremi Schtadt!*
Do hen sie nix zu fresse ass Rockelbrot,
Un sell net halwer satt.

Oh, Berlin, you poor city! There they have nothing to eat except rye bread, and that not half enough.

52. *Du bist furicht mein kind*
Du meis noch Berlin
Wo die furichten sind.
Da geherst du hein.

You are crazy, my child, you must go to Berlin, where the crazy people are. There you must go.

53. *Heidelbarriyer buuva*
Drawga griena reck.
Geena karrassiera;
Ferschteena aw ken dreck.

The boys of Heidelberg Township wear green coats to go courting; they don't know the first thing about making love.

54. *Reading, du awrmi schtatt,*
Drucka broot, un des net satt.
Kutztown, du reichi schtatt,
Jelly broot un allfatt satt.

Reading, you poor place, nothing but dry bread and not enough of it to satisfy. Kutztown, what a princely place: bread with jelly and enough to eat for everybody.

55. *Maxatawny, du eedler fleck,*
Kutztown leit im dreck.
Kercherschteddel desgleicha.
S hot fiel mee awrma drin ass reicha.

Maxatawny, what a princely place. Kutztown is full of mud and so is Hamburg, which has many more poor people than rich.

56. God made the Irish;
He also made the Dutch.
But when he made the Irish,
He didn't make much.

Personal Rhymes

57. *Die Lissie Rebecca*
Schpringt in die hecka
Mit ma groosa schtecka
Far die hawsa ferschrecka.

Lizzie Rebecca runs in the briers with a big stick to scare the rabbits away.

58. *Nau was iss tsu denka*
Fum Solomon Reddich?
So lang er net heiert
Doo iss er noch leddich.

Now what do you think of Solomon Reddich? As long as he doesn't marry, he will stay single.

59. *Hansel von Bach*	Johnny of the brook
Hat lauter gut sach	Has good things plenty,
Hat stiefel und schporra	Has spurs and booth,
Hat alles verlora	Has gone to the duce;
Hat kugele gegusa (gegossen)	Bullets he's molded,
Hat Soldada todt gshusa	Soldiers he's shot,
Hat's Heisle verbrennt	Houses he's burned
Hat lumpa drum g'henkt.	And dresses in rags.

60. *John, John, der Lumbamann*
Schteckt sei naws in die kaffi-kann.
Der kaffi wawr hees,
Der John wawr bees.
John, John, der Lumbamann.

John, the ragman, sticks his nose in the coffee pot. The coffee was hot and John got mad. John, the ragman.

61. *Peder Kutz wū wid du hin,*
Geld du suchscht farrekta ki?
Wan du farrekta ki wid sucha,
Musht du net därt nuffa gukka;
Därt drunna im dem waida ek
Därt lait 'n kū di is farrekt;
Selli kū di hot 'n waiser kop,
Peder Kutz du ârmer drop.

Peter Kutz, where are you going,
Are you hunting for dead cows?
If you wish to search for dead cows
You must not look up that way;
Down there in the willow copse,
There lies a cow that has expired.
That cow has a white head,
Peter Kutz, you miserable fellow.

Nonsense Rhymes

62. *Mariyeds wann ich frie uff-schtee,*
No schau ich noch da wolka.
Mammi iss die supp gekocht
Un iss der bull gemolka?

When I get up very early in the morning I always look up in the sky. I ask my mother whether the soup is ready and whether the bull has been milked.

63. *Alte wind muhl*
geh die strass naus,
Hol die kuh ham,
Trieb die schof naus.
Werst net n'ouf gekratelt
Wer'st net nunta g'falla.
Hets mei Schwester g'heirt
Wer'st mei Schwoger wara.

Old windmill,
go up the road,
bring the cow home,
drive the sheep out.
If you don't climb up
you won't fall down.
If you marry my sister,
you'll be my brother-in-law.

64. *En alti grapp, die wawr so mied*
Un hockt sich uff'n scholla.
So bin ich nau am end fum lied,
Un doo iss nix tsu wolla.

An old crow was so very tired that he sat down upon a clod. And this brings me to the end of my song; there's nothing to do about it either.

65. Stirrum, stirrum with a spoon,
Old women eat a lot.
The young get nothing.
The bread lies in the drawer.
The rooster sits on the roof;
The rooster laughed himself into a hump.

66. *Fadder unser, der du bischt,*
Marriya fawra mar unser mischt.
Ivver-marriya noch en load
No schlagga mar der schimmel doot.

Our Father, that Thou art, tomorrow we'll drive a load of manure out in the field; the following day we'll take another and then we'll club our white horse to death.

67. *Unser Harrgott, wie du bischt.*
Tswae load schtroo macht ae load mischt.
Our Lord, as Thou art, two loads of straw make one load of manure.

Toasts

68. Eat when you're hungry,
Drink when you're dry;
If nobody kills you,
You'll live till you die.

69. *So drink ich, so stink ich;*   If I drink I stink;
drink ich net, so stink ich doch,   If I don't drink I stink anyway,
so ist besser gedrunka und gestunka   So it's better to get drunk and stink
os net gedrunka und gestunka doch.   Than not get drunk and stink
    anyway.

70. Here's to the bull that roams the wood
And does the cows so much good.
If it wouldn't be for him and his big, red rod,
We wouldn't have no beef, by God.

Weather Rhymes

71. *Wann der hawna graet eb er schloofa gaet,*
So raert's em uff der schwantz eb er uff-schtaet.
If a rooster crows before he goes to roost, it will rain on his tail before he wakes.

72. *Dansen in Januar die mucka,*
So muss der bauer noch sei fuuder gucka.
If flies dance in January the farmer must take a look at his fodder.

73. *Wann es gwittert in die darra wald,*
Dann watt's noch sicher kalt.
If there is lightning when the forests are still bare there will follow considerable cold weather.

74. *Ken schnae heifa,*
Ken hoi heifa.
If there are no snow banks in winter there will be no hay piles in summer.

The Zodiac Rhyme

75. *Der widder der staised,* The weather butts;
Die kinner sin base the children are angry;
Der labe, der brilled, the lion roars;
Die woke die gilt. the scales weigh.
Der shits der sheesed, The hunter shoots;
Der wasserman giesed. the waterman pours;
Der fish, der schwimmt, the fish swims;
Der steinbuck springt. the goat leaps.
Der scorpian sticht, The scorpion crawls;
Die yungfrau spricht, the maiden talks;
Der greps, der shot, the crab scratches;
Der ox, der blatt. the ox lows.

Epitaphs

76. *Christian Hebel heise ich* My name is Christian Hebel,
gegen himmel reise ich; I am bound to go to heaven.
ich sage gude nacht I say, "Good night."
Ich folge desen ruhf I follow the call
Der ueber uns alle wacht. of He who watches over all.

Gravestone in the Benders Lutheran Church cemetery, Heidlersburg, Pennsylvania, showing symmetrical, stylized Germanic heart and tulip symbols.

Gravestone in the Benders Lutheran Church cemetery, Adams County, Pennsylvania, portraying a radiant shield at the top and a crescent moon and starbursts to one side.

77. Matilda Brong is my name,
America is my station,
Allentown my dwelling place
And Christ, my salvation.
The rose is red, the grass is green;
The days are past which I have seen.
When I am dead and in my grave,
And all my bones are rotten,
Just look at this and think of me
When I am quite forgotten.

78. *Do leit mei Weib*   Here lies my wife,
Gott Lob und Dank!   Thank and praise God:
Hot lang gelebt   She lived too long
Un fiel getsankt.   And nagged too much!
Mei liewe Leit   My beloved friends,
Geht weck fun hier   Go away from here,
Schun schteht sie uff   Else she'll stand up
Un tsankt mit dir!   And nag you!

79. *Hier liegt ein Kleines Oechselein*   Here lies a little baby Ox
Dem alten Ochs sein soehnelein;   A son of elder Mr. Ox.
Der liebe Gott hat nicht gewollt   The dear Lord did not intend
Dass er ein Ochsen werden sollt.   The child its life as ox should spend.

80. Remember me as you pass by;
As you are now, so once was I.
As I am now, so you must be;
Prepare for death and follow me.

81. The strongest man that ever lived on earth
At last did quietly yeild [sic] up his breath;
This fate is sure to all to you and I
Come then prepare for death before you die.

Graffiti

82. *Solomon, der Weise, spricht:*
Die lauten Furzen stinken nicht,
Aber die Leisen
Die dreimal das Argeloch kreisen.
Behüte dich,
Die stinken fürchtenlich.

Solomon, the wise, spoke: The loud farts don't stink, but the soft, gentle ones cause three times as much mischief. Watch yourself; they stink dreadfully.

83. *Auf diesem Lokus sitzt ein Geist,*
der jedem, der zu lange scheisst,
von hinten in der Eier beisst.

In this place sits a ghost who bites anyone who shits too long from behind on his eggs (testicles).

84. To be is to do—Nietsche.
To do is to be—Hegel.
Do be do be do—Sinatra.

Frau Wirtin Rhymes

85. *Frau Wirtin hatte einen Sohn,*
Der hatt' ein Ding von Eisen;
Um dieses zu beweisen,
Legt' er es auf den Schienenstrang
Und liess den Zug entgleisen.

Frau Wirtin had a son, he had a thing of iron; and to prove that, he laid it on the railroad track and derailed the engine.

86. *Frau Wirtin hatte einen Sohn,*
Der konnt' es mit zwölf Jahren schon:
Er füllt' das Zeug in Flaschen
Und liess zur holden Weihnachtszeit
Die Tanten davon naschen.

Frau Wirtin had a son; he knew how to do it already at twelve years of age. He filled a flask with juice, and during the Christmas season let his aunts all have a taste.

87. *Frau Wirtin hatte 'nen Student*
Der war in furzen ein Talent.
Er furzt' "Die letzte Rose";
Doch als der Sang an Aegir kam
Da schiss er in die Hose.

Frau Wirtin had a student who was a real talent at farting. He farted "The Last Rose of Summer"; however, while he was singing, an impulse came and he shit in his pants.

88. *Frau Wirtin hatte einen Traum.*
Es rannte ein Mann um einen Baum.
Doch wollt' es ihm nicht glücken,
Trotz rasender Geschwindigkeit
Sich selbst im Arsch zu ficken.

Frau Wirtin had a dream. A man ran around a tree. However, no matter how fast he ran, he was not lucky enough to fuck himself in the ass.

89. *Frau Wirtin hat auch eine Magd,*
Die hat noch niemals nein gesagt.
Nur zu dem Fuhrmann Hancke,
Bei dem der Tripper grünlich floss,
Da sagte sie, nein danke!

Frau Wirtin also had a serving maid, who never had said no. Only in the case of sailor Hancke, whose clap flowed green, did she say, "No thank you!"

Miscellaneous

90. *Police, police,*
Schtinka fiess.

Police, police,
Stinky feet.

91. *Wann die hinkel iera oier im fammidawg leega*
Un die weibsleit hossa treega,
Dann will ich nimmi leeva.

When chickens lay eggs in the afternoon and women wear pants, then I don't care to live any longer.

92. *Du bischt der schreiner.*
Du machscht die wieg fer die gleina,
Avver die gleina mach ich.

You are the carpenter. You make the cradle for the little ones, but I make the little ones.

93. *Der Sandman ist da,*
Der Sandman ist da,
Er hat so schoenen weissen Sand,
Drum ist er auch so wohl bekannt!
Der Sandman ist da.

Sandman, Sandman, here comes the Sandman, he has such pretty white sand; that's why he is so well-known. Here comes the Sandman.

94. *Mein Mutter hat gesagt,*
"Heirat keine Bauersmagd,
Heirat eine aus der Stadt,
Die die Tasch' voll Geld hat."

My mother said, "Don't marry a farmer's daughter; marry one from town who has her purse full of money."

95. *Meedel, wann du heiera witt,*
Dann heier du im Moi.
Wann die kascha tseidich sin,
Noo back ich dier en boi.

Maiden, if you wish to get married, marry in May when the cherries are ripe, and then I'll bake you a pie.

96. *Sah ein knab' ein Röslein stehn,*
Röslein auf der Heide,
war so jung und morgenschön,
lief er schnell es wahr zu sehn sah's mit vielen Freuden,
Röslein, Röslein, Röslein, rot,
Röslein auf der Heide.

A boy saw a little rose, a rose in the field. It was young and beautiful like the morning and he ran quickly and saw it with pleasure. Little rose, little rose, little red rose in the field.

97. *Soo duun die bauera buuva un soo dunn sie.*
Sie reita die hivvla uff un ab,
Sie reita da geil ier hels schier ab.

Soo duun die bauera meed un soo duun sie.
Sie grieya en kivvel un melka die kuu,
Sie tsuppa die ditza uff un tsuu.

Soo duun die alta leit un soo duun sie.
Sie grieya en buch un leesa soo schee,
Un Sundawgs geena sie in die gmee.

So do the farmer boys and so do they. They ride up and down the hills; they ride their horses' necks nearly off. So do the farmer girls and so do they. They get a milk pail and milk the cows; they pull the teats up and down. So do the old people and so do they. They get a book and read and on Sunday they go to meeting.

CHAPTER FIVE

Songs

The study of folk music is complicated by the tendency that songs have to move from one culture to another. Academic musicians frequently draw on folk materials for inspiration; popular songs often move into a traditional form known by all and learned by listening rather than from the printed score; and folk performers occasionally borrow a classical or popular tune to set their improvisations against. Collectors of music among ethnic groups quickly discover that their informants are likely to intermingle true folk items like lullabies and playground songs with songs taught in school, which are not truly folkloric because they are learned from print and exist in a single form lacking the variants that generally occur in oral transmission.

Among the eighteenth-century migrants a few traditional folksongs survived transplantation into the New World. However, most of the songs they sang were religious music, usually of literary rather than folk origin. Still, some secular songs persisted into the twentieth century. The Pennsylvania Germans in their everyday music reveal the same earthy humor that was found in medieval German folksongs. A few border on the risqué, but as the singers usually note, they're not really dirty unless you translate them. Some German songs are creations indigenous to the United States, composed about local people or events, but usually set to familiar tunes. Then too, numerous attempts have been made during periods of ethnic enthusiasm to translate or adapt English popular songs to standard or dialectal German. These attempts, though amusing, were not always successful, and few of them have entered the folk tradition.

One curious hybrid is a familiar or newly composed rhyme in

"Dutchified English." These songs are characterized by English words pronounced with a German accent, standard English verb forms with German infinitive and participial affixes, and lots of "mits" and "unds" thrown together with the indiscriminate use of the article "der" for any case and gender. "Dunderbeck's Machine" below is such a song.

Nineteenth-century immigrants often brought with them the type of song associated with German beer-halls and Oktoberfeste. Most of these songs are still to be found in the *Allgemeines Deutsches Kommersbuchen* (student songbooks) published at regular intervals throughout Germany. Singing schools and *Gesangvereine* (singing societies) kept German music alive throughout the regions where these people settled. *Sängerfeste* (singing meets) were frequently organized to raise nationalistic pride and to provide a unifying element for scattered groups of settlers (see LaVern Rippley, 294–96).

German-American music has not been systematically collected or studied. Good collections of Pennsylvania German materials exist— *Songs along the Mahantongo,* edited by Walter Boyer, Albert Buffington, and Don Yoder (Lancaster: Pennsylvania Dutch Folklore Center, 1951; reprint Hatboro: Folklore Associates, 1964); Albert Buffington, *Pennsylvania German Secular Songs,* (Breinigsville, Pa.: Pennsylvania German Society, 1974). Religious music has been examined by Bruno Nettl ("The Hymns of the Amish," *Journal of American Folklore* 70 [1957]: 323–28) and Don Yoder (*Pennsylvania Spirituals* [Lancaster: Pennsylvania Folklife Society, 1961]). Occasional songs appear in local folklore journals and collections like those of Mary Jo Meuser (*German Rhymes and Songs* [Privately printed, 1978]), William A. Owens, (*Texas Folk Songs* [Austin: Texas Folklore Society, 1950]), and Gilbert Jordan (*German Texana* [Austin: Eakin Press, 1980]).

Unlike other aspects of folk culture, folk music is in danger of disappearing in a single generation. If transmission is not continuous, folksongs are quickly forgotten or corrupted. Much German folk music today is already revivalist in nature, learned from printed sources, performed by professional musicians, and taught in a manner unlike that of an aural-oral folk situation. It would be nice to say that this music has been completely collected, transcribed, and recorded and is available permanently for study and research, but such is not the case.

1. *Schlof, Bobbli, Schlof*

a. *Schlof, Bobbeli, schlof,*
Der Daadi hiet die Schof,
Die Mammi hiet die Lemmer,
Schlof en Schtundli lenger.

Sleep, baby, sleep,
Daddy's tending the sheep,
Mamma's tending the !ambs,
Sleep an hour longer.

b. *Bei-o, Bobbeli, schlof,*
Der Daadi holt die Schof,
Die Mammi melkt die Millich Kieh;
Sie kummt net haem bis Marriye frieh!

Bye-o, baby, sleep,
Daddy's tending the sheep,
Mamma milks the milk-cow;
She won't be home until early
    tomorrow.

c. *Schloof, bobbli, schloof,*
Der dawdi hiet die schoof,
Die mammi hockt unnich'm
   hollerschtock
Un macht m bobbli n unnerrock.

Sleep, baby, sleep,
Daddy's tending the sheep,
Mamma sits under an elderbush

And makes her baby a petticoat.

d. *Schlof, Bewi, schlof!*
Der Vadder hiet die Schof,
Die schwaze un die weisse,
Ass sie dich net beisse.

Sleep, baby, sleep!
Father is tending the sheep,
The black ones and the white ones,
So that they don't bite you.

e. *Schloof, kindschen, schloof!*
Drauss geen tswei Schoof,
Eens iss schwarz un eens iss weiss,
Und wann dess kind ket schloofa will
Dann mummt das schwarz und beisst's.
Ssh, schloof, kindschen, schloof!

Sleep, little child, sleep:
Two sheep go outside,
One is black and one is white,
And if this child won't sleep
The black one comes and bites it.
Sleep, little child, sleep!

f. *Schloof, bobbli, schloof.*
Der dawdi hiet die schoof.
Die mammi hiet die darra kie.
Sie bawt im dreck bis an die gnie.
Sie kummt net heem bis mariya frie.
Schloof, bobbli, schloof.

Sleep, baby, sleep.
Daddy's tending the sheep.
Mamma's tending the skinny cows.
She wades in muck up to her knees.
She won't be home until early morn.
Sleep, baby, sleep.

g. *Schloof, bobbli, schloof,*
Die mammi hiet die schoof,
Der dawdi iss uff da glebberyacht
Un kummt net heem bis middernacht.

Sleep, baby, sleep.
Mamma's tending the sheep,
Daddy's off on a gab-fest
And won't be home until midnight.

h. *Schlaf, Kindchen, schlaf,*
Der Vater hut't die Schaf,
Die Mutter schuttelt's Baumelein,
Da fallt herab ein Traumelein;
Schlaf, Kindchen, schlaf.

Sleep, little child, sleep,
The father watches the sheep,
The mother shakes the little tree,
Down there falls a little dream;
Sleep, little child, sleep.

2. Des Bucklich Mennli

Maryets wann ich uff schtee,
Guck ich in die wolka;
Mudder, iss die supp gekocht?
Sin die kie gemolka?

When I get up in the morning,
I look up at the clouds [and say],
"Mother, is the soup ready?
Are the cows milked?"

Wann ich in mei kie-schtall kumm
Far mei kuu tsu melka;
Schteet des bucklich mennli datt
Un fangt aw tsu schelda.

When I enter my cow-stable
To milk my cows,
The little hunchback stands there
And begins to scold.

Wann ich in mei gawrda kumm
Far mei blumma blansa;
Schteet des bucklich mennli datt
Un fangt aw tsu dansa.

When I enter my garden
To plant my flowers,
The little hunchback stands there
And begins to dance.

Wann ich in mei kichli kumm
Far mei essa macha;
Schteet des bucklich mennli datt
Un fangt aw tsu schaffa.

When I enter my kitchen
To make my meal,
The little hunchback stands there
And begins to work.

Wann ich in mei keller kumm	When I enter my cellar
Far mei millich seia;	To strain my milk,
Schteet des bucklich mennli datt	The little hunchback stands there
Un fangt aw tsu geiga.	And begins to fiddle.
Wann ich in mei schpeicher kumm	When I go upstairs
Far mei bett tsu macha;	To make my beds,
Schteet des bucklich mennli datt	The little hunchback stands there
Un fangt aw tsu lacha.	And begins to laugh.
Wann ich in mei schtuvvli kumm	When I enter my room
Far mei schtuvvli keera;	To sweep it out,
Schteet des bucklich mennli datt	The little hunchback stands there
Un fangt aw tsu weera.	And begins to hold me back.

3. Das Mannlein [The Little Man in the Wood]

Ein Mannlein steht im Walde	A little man stands in the wood
Ganz still und stumm.	All still and mute.
Das hat von lauter Purpur	He has a little mantle on,
Ein Mantlein um.	All of bright purple.
Sagt da steht im Wald allein	I saw him standing there alone
Mit dem purpurroten Mantelein?	In the wood with his purple-red cape.

4. Die Frösche

Die Frösche, die Frösche, die sind ein lustig chor,
Die brauchen sich nicht zu kämmen, die haben keine Hoar.
The frogs, the frogs, they are a lusty choir,
They don't have to comb themselves, because they haven't any hair.

5. Du, du, liegst mir im Herzen

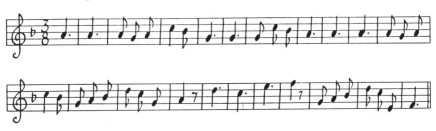

Du, du, liegst mir im Herzen,
Du, du, liegst mir im Sinn.
Du, du, machst mir viel Schmerzen,
Weisst nicht, wie gut ich dir bin.
Ja, ja, ja, ja, weisst nicht, wie gut ich dir bin.

So, so, wie ich dich liebe,
So, so, liebe auch mich.
Die, die, zärtlichsten Triebe.
Fühle ich einzig für dich.
Ja, ja, ja, ja, fühle ich einzig für dich.

Doch, doch, darf ich dir trauen,
Dir, dir mit leichtem Sinn?
Du, du, kannst auf mich bauen,
Weisst ja, wie gut ich dir bin.
Ja, ja, ja, ja, weisst ja, wie gut ich dir bin.

Und, und wenn in der Ferne
Mir, mir dein Bild erscheint,
Dann, dann wünscht ich so gerne,
Dass uns die Liebe vereint.
Ja, ja, ja, ja, dass uns die Liebe vereint.

You, you are in my heart, you, you are in my mind. You don't know how much I love you. Yes, yes, yes, yes, you don't know how much I love you.

So, so, how much I love you, so, so, how much you love me. The tenderest instincts are what I have for you. Yes, yes, yes, yes, what I have only for you.

Still, dare I trust you, you with the fickle mind? You can count on me; you know how much I love you. Yes, yes, yes, yes, you know how much I love you.

And when in the distance your image appears, I wish so willingly that love will unite us. Yes, yes, yes, yes, that love will unite us.

6. *Dunderbeck's Machine*
Der vass a good old German man
His name vass Dunderbeck.

He vass very fond of poodle dogs
And sauerkraut und speck.
He had a great big butcher shop,
Der nicest ever seen.
He got him up a patent
To make sausages by steam.

Chorus: Oh, Mr. Dunderbeck, how could you be so mean?
You'll be sorry you invented dot wonderful machine.
Now pussycats and long-tailed rats
No longer will be seen.
You grind them up to sausage meat,
Mit Dunderbeck's machine.

Von day I vent out valking,
I valked into a store,
I saw a pound of head cheese
Dat vass dancing round der floor.
And vile I dere vass vaiting,
I vistled up a tune;
Dem sausages began to dance
And jump around the room.

Von day dere vass something der matter,
Dat machine it vouldn't go.
Old Dunderbeck he crawled inside
To see vat vass der trouble you know.
His vife she got der nightmare,
Vent valking down the street,
She gave dot crank von awful yank,
And Dunderbeck vass meat.

7. I woke up this morning and looked upon the wall.
The bedbugs and roaches were having a game of ball.
The score was nineteen to twenty; the roaches were ahead.
The bedbugs hit a home run and knocked me out of bed.
I went down to the gas station to get a drink of water,
And out came Sweeney and kicked me in the . . .
Do take care of the bumblebees, for they surely sting.

8. *Kommt ein Vogel Geflogen*

Kommt ein Vogel geflogen,
Setzt sich nieder auf mein'n Fuss,
Hat ein'n Zettel im Schmabel,
Von der Mutt ein'n Gruss.

A bird comes flying,
And it's settling on my leg,
And it has a little letter
Saying hello from my Mom.

9. *Meedli, witt du heiere?*

Meedli, witt du heiere?
Ya, vaader, ya.
Meedli, wann du heiere wett,
Heierscht du en Bauer?
Nee, en Bauer will ich net;
Kiehschtall mischde gleich ich net.
Nee, vaader, nee.

Daughter, will you marry?
Yes, father, yes.
Daughter, when you would marry,
will you marry a farmer?
No, a farmer I will not.
I don't like cleaning stables,
No, father, no.

Meedli, witt du heiere?
Ya, vaader, ya.
Meedli, wann du heiere wett,
Heierscht du en Dockder?
Nee, en Dockder will ich net;
Leit vergifde gleich ich net.
Nee, vaader, nee.

Daughter, will you marry?
Yes, father, yes.
Daughter, when you marry,
will you marry a doctor?
No, a doctor will I not.
I don't like poisoning people,
No, father, no.

Meedli, witt du heiere?
Ya, vaader, ya.
Meedli, wann du heiere wett,
Heierscht du en Schulmeschder?
Nee, en schulmeschder will ich net,
Kinner dresche gleich ich net.
Nee, vaader, nee.

Daughter, will you marry?
Yes, father, yes.
Daughter, when you marry,
Will you marry a schoolteacher?
No, a schoolteacher I will not.
I don't like beating children.
No, father, no.

Meedli, witt du heiere?
Ya, vaader, ya.
Meedli, wann du heiere wett,
Heierscht du en Parre?
Nee, en Parre will ich net,
Windel wesche gleich ich net.
Nee, vaader, nee.

Daughter, will you marry?
Yes, father, yes.
Daughter, when you marry,
Will you marry a preacher?
No, a preacher will I not.
I don't like washing diapers.
No, father, no.

Meedli, witt du heiere?	Daughter, will you marry?
Ya, vaader, ya.	Yes, father, yes.
Meedli, wann du heiere wett,	Daughter, when you marry,
Heierscht du en Loiyer?	Will you marry a lawyer?
Nee, en Loiyer will ich net,	No, a lawyer will I not,
Leit bedriegge gleich ich net.	I don't like cheating people.
Nee, vaader, nee.	No, father, no.
Meedli, witt du heiere?	Daughter, will you marry?
Ya, vaader, ya.	Yes, father, yes.
Meedli, wann du heiere wett,	Daughter, when you marry,
Heierscht du en Geiyer?	Will you marry a fiddler?
Ya, en Geiyer will ich, yo,	Yes, a fiddler, sure I will,
Singe un danze gleich ich so.	I like singing and dancing so.
Ya, vaader, ya!	Yes, father, yes!

10. *Muss I Denn*

Muss i denn, muss i denn zum Städtele naus [Städtele naus],
Und du, mein Schatz, bleibst hier?
Wenn i komm, wenn i komm, wenn i wied'rum komm [wied'rum komm],
Kehr i ein, mein Schatz, bei dir!
Kann i gleich net allweil bei dir sein,
Hab i doch mein Freud an dir.
Wenn i komm, wenn i komm, wenn i, wied'rum komm [wied'rum komm],
Kehr i ein, mein Schatz, bei dir!

Must I leave this town and you, my dear, stay here? When I come back
again, I will stay here with you, my dear. Even though I cannot be with

you just now, I still have joy in loving you. When I come back again, I will stay here with you, my dear.

11. My sweetheart's the mule in the mine,
I can drive him without any line.
On the bumper I stand
Without a sprag in my hand.
My sweetheart's the mule in the mine
I can drive him without any line
Tobacco I spit
All over the mule's behind.

12. *Schpin, Schpin*

Schpin schpin my lieve dochter,
No kauf ich der n frock.
Ya ya my lieve mammi avver ainer mit n sock.
Ich kan nimmi schpinna, my hend g'schwilla immer,
Un oh! sie dien mer so way!

Schpin schpin my lieve dochter,
No kauf ich der n shotz.
Ya ya my lieve mammi avver net zu katz.
Ich kan nimmi schpinna, my hend g'schwilla immer,
Un oh! sie dien mer so way!

Schpin schpin my lieve dochter,
No kauf ich der shoe.
Ya ya my lieve mammi, un bendel datzu.
Ich kan nimmi schpinna, my hend g'schwilla immer,
Un oh! sie dien mer so way!

Schpin schpin my lieve dochter,
No kauf ich der n'hund.
Ya ya my lieve mammi avver net zu rund.
Ich kan nimmi schpinna, my hend g'schwilla immer,
Un oh! sie dien mer so way!

Schpin schpin my lieve dochter,
No kauf ich der n koo.
Ya ya my lieve mammi, un n kivel datzu.
Ich kan nimmi schpinna, my hend g'schwilla immer,
Un oh! sie dien mer so way!

Schpin schpin my lieve dochter,
No kauf ich der n macheen.
Ya ya my lieve mammi, ainy mit gasoline.
Ich kan nimmi schpinna, my hend g'schwilla immer,
Un oh! sie dien mer so way!

Spin, spin, my dear daughter, I'll buy you a dress. Yes, yes, my dear Mommy, but one with a pocket. I can't spin any more, my hand always swells, and, oh! it hurts me so much!
Spin, spin, my dear daughter, I'll buy you an apron. Yes, yes, my dear Mommy, but not too short. I can't spin any more, etc.
Spin, spin, my dear daughter, I'll buy you a shoe. Yes, yes, my dear Mommy, and laces too. I can't spin any more, etc.
Spin, spin, my dear daughter, I'll buy you a hound. Yes, yes, my dear Mommy, but not too round. I can't spin any more, etc.
Spin, spin, my dear daughter, I'll buy you a cow. Yes, yes, my dear Mommy, and a bucket, too. I can't spin any more, etc.
Spin, spin, my, dear daughter, and I'll buy you a machine (car). Yes, yes, my, dear Mommy, one with gasoline. I can't spin any more, my hand always swells, and, oh! it hurts me so much!

13. She promised to meet me at the stockyard seventeen
about three miles out of town,
where the pig ears and pig tails are scattered all around
and the beefsteak is forty cents a pound.
Oh, she's my darling, she's cock-eyed and she's crazy;
people say her teeth are false
just from gargling applesauce.
She's my humpback, consumption, Mary Jane.

14. Tsu Lawderbach

Tsu Lawderbach havvich mei schtrimp ferlora,
Un unna schtrimp kann ich net heem.
Do geen ich dann widder uff Lawderbach tsu,
Un kawf mier'n pawr schtrimp tsu mei been.

Tsu Lawderbach havvich mei hats ferlora,
Un unna hats kann ich net leeva,
Dann geen ich als widder an Lawderbach hie,
Un des meedli muss ieres mier gevva.

In Lauderbach I forgot my sock and without a sock I can't go home. So I'm going back again to Lauderbach to buy a pair of socks for my legs. In Lauderbach I forgot my hat, and without a hat, I cannot live. Then I'm going again to Lauderbach and the girls must give me one.

15. Winterlied

Nach grüner Farb mein Herz verlangt in dieser trüben Zeit.
Der grimmig Winter währt so lang, der Weg ist mir verschneit.
Die sussen Vöglein jung und alt, die hört man lang mit meh;
das tut des argen Winters Gwalt,
der treibt die Vöglein aus dem Wald
mit Reif und kaltem Schnee.

Er macht die bunten Blumlein fahl im Wald und auf der Heid.
Dem Laub und Gras all überall, dem hat er widerseit.
All Freud und Lust wird jetzo feil, die uns der Sommer bringt.
Gott geb dem Sommer Glück und Heil,
der zieht nach Mittentag am Seil,
dass er den Winter zwingt.

My heart longs for the green in this sad time. The grim winter lasts so long and my way is covered with snow. The sweet little birds, young and old, have not been heard for a long time. Thus is winter's power. It drives the little birds from the woods with frost and snow.

It makes the flower's colors fade in the woods and on the meadow. Everywhere it has turned against the leaves and grass. All happiness and desire that the summer brings us is gone. God gave the summer joy and peace, that he brings together at midday and overcomes winter.

CHAPTER SIX

Folk Narrative

German culture has provided the western world with a wealth of folk narrative material. Jacob and Wilhelm Grimm's publication in 1812 and 1815 of their two-volume collection of *Märchen,* which in English are usually called "fairy tales," has influenced children's literature ever since. The publication of the Baron von Münchausen's facetious stories in 1785 affected the development of the tall tale not only in Europe but in the New World as well. And the migration of the character Till Eulenspiegel from the pages of late medieval chapbooks and Renaissance jestbooks into oral literature still leaves its traces in the story repertory of Germans in America well into the twentieth century.

In those social settings in which stories are told, whether around a general store's cracker barrel or during a factory work break, a great variety of narrative forms is included. Some stories are based on fact, while others are obviously jokes that have been circulating for years. Many of the stories are what folklorists call *memorates*—narratives of personal experiences. One result of this is that stories repeated by a narrator are later retold as having happened to him, especially if he is the type of raconteur who localizes his tales to a more familiar setting. In just such ways are legends born.

Legend is akin to myth. It is often the attempt to explain a local custom, phrase, or belief. Narrators of legends usually try to convince their listeners of the truth of what they say, so legend often has a moral to it. By its nature, legend also leads to the development of antilegend, a story which is obviously not true but which makes fun of the legend genre or the seriousness with which people regard legends. Such a tale is

No. 4 below, purportedly explaining why dogs sniff each other. Some antilegends which are true are told to debunk a previously reported legend.

Ghost stories are a form of legend, often attempting to explain why no one lives in a deserted house or giving evidence that there is life after death and punishment for the wrongs done in this life, as in No. 5, "The Ghost and the Drunk," below. Some ghost stories are also antilegends and dwell on the humorous result of mistaking natural events for supernatural occurrences (for example, No. 7 below).

Preacher stories are very popular among German-Americans, not surprisingly, considering the importance of religion in their lives. Some of the stories reflect the affection and fond regard in which the preacher is held, but most dwell on hypocritical or uncharacteristic behavior, as if to remind us that preachers are subject to the same emotions and passions as normal people.

And finally, the joke is a significant narrative form, because it reveals a great deal about the teller and the culture in which he lives. Jokes, psychiatrists tell us, are a way of relieving tension. We joke about things over which we have no control, as an attempt to ascribe some logic to them or perhaps to suggest that they are not really worth worrying about.

Legends

1.   It is said, many years ago there was a countess who lived in the Rhine region. She was a very beautiful maiden, her hair was like gold and came down to the waist.

All men liked to look at her; however, she did not care for any of them. Her only desire was to go to a convent. One day when she arrived at a convent, and asked for reception, the Mother Superior was afraid to take her because of her beauty. She thought the girl might be as sinful as she was beautiful.

The maiden was very sad about it, and did not know what to do. Finally she climbed a mountain called Lorelei; it is very steep, and came right out of the Rhine River. On this place the Rhine is quite narrow, and all the boats which pass there are in danger of being wrecked.

The maiden sat on the cliff day and night combing her hair and singing a lovely song. All the sailors who passed this place looked up to the mountain top to see the beautiful maiden, and they listened to her song. The appearance of the girl and the sound of her voice was like magic to them. They could not turn their eyes away from her, and did not watch out for the dangerous cliff. So it happened that every man met his death where his boat reached this place.

2.   Among the early settlers in that district was a family who had a daughter of about four years of age. As it was in the busy season of hay and harvest, they worked much abroad in the fields. The little girl was in the practice of spending much of her time in play by a copse below the garden daily in fine weather, with a cup of bread and milk. One time as she was staying longer than usual, her father went after her and first observed her there through the branches, at the same time saying, *"Esz auch die brocken"* (Eat the crumbs too). On going nearer he beheld, to his horror, a large black snake taking milk from the cup in his child's hands, who at the same time was repeating, "Esz die brocken," as she was patting the snake's head with the spoon. The anxious parent with a stick finally dispatched the snake. The child with sympathy for the snake said it had often partaken of her bread and milk. Not long after the child became unwell and died, and it became the belief of the neighborhood that fate decreed their lives to be linked together, and that the destruction of the snake involved that of the child. The parents ever after deeply regretted it, and believed the child's death was occasioned by killing the snake.

3. *Why Pigs Have Curly Tails*

Once upon a time there was a very prosperous English farmer who came to America. He had everything he wanted, he had a loving wife, three strong sons, an abundance of land and healthy crops; but he was not happy. The Englishman dreamed of mouthwatering ham and crispy bacon, but there were no domesticated pigs in America—only wild boars. This fact made the Englishman very unhappy and grumpy; because the only thing he thought about were pigs.

One night a fairy came to his bedroom and she granted him one wish, and of course he wished for pigs in America. The fairy was very cunning, and she had grown tired of his constant complainings, so she devised a scheme.

That night as the Englishman lay in bed, he had a sudden craving for corn cobs and garbage. He arose from his sleep, and to his horror his legs were turning pink and he was sprouting bristles. He felt something protruding from his lower back, and to his panic it was a tail about twelve inches long. He tried desparately to rid himself of the tail; he tried pulling, he tried twisting it, finally in desperation he left the tail alone. Due to his twisting and pulling, he was now left with a short curly tail, which was uglier than the original one. The Englishman converted totally into a pig as did his wife. That is how pigs got curly tails, and became a part of America.

The moral of the story is: Be happy with what you have.

4.   Harry Kramer used to tell about the dogs all going into a dog vaudeville show and they had to hang their holes up at the door because they didn't have hats. When they were inside somebody hollered, "Fire," and they all ran out and grabbed a hole without looking. Ever since they go around smelling each other's hole trying to find their own.

Ghost Stories

5. The Ghost and the Drunk

Es hot moll so n fratsicher en eck-schtickel geroppt un hot en weider nivver uff em annera mann sei land gschteckt. Sella weeg hot s iem no en fiel schenner feld gevva, un mee land.

Endlich iss der raugdierrisch no moll ee dawg umkumma. Un glei denooch hot s evva keesa, dass am sellem eck deet's gschpucka. Deel hen geclaimed sie hetta en mann gseena unna kopp un er hett als gsawt, "Wuu soll ich s hie duu, wuu soll ich s hie duu?"

Fiel leit solla s gseena un keert havva, avver sie wawra all ferschrocka un bang. So iss des ding evva fer yawra lang fatt ganga.

Endlich iss no mol kappend ass so n alter saufloodel der weeg kumma iss, un eb er fremm wawr adder im suff, net gwisst hot wuu er iss, avver ennich-how, wie er an den blatz kumma iss, hot des gschpuck evva widder awgfanga, "Wuu soll ich s hie duu, wuu soll ich s hie duu?"

Dann bleibt der saufloodel moll schtee. No sawgt er, "Ei du ferflammter ox, duu es hie wuu du es grickt hoscht."

No hot des gschpuck gsawgt, "Sell sin grawd die watta was ich schunn fer langa yawra am warta bin fer tsu heera. Nau kann ich aw widder ruu griega."

Un sell hot do die gans gschpuckerei gfixt.

Years ago there was a farmer who moved one of his boundary stones a considerable distance on to his neighbor's field. This made his own a much more desirable piece of land, as well as a larger one.

Some time later this same farmer lost his life in an accident. Soon it was rumored that there was a spook haunting the vicinity where the boundary stone had been moved. Some people claimed they saw a man without a head, whenever they passed there at night. The headless man kept asking, "Where shall I put it, where shall I put it?"

Not a few reported seeing and hearing the ghost. But each time the person who saw it was too frightened to think of answering the question. The spook continued to be seen thereabouts for many years.

Finally, one day, a drunkard happened to pass by the place where the boundary stone had been moved. As always, the ghost appeared, mumbling, "Where shall I put it?" Too far gone to be afraid of anything, the drunkard stopped, turned to the apparition and said, "You fool [damned ox], put it where you got it."

"I waited long years for an answer to my question. Now that I have it I'll be able to find peace at last," said the ghost and disappeared. And nobody ever saw the ghost again.

6.   Dad also used to talk about this ancestor of ours, a cousin or something, his name was Poulder Klahn. He thought he could talk to the devil and spirits.

There was a man had a big old house he rented. People were always moving in and moving right back out right away because they said there was a ghost in the house. Old Poulder thought he'd find out who this ghost was, so he took a gun and a bullet that he'd put a dime in, because he thought you could kill ghosts with silver. He went in the house at night and waited. Pretty soon he heard something clanking coming toward him. He told it to stop two or three times and asked who it was. This thing just kept coming so Poulder shot it. It was the landlord. He'd been collecting the rent and then scaring out the people and renting it again.

7a.   There was two fellas, they were out fishin' an' they caught a whole bunch of fish, and on the way home they passed a cemetery. And they had two big fish an' they left them lay at the gate. Left them lay at the gate an' went into the cemetery with the rest of the fish. An' two people come along an' they heard these two fellas in the cemetery dividin' the fish, "One fer me and one fer you; one fer me an' one fer you," till they were done dividin' the fish. Then they said, "Now we'll git them two at the gate." An' the two people at the gate thought it was the Lord and the Devil dividin' and they were comin' to git them.

b.   Some boys stole some hazelnuts one night. They climbed over a cemetery fence when they were running away; and they tore their bags and spilled some. So they decided to sit down and divide them up. They were counting: "One for you and one for me," and then, "Let's get them two outside the fence." Two colored guys were walking home from work at the brickyard and heard them. These guys thought it was ghosts talking and ran like hell.

Märchen

8. *Jorinde and Goringel*

Two lovers who liked to walk in the woods were from a village where many young girls had disappeared. This was presumably the work of an evil witch. One day the couple was on a promenade through the woods on a beautiful spring day. They were so lost in each other that they paid no attention to where they were going. Jorinde said it was time to go home, but they discovered they were lost. They wandered around until dark and then through the trees they saw the walls of an old castle. They saw an owl flying around them and this gave them an evil foreboding. The owl flew into a grove of trees and suddenly the old witch appeared. The couple tried to run but found they were rooted to the spot. The witch dragged the girl away by her hair and the boy could not follow. After the witch disappears the boy is able to move. He looked for a way out of the woods until he drops to sleep under a tree. He dreams of a blue flower which is a powerful, magic flower. The possessor of the flower can destroy evil and overcome obstacles. The boy awakes and searches for such a flower. After three days he finds a meadow like the one in his dream and in the meadow is the blue flower.

The boy returns to the castle and again sees the owl flying. He lifts the blue flower up and the owl screeches and flies away. The boy gets into the castle and finds himself in a huge room, which is crowded with bird cages. He realizes that these are the victims of the witch. The boy looks for his beloved but can't find her. While looking he notices the witch pick up one cage and try to sneak out of the room. The witch is stopped with the flower (he touches the witch with the flower and the witch is turned to stone). He then realizes that this bird must be his girl. He touches the bird with the flower and the enchantment is broken. They fall into each other's arms and then decide to open all the cages and touch all the birds. All the birds are then changed into the missing girls and they all return to the village where there is great rejoicing. The boy is greatly honored by the village and may marry Jorinde and if they haven't died they'll be living today.

9. *Frau Holle*

Once there was a good girl whose mother had died and she lived with a stepmother and stepsister. The good girl was hardworking and industrious, but the stepmother treated her very badly. Finally, the good girl ran away to look for work. By and by she passed an apple tree. The apple tree cried out, "Shake me down, shake me down." She shook the apples from the tree and went on. By and by she passed a baking stove (community baking oven). The bread in the stove cried out, "Let me out. We are baked through." She pulled the bread out of the oven and went on. She came to Frau Holle's house and got a job there. Her job was to keep house and especially to shake the beds out; for Frau Holle was Mother Winter and the shaking of the beds caused the snow.

The good girl stayed for a year and did a good job, but after a year she became homesick and told Frau Holle that she would like to return home. Frau Holle told her that she had been a good worker and would let her go home. Frau Holle also told the girl that she would receive a present but she wouldn't find out what it was until she got home. The girl went home and as she came home, the cock crowed and gold fell all over her. People said, "Here comes Gold Marie."

When the stepmother saw the gold, she wanted her daughter to go and get a job with Frau Holle. So the real daughter, who was lazy, started out to look for work. She also passed the apple tree, but when it cried out to be shook the lazy girl said, "Shake yourself, it's not my business." She went on and when she passed the oven and the bread cried out, the lazy girl said, "It's none of my business. Get yourself out." The lazy girl also got a job with Frau Holle. She worked for a while, but then she got to loafing whenever Frau Holle turned her back.

After a year the girl told Frau Holle that she wanted to go home and she wanted a present. The girl went home and when she got there, the cock crowed and black pitch fell over her. People called her "Tar Girl" and made fun of her.

10. *Cinderella*

I noticed that here in the United States there's a different version of Cinderella than there is in Germany. I won't go through the whole story, but I'll say that the end in German is a little more gory. For instance, the prince and one of his men go and they look to see what young lady will be his wife if her foot fits the shoe. And so he finds one of the stepsisters and she cuts off her heel because she wants to fit into the shoe, and he takes her home on his horse because he didn't realize that he'd been cheated. And on the way the pigeons, or the doves, say, *"Koo koo, kookity*

110

koo, Blut ist im Shue," which means something like "Coo, coo, there's blood in her shoe." So he takes her back and says that just won't do, so he gets the other one, the other stepsister, and she cuts off her toes, and so as the prince is taking her home, the doves again say, "Coo, coo, there's blood in her shoe," and he looks and sure enough, he's been cheated again. So he goes a third time and at last Cinderella has a chance to try on the shoe, and then the story ends just the same way.

11. *Mouse and Sausage*
A mouse being pursued by a cat hid among the sausages. He became good friends with a big frying sausage. They decided to live together and take turns going out to work. The other would stay at home and cook. Time went by. Kale season came along.

One evening the mouse came home from work and smelled such a wonderful meal cooking. It was kale, and the seasoning was delightful. He asked the sausage how she had done it. She told him that she had fried herself a little and then passed herself three times through the kale.

The next day when the sausage came home she found the little mouse sitting by the door all huddled up and red, without any hair. She asked what had happened and the mouse told her that he had passed himself just once through the cooking kale—and look what had happened.

Numskull Tales

12. *Hans in Glück [Lucky Hans]*
Sometimes even today people in Germany will say, *"Er ist der Hans in Glück,"* which means, "He is Hans, the lucky one." But actually this is meant ironically, because the story of Hans goes like this.

One day poor stupid Hans was told by his mother that he must seek his fortune. So he worked for many, many years as an apprentice and later as a craftsman with some man, and, I guess, earned a considerable sum. Finally he decided it was time to go home and make a good life for his mother in her old age.

As he goes along with his huge sackful of gold, a man comes up with a beautiful white horse, and Hans, who has never owned a horse, wants it very much. So he gives him all his gold for this horse, which of course is about twice as much as the horse is worth. But Hans doesn't know how to ride the horse, so he leads him by the bridle, and passes down the road until he comes to a man with a nice, really fine, cow. Hans decides that probably his mother would like a cow better than the horse, so he trades the horse for the cow, again losing somewhat. But the cow proves to be very unmanageable, and he goes further down the road until he meets this man with a very fat hog, which is just as docile as it can be. So he trades the cow for the hog. But then he decides that the hog just smells too bad, and his mother wouldn't like that, and so as he goes down the road he trades the hog for a cat, because he thinks that his mother will probably want a nice pet. As he goes down the road again, he sees a man with a fine white goose, and he thinks of all the times that his mother has wanted a goose dinner and has never been able to have one. So he trades the cat for the goose. As he passes further down the road, some evil man with a beautiful wrapped box comes along and it's so beautiful that he thinks it must hold a great treasure inside, and so he trades the goose for the box. He opens the box, and inside is nothing but a large heavy stone, and he is so angry that he throws it away, so when he comes home, he has nothing after seven years of hard work.

And so, even today, people will say, *"Er ist der Hans in Glück"* (He is the Lucky Hans), and by that they mean that he just can't seem to get along in the world; he's just too generous, I suppose, or too foolish.

13.   There once was a lady who went to Offenbade in Germany. She was walking down the street and all of a sudden a dog started to chase her. While running down the street she saw a rock and bent down to pick it up, but it was stuck in between two cracks and she could not get it loose. With disgust she said, *"Grete grenk."* These are senseless words, but she meant, "You let your dogs run loose, but you keep your stones tied down."

14. *Knows His Drinks*
Es wawr moll en kall fum barrick ass moll ee dawg ins schteddel ganga iss. Er seent en groossi sign ass drauss am weg hengt. Es leest: Billiards and Beer. *Well, er wawr daschdich, so schtoppt er un geet neit.*

"Geb mar en glaws billiards," sawgt er.

"Ei was," sawgt der mann.

Widder sawgt er, "Geb mar n glaws billiards."

Der mann hot moll wennich gedenkt, no iss er hinna naus ganga. Doo wawr n groosser tsuvver wesch-wasser. So grickt er n glawsfoll defun, nemmt es nei in die bier-schtupp un gebt es tsu dem barriyer. Der barriyer dutt's nunner in eem schluck. Er huuscht wennich, guckt der bar-mann aw un sawgt, "Wann ich net n alter billiard saufer weer, dann deet ich ferdeiveltsei sawga, ass sell wesch-wasser wawr!"

112

There was once a fool from the mountain who went into town one day. He saw a big sign that hung outside on the street. It read: **Billiards and Beer**. Well, he was thirsty, so he stopped and went in.

"Give me a glass of billiards," he said.

"Say what?" said the man.

Again he said, "Give me a glass of billiards."

The man thought a little, then he went out back. There was a big tub of wash-water. So he took a glassful from it, put it in a beer-mug and gave it to the mountaineer. The mountaineer drank it down in one swallow. He coughed a little, looked at the barman and said, "If I wasn't an old billiard drinker, then I would sure as the devil say that that was wash-water!"

15.   A schoolmaster in a Lancaster county public school was drilling a class of youngsters in arithmetic. He said to them: "If I cut an apple in two what will the parts be?" "Halves!" was the answer. "If I cut the halves in two what would you call the parts?" "Quarters!" "If I cut the quarters in two, what would the parts be?" Answer (unanimous): *"Snits!"*

16.   This fellow gathered up a bunch of rabbit dirt and he told this other fellow, "They're smart pills." So he bit into one, and said, "You know, I think they're rabbit pellets," and he said, "See, you're gettin' smart."

17.   There once was a rather stupid family who lived in Huenstein, a section of Germany. They lived in a cave. One day they decided to go on a vacation. They didn't want any of their things to be stolen from their cave, so they took the cave door with them thinking that no one could break in if the door wasn't there. Today there is a huge rock in Huenstein that everyone says is the cave door.

18. *The Schwabians and the Town Hall*

When I was a little girl there used to be these stories, and I think they were very old stories, nobody really knows where they came from, of the Schwabians, and I guess the Bavarians looked down on the people of the Black Forest, who were the Schwabians. One story I remember in particular is the story that the townspeople of Schwabia, of some village in Schwabia, were going to build a large town hall, and so they built it, and they didn't put in any windows. So they decided that they had to have some light in it. So they hire all of the men of the village, and they go out in the broad daylight and take these huge sacks with them and catch the sunlight and carry it into the town hall. Well, they work at this for several months and obviously they make no progress, so that's just one of the stories to illustrate the stupidity of the Schwabians.

19. *The Schwabians and the River*

There's another story about the Schwabians. Let me explain first; in Germany the word *wat* means "wade" like wade in a stream, but *wart* means "to wait," and it's also a sound that's attributed to frogs. You know, like we say frogs go "croak," well in Germany the frogs go "wart."

So the Schwabians come to this huge river, and they didn't know how to cross it. It certainly looked deep, but they didn't know, so they decided they'd just wait around and see if anybody in the neighborhood would tell them how deep it was, so they'd know whether or not they could walk across it. So while they're waiting around they hear the frogs say, *"Wart, wart,"* so they think that someone is saying, *"Wat, wat,"* and they say, "Well, if it's not that deep we'll just wade across it, and so they do, only they never get to the other side, and I guess that's just another example of the stupidity of the Schwabians.

20. *Der Babbegoi [The Parrot]*

Es hen moll leit en babbegoi katt, ass arrick guut schwetza hot kenna. So moll ee dawg wawr der babbegoi leenich im haus, un's kummt en mann an die dier un ruuft nei: "Breicht der hols?" Dann secht der babbegoi: "Sure, lawd's ab."

Noo wie der mann s about abgelawda hot katt, is die fraw heem kumma. Noo secht sie: "Ei, mier hen ken hols geaddert."

Noo secht der mann: "Well, ebber hot; ich wawr uscht an de dier un hab gfroogt, eb ich's schtarda hab ablawda."

"So!" sawgt die fraw, "des wawr dann der ferflucht babbegoi, was es geaddert hot."

"Well," secht der mann, "es hot ebber gsawt: 'Sure, lawd's ab.' "

Dann is die fraw ins haus un hot der babbegoi moll gedichdich abgedroscha; noo hot er sich ferschluppt hinnich ebbes.

Noo hot die fraw rawm adder ebbes katt un hot's gschwind uff die bank gschtellt fer noch ebbes schunnscht schnell duu; dann wie sie tsurick kumma is, dann wawr ferhaffdich sei die katz datt draw.

Noo hot sie die katz dann aw noch guut abgegarrebt. Noo hot selli sich aw ferschluppt un is grawd tsum babbegoi kumma.

Dann froogt der babbegoi die katz so gedrooscht-miedich: "Hoscht du aw hols kawft?"

There was once a family with a parrot that could talk rather well. One day, when no one was at home, a man knocked at the door and called: "Do you need any wood?" The parrot answered, "Sure, go ahead and unload it."

Just as the man was about finished unloading it, the woman of the house returned home. She said: "We didn't order any wood."

The man answered: "Well, someone did. I asked at the door and was told to unload it."

"That must have been the damned parrot that ordered it," said the woman.

"Well," said the man, "at any rate, someone said, 'Go ahead and unload it.' "

Angered, the woman went in the house and gave a severe drubbing to the parrot, which then crawled in a corner to hide.

While all this was happening, the cat went and ate the cream which the woman had standing on a bench. And then the cat got a good beating, too. Like the parrot, the cat sought out a corner to pout in, a corner not far from the sulking parrot.

After some minutes of silence, the parrot asked the cat in a very meek voice: "Did you order a load of wood, too?"

21.   My father was a tailor years ago. He used to tell how Eichelspiel called all the tailors together for a conference and he told them, "Now if you don't put a knot in the end of your thread, the first stitch won't be any good."

22. *Eilespigle*

It seems when Eilespigle was a small boy he was very observing, also sometimes very outspoken, and frequently embarrassed his parents. On one occasion the family were having the preacher for Sunday dinner. And the preacher had a very large, protruding nose, which could hardly go unnoticed by anyone.

To avoid embarrassment, the parents warned Eilespigle not to make any remark about the preacher's nose. The dinner was nearly over and all seemed to be going well, when the mother noticed Eilespigle casting sly glances at the preacher's nose and became very uneasy. After a while Eilespigle leaned over to another youngster at the table and said, in Pennsylvania Dutch: *"So'n naws, un mer darf nix sawga"* (Such a nose and one may say nothing about it).

23.   My daddy used t' tell me about a little boy that went t' the store, an' he bought a punkin. An' he didn't know what they were, so the storekeeper told him, he said, "They're mule eggs." So he started home with it,

an' he got to the top of the hill an' set it down, an' it went rollin' down the hill. An' it scared a rabbit out of the brush an' he went runnin' away from 'im, and the boy come runnin' after an' he said, "Hey, stop, here's your mommy."

Tall Tales

24. *Der Warri Mess geet oftmools fischa, avver wie geweenlich fangt er net fiel. Datt hockt er ee dawg an da grick un wawrt uff n beiss. No kummt n mann aus da hecka raus un froogt: "Well, bruuder, wie machscht aus?"*

"Gans guut," sawgt der Warri, "ich hab schunn elf schwatsa bass, tswan-sich sunnafisch, nein katsafisch un ..."

"Halt a mool. Weescht du tsu wem du schwetzscht? Ich bin der fisch-warden."

"Ei, ich bin der greescht liegner in Barricks Kaundi," secht der Warri.

Warri Mess often goes fishing, but he usually doesn't catch much. He's sitting there one day at the creek waiting for a bite when a man comes out of the brush and asked: "Well, brother, how are you making out?"

"Pretty good," said Warri, "I already have eleven black bass, twenty sunfish, nine catfish and ..."

"Wait once. Do you know who you're talking to? I'm the fishwarden."

"Well, I'm the biggest liar in Berks County," says Warri.

25. *The Fog Thickens*
Ae marya letsht wuch bin ich un de arvet. We ich ivver de Konestoga grick bin, hut ebbis my windshield gedruffa. Ich hop gschtuppt tsu gucka un datt licht n grosser katza-fish uff'm fender. Ich hop oom mich room-gegookt. S wawr n shaener mess suckers un katzafish im car. De fish wawra uvvich m wosser un wawra im nevvel um schwimma.

One morning last week I was going to work. While I was crossing the Conestoga creek, something struck my windshield. I stopped to look and there lay a big catfish on the fender. There were a whole mess of suckers and catfish in the car. The fish were out of the water and were swimming around in the fog.

26. I was tellin' them over there at the barber shop. Me and my brothers was huntin' down there at that cabin, an' I dropped a lantern in

the stream. An' when we come back about eleven years later it was still lit, so I got a stick and an' hooked it an' pulled it out. He didn't say anything at first an' then he said, "Well, there must a been a lot a oil in it."

27.   This ol' guy used to rip off s' many lies, and they seen him, he was goin' down the road one day hell-bent for election, an' they said, "Charley," or whatever his name was, "tell us a good one." An' he said, "I ain't got time. There's a fire or an accident down the road and I want a get down there an' watch, or see." So they all jumped in their wagons an' went down there right away, but there wasn't anything. They asked him fer one an' he told them one. That's supposed to be true.

Memorates

28. *Winanosa*
This is an old Pennsylvania Dutch word. My mother-in-law would be in the kitchen cooking and my husband was just a little boy at the time. He and his brother would always ask my mother-in-law what everything was. She got tired of answering him all the time and used the old word "Winanosa," which means "None of your business." Somehow my brother-in-law associated the word with "applesauce" because he asked one day what applesauce was and she said, "Winanosa."

One day their grandparents (not Pennsylvania Dutch) took the two boys out to eat. When Randy was asked what he wanted he said, "Winanosa," meaning "Applesauce." The grandparents, my husband and the waitress all had to go through the whole menu to find out just exactly what the kid wanted.

29. *Kannitverstan*
A German businessman, who knew very little Dutch, went to Amsterdam. The first thing he saw in Amsterdam was a big beautiful house. He asked a passer-by who the house belonged to. The Dutchman understood hardly any German, answered, *"Kannitverstan,"* which literally means, "Can't understand." The German thought that Mr. Kannitverstan must be a mighty wealthy man to own such a beautiful house. Next, he walked to the river and saw a marvelous ship. He asked a man at the pier whose ship that was, and the man replied, *"Kannitverstan."* The German thought that Mr. Kannitverstan must truly be a wealthy man to own such a huge ship and wonderful house. Finally, he saw a funeral procession and asked one of the mourners who the dead man was. His reply was *"Kannitverstan."* Now the German thought to himself that this wealthy Mr. Kannitverstan has the same ending as a poor man like himself.

30.   Two women were driving home from a grocery shopping trip on a narrow winding road. As luck would have it, they got behind a man in a horse and buggy. The pace was unbearably slow, but there was no way to pass him, and he wouldn't pull over to let the women by. Finally, a straight stretch of road appeared. As they passed him, the woman on the passenger's side, now infuriated, rolled down the car window and tossed two eggs at the man. Suddenly, he whipped the horse and began a swift chase after the women. To their amazement, he caught up to the car, pulled up beside it, and yelled, "Fool women! What are you wasting good food like that for?"

31.   Mr. Bull lived near the old post office known as Restmont in Dover Township [York County, Pennsylvania]. Some of his witty sayings have been used many times and a long time since his death. The one used most frequently is, *"Mier vella in's bett, Die leidt vella heem gee"* [We must go to bed, so these people can go home], which he used when his neighbors who paid him a friendly visit during an evening stayed longer than Mr. Bull thought they should.

You can be quite certain that those neighbors did not need a second hint, but that it was time for them to say, "Good night." And that even if the joke was on them, this was too good to be kept to themselves. This technique is used locally, even today when hosts become bored.

Preacher Stories

32. *A Boy's Tears*

A minister in entering a home of a church member heard the wife say, "Here comes the minister. This visit does not suit me at all." She welcomed him, however, and urged him to stay, saying she would prepare a chicken dinner.

He stayed. Dinner came with chicken. On leaving, he passed a boy of the family sitting by a hen coop sobbing and petting a young chicken. To inquiries, the boy replied, *"Ei, des biebli hot ken mam mee; du hoscht sie gfressa far middawg"* (Oh, this baby has no mamma; you ate her for lunch).

33.   One Sunday a minister whose name I do not recall delivered a sermon in the Host Church. During the sermon, he said these words, *"Im mein Fawder's Hausa sin fiela wuuning, wenn es nicht so weer, hett ich es net gsawt"* (In my Father's house are many mansions; if it were not so, I would not have said it).

At that moment a young chap seated on the gallery rose to his feet and said, *"En ferdammti lieg; ich hab dei fadder guut gekennt. Er hot yuscht in so ra alda block-hitt gewuunt"* (That's a damned lie—I knew his father well. He only lived in an old log house).

34.   There was a certain preacher who did not quite satisfy his congregation as to the texts he chose. So his members asked him whether he would deliver a sermon if they would choose a text. He replied that it would be satisfactory to him, and he would preach from whatever text they would choose. The next Sunday he found the Bible on the pulpit opened where the text was written with a slip of paper noting the name of the book with the chapter and verse or verses. He delivered the sermon with satisfaction to his congregation. Then every Sunday thereafter for a long time he had the text chosen and all went well. One time the members agreed not to choose a text and laid the Bible on the pulpit closed.

When the preacher went on the pulpit that Sunday he saw the Book was closed. He opened the lid, paged partly through it, he found no note, and said, *"Hiir ischd nix"* [Here is nothing], turned the Bible around to see if nothing was under it and found nothing, and said, *"Un daw ischd nix; un aus nix hut Gott die Weld arschaffe"* [And there is nothing, and out of nothing God made the world]. He gave them the best sermon that he ever preached from the pulpit.

35. *A Hired Man's Prayer*
This happened many years ago, at a place where they always had some kind of potatoes for their meals. The hired man got tired of this and as luck had the Boss asked the laborer to pray at a meal. He did; this is what he said in German:

Morgiet, grumberia un dee free,
Meddags, grumberia un dee free,
Obets, grumberia un dee s'teit,
Does war't bus in allus aiches keit.

For breakfast, potatoes in the morning,
For dinner, potatoes [again],
For supper, always potatoes,
Always until eternity.

36.   The sainted Rev. Moses Dissinger came to my grandparents' home on a Monday at 11:00 a.m. one time.

Grandmother, busy with her washing, informed Mose that he was welcome to stay for dinner but that she was sorry she had nothing to offer but sour kraut and speck.

Said Mose, *"Aenich epper dass sauergraut net gleicht, sott gawr nix havva un der Mose bleibt fer middawg"* (Anyone that does not like sour kraut shouldn't have anything and Mose is going to stay for dinner).

37.　　*Fritz Reuter kommt an einem Sonntag in ein kleines norddeutsches Dorf und geht in die Kirche. Nach der Predigt geht er zu dem Pastor und sagt: "Es war eine schöne Predigt, aber ich habe zu Hause ein Buch, und in dem Buch steht diese Predigt, Wort für Wort."*

Der Pastor wird rot und sagt: "Es war meine Predigt. Ich habe sie geschrieben. Könnten Sie mir das Buch schicken?"

"Ich schicke es Ihnen morgen," sagt Fritz Reuter.

Am nächsten Tag bekam der Pastor mit der Post ein Wörterbuch.

Fritz Reuter comes on a Sunday to a small north German town and goes in the church. After the sermon, he goes to the preacher and says: "It was a nice sermon, but I have at home a book, and in the book is this sermon, word for word."

The preacher turns red and says: "It was my sermon. I have written it. Can you send me that book?"

"I send it to you tomorrow," says Fritz Reuter.

The next day the preacher received through the mail a dictionary.

38.　　Did you ever hear the joke about the preacher who didn't believe in ghosts and thought his members shouldn't either? He devoted a part of a sermon to arguments against believing in these creatures. To cap the argument he rhetorically asked, "Who ever heard of anyone having intercourse with a ghost?" A little old fellow in the back said he had. "You know of someone who had relations with a *ghost*?" the preacher asked. "Not with a ghost," the fellow said, "I thought you said goat."

39.　　Evangelicals were having a meeting. There was an attractive girl in the audience again and again, but she never came to the mourner's bench. She averred to the young preacher that the spirit just was not moving in her, that there must be something wrong. He said he would fix that. So one evening, Bible in hand, he took the girl for a stroll in the woods area. When they came to a spot distant from the meeting, he placed the Bible on the ground and directed the girl to lie down and put her head on the Bible. Both undressed. He finally addressed her as follows:

The Word of God is under you,
The Son of God is on top of you.
The Gospel Pole is in your hole.
Now work your ass to save your soul.

Jokes

40.   These two fellows, the one chewed tobacco and the other one didn't. He thought it was a waste of money. So they didn't see each other for a good while, ya know, and he met him on the street one day and he said, "Say, do you still chew tobacco?" He said he did. So he said, "You know, if you hadn't chewed tobacco all your life you could own that big building over there." He said, "Which one do you own?"

41.   All the old Germans from the north-east end (of LaSalle) were real good beer-drinkers. They could kill off a barrel in no time, just a few of 'em. I can remember when I was a kid sitting in on some of their card and beer parties so I could be sent for more.
    One time one old man was really soaking it up and the others began kidding him and saying, "Pete, if you drink one more glass beer you're gonna bust."
    But Pete he just grins and says, "So pass the beer and get outta the way."

42.   During World War II, there was a group of German soldiers who'd been stuck in the desert for months and months. They were dirty, filthy, disgusting, 'cause they'd been wearing the same clothes for months and months. One day, the German captain climbed into the bunker and said, "I haf goodt noos undt I haf bad noos. Zee goodt noos . . . vee all get to change clozes today, zee bad noos . . . Hans, you change viss Fritz; Fritz, you change viss Adolf; Adolf, you change viss . . ."

43.   Shortly after one of the wars a girl married a soldier just returned. It was a hurry-up wedding. The morning following the wedding night the mother asked the girl how she fared with her husband (sexually, she meant of course). The girl cried, "Oh mother, he's got only one foot."

"Daughter," replied the mother, "you're well off. Your father only had six inches."

44.   *En Zebra is mool aus em zuu gebrucha un is in en scheierhoof kumme un hut en hinkl oo gedruffe. Noo saagdt da Zebra tsum hinkl, "Was bischd duu?" "Ich bin en hinkl." "Was duuschd duu?" "Ich leeg oier." Noo kumpd da Zebra tsuerre koo, un frookd, "Was bischd duu?" "Ich bin en koo." "Was duuschd duu?" "Ich geb millich." Es neegschd dreft aar en bull oo, un frookd, "Was bischd duu?" "Ich bin en bull." "Was duuschd duu?" Saagd da bull, "Nem dei schdreeffi pajamas ab, noo weis ich der was ich duu!"*

A zebra has gotten out of a zoo and is in the barnyard where he came upon a hen. So the zebra said to the hen, "What are you?" "I'm a hen." "What do you do?" "I lay eggs." So he came to the cow and asked, "What are you?" "I'm a cow." "What do you do?" "I give milk." He was curious about the bull and asked, "What are you?" "I'm a bull." "What do you do?" "Take those striped pajamas off, and I'll show you what I do!"

45.   An elderly couple were out on their farm one day. It was the same place where they had spent their courtship days. The two said, "Let's try to compare then and now." The husband finally volunteered, "Well, Mary, *sell tseit havvich mei bibber unnich der riggel duu missa, so ass er mer net ins gsicht gschlagga hot; net muss ich n uff der riggel leega, so ass er net uff die schtiffel seecht"* (That time I had my peter under the rail to keep from wetting my face; now I must lay it over the rail to keep from wetting my boots).

46.   *Ein alternder General lebt mit seiner jungen Frau in einer einsamen Villa. Vor dem Haus sind zwei Wachposten postiert, die das Paar vor Eindringlingen schützen sollen. Eines Abends brennt im Schlafzimmer verdächtig lange Licht. Die Wachposten sind beunruhigt, schleichen sich an das Fenster und schauen vorsichtig hinein. Da sehen sie die Frau des Generals nackt auf dem Bett liegen, während er, ebenfalls unbekleidet, mit einer Pistole in der Hand herumläuft, an seinem Körper herabblickend und brüllt: "Stehen bleiben oder ich schiesse."*

An aging general lives with his young wife in a lonely villa. In front of the house two guards are posted, who are supposed to protect the pair of them from intruders. One evening the light burns suspiciously long in the bedroom. The guards are disturbed, so they slip up to the window and look cautiously inside. There they see the general's wife lying naked on the bed, while he, likewise undressed, with a pistol in his hand, is running around, looking down at himself and shouting, "Stand or I shoot."

47.   There was a government official came up here from Washington during the war and he saw some goats, but he'd never seen any before so he called up Washington and said, "I ran into some things here that have beards, hard heads and stink. What should I do?" And they told him, "Let them alone! They're Amish."

48.   The difference between a High and a Low German is the Low German lets his kids play with Polacks.

49.   Churchill, Roosevelt, and Stalin were holding an international conference when a thunderstorm came up and they had to take refuge in a pigpen. After an hour, Roosevelt says, "I can't stand this any more," and he comes out. After another hour, Churchill says, "I can't stand this any more," and he comes out. After another hour, the pig comes out.

50.   Didn't I ever tell you that joke? It's told all over Germany. There's a big dance and the mayor's daughter is there. She's a real cutie, so everyone wants to dance with her. One fellow says, "Did you dance with the mayor's daughter?" And the other says, *Das Schwein habe ich noch nicht gehabt"* (That luck [pig] I haven't had yet).

CHAPTER SEVEN

Games

The role of games in the life of children has changed considerably in the past generation. Once an essential part of the educational and social process, the game is now an incidental form of entertainment. This change is largely the result of the disappearance of the one-room school, where recess provided an opportunity for children of various ages to learn the community's games in a traditional setting. Most of the games recorded here were learned in such an environment, and the informants who remembered them recalled nostalgically how much fun they were.

With the consolidation of small schools into larger, supposedly more efficient units, the child's life is more highly regimented, the games played are organized sports taught from rule books by professional game-players, and the toys used come from stores rather than from the child's imagination. Simon Bronner recently noted that "companies . . . attempt to control the material culture of children and discourage the supposedly jerrybuilt folk culture. Often, folk products like the stickball bat, go-cart, and wooden puzzle are usurped and repackaged. The stickball bat I made as a kid out of an old broom now sells for $12.95 and comes in 'official' and 'professional' models" (*Grasping Things* [Lexington: University Press of Kentucky, 1986], 90). Even the child's leisure-time activities are related to the electronic medium and its adjuncts, the computer-game and the television-inspired toy. This may be an improvement over "the good old days," but the repertory of games that today's child plays pales by comparison with the long lists remembered by his ancestors.

The function of games in the German-American culture has not been well examined. William W. Newell mentioned a few games in his pioneering collection *Games and Songs of American Children* (New York: Harper, 1883). A few regional collections exist, mostly of Pennsylvania German games: Morton L. Montgomery's scrapbook of games played in Berks County, Pennsylvania, in the 1850s; Ely J. Smith's "Games and Plays of Children" and A. Eugene Laatz's "German Games and Plays" (*Bucks County Historical Society Papers* 4 [1917]: 1–6, 30–34); George L. Moore's "My Childhood Games" (*Pennsylvania Folklife* 13.4 [1964]: 42–57); and Paul R. Wieand's *Outdoor Games of the Pennsylvania Germans* (Plymouth Meeting: Mrs. C. Naaman Keyser, 1950). Julia Estill collected "Children's Games" in Fredericksburg, Texas (*The Sky Is my Tipi,* ed. Mody C. Boatright [Dallas: Southern Methodist University Press, 1966], 231–36), and Gilbert C. Kettelkamp published a collection of "Country School Games of the Past" (*MidAmerica Folklore* 8 [1981], 113–23), compiled among Germans of south-central Illinois.

Any attempt to classify games must be of necessity arbitrary. The present collection does not constitute a large enough body of material to arrange in any significant manner, so the games are listed alphabetically in three groupings: games played primarily by young children in playground settings, games played by children and adults in party situations, and tricks or pranks played primarily by adults. Even then, many of the tricks are obviously party games. Some games have a strictly seasonal association and are discussed in the appropriate section of the next chapter.

Playground Games

1. Anty-Over
Two teams are chosen and stand on opposite sides of a building, such as a schoolhouse. One team throws a ball over the roof and if someone on the other team catches it, he can run around the building and hit one of the opposite team with it. Anyone so hit changes teams, and the game continues until one team is depleted.

2. Baking Bread (Broot Backa)
Baking Bread is a game for little children. Two of the taller ones are the bakers; the rest are the bread and sit in a line with their hands clasped under their knees. The bakers then put salt and pepper on the bread, using one fist to represent the shaker and the other to tap the shaker. The

bakers then walk a short distance away while the bread bakes. If they go too far the bread burns and hisses and the bakers come running back to see how many loaves are baked.

They test the bread by pushing the index finger against the forehead of the bread. If they are baked, they fall over, and if not, they remain in the same position. The baked bread is tested to see if it is sweet or sour. As the bread clasps hands beneath its thighs, the bakers swing it by the arms, saying, "Slop barrel, slop barrel, you go into the slop barrel," if the bread laughs, or "You go into the sugar barrel" if the bread keeps a sober face. The game continues until all the bread is baked and tested.

3. Bean Bag (Boona-sock)

All the players sit on a long bench, as close together as possible, with their hands behind their backs. We had a cloth bag holding perhaps a half-pound of dried lima beans. The bean bag was passed from one to another and the object was for the one who was It to retrieve it by feeling along each person. If he got the bag he took the place of the one who held it, who in turn became It. The fun of the game was if you were maybe two or three away from the fellow who had the bag, and he would give you a resounding whack on the seat. This would also give you a clue as to where the bag was.

4. Blummsack

A large knot was tied into the closed end of a two-bushel grain sack. The players then knelt closely at a long bench facing the blackboard. The socker (the one who was It) tossed the bag to the players, then faced in the opposite direction and counted to fifty aloud, while the players shifted the bag from one to another. After the count the socker came up right behind the bench and tried to discover who had the bag, which was supposed to be kept in motion. If he chose correctly, the one who had the bag was obliged to hand it to the socker, who took a hefty swing and socked him on the rear end with the knot. The one who was socked was out of the game. If the socker guessed wrong, then that player became the socker and the original socker took his place at the bench.

5. Corner Ball

In corner ball, four boys would station themselves at equal distances from each other, two on one side of the street and two on the other. Our ball ground was almost entirely on the street. Then we would throw the ball around from one to the other, either to the right or to the left. Sometimes we would pretend to throw one way and then suddenly throw another, to try to catch one napping. We generally started slowly, and wound up by throwing as rapidly as we could. Frequently we had a fifth player, who took to the street to run after a "fly" ball. If anyone missed a catch or threw a bad ball he had to take the street.

6. *Crack the Whip (Schwinge)*

A common game with the boys in the evening was "crack the whip." Any number of boys would take hold of each other's hands, generally six or eight, and stand in a row across the street, then the leader would start running and the others would follow for a short distance, twenty or thirty feet, when he would describe a short curve quickly and the last boy in the row would have to stretch his steps to keep up, or go sprawling in the street. By anticipating the curve and hugging the row towards the leader he could overcome the motion to a considerable extent. Each boy would take a turnabout as a leader, and in this way each one became the "cracker" at the end.

7. *Dollar, Dollar*

This is a guessing game in which a silver dollar is passed from hand to hand, accompanied by the singing of:

Dawler, dawler, du musscht wandeln	Dollar, dollar, you must wander
Fon einer bis tsum andern.	from one to the next.
Ei, das weer doch gawr nicht scheen	It isn't pleasant
Kann man dich nicht sehen.	not to see you.

8. *Donkey-on-the-Rock*

A group of six or seven players is the ideal number for a lively and interesting game. It is played on an area about the size of a tennis court. In the center of this playing area is placed a stump or a large stone about twelve inches high with a flat top.

Each player must possess a rock about the size of an orange. One player is chosen from the group to act as the Donkey. He places his rock, which is the target, on the stump and stands aside. The others stand about fifty feet from the target. It is their objective to knock the target off the stump by tossing their rocks at it, in order that they may return to the starting line. After this is attempted and if no one has succeeded in doing so, the Donkey has the privilege of giving a penalty to each unsuccessful player.

Two of the penalties which may be imposed are balancing the rock on the head or balancing it on the back of the hand with arms extended until the player reaches the starting line. Other penalties may be used, but these two are the most common. The first player that fails to carry out the penalty becomes the Donkey, unless he is able to "chance a steal" by running to the starting line with his rock without being tagged by the Donkey.

9. Don't Got None
One child is Witch and one child is Mother. All the other children are her children. Mother gives each child the name of a color. Mother goes away.

Witch comes in and calls out the name of a color. Then Witch takes child who has that color name and child goes to Witch's house.

Mother comes back and says, "Where's my child?"

Children yell, "The witch took her." Mother spanks them all.

This is repeated until the witch has taken all the children.

After all the children are gone the Mother goes to the witch's house and says, "Where are my children? I'll spit on your floor if you don't tell me where my missing children are."

Witch says, "At Mississippi" (or any place).

Mother goes and looks, then comes to Witch again and says, "They aren't there."

This is repeated many times (different place mentioned each time), then Mother spits on the witch's floor.

Witch says, "Wipe it up with . . ." this, that and the other thing. At each thing the witch says to wipe it up with, the mother says, "Don't got none." Finally the witch mentions something the mother has, like feet. Then the mother wipes it up. Then all the children come running out.

10. Hat Ball
The players place their hats in a row, and the one who is It drops a ball into one of them. Everyone runs except the player whose hat that is. He must quickly pick up the ball and try to hit one of the other players with it. The one who is hit becomes the It player for the next round.

11. Hawk and Hen (Gluck un Hinkelwoi)
One child is the *Gluck* (Mother Hen) and one is the *Hinkelwoi* (Chicken Hawk). The rest are baby chicks, and all stand in a circle around the Hawk, who is digging in the ground. A dialogue ensues:

Gluck: Hinkelwoi, was grawbscht du so?	Chickenhawk, what are you digging for?
Hinkelwoi: Noodel sucha.	Looking for needles.

Gluck: Was witt mit da noodel?	What do you want with the needles?
Hinkelwoi: En sack macha.	To make a sack.
Gluck: Was witt mit em sack?	What do you want with a sack?
Hinkelwoi: Koola nei duu.	To put coal in.
Gluck: Was witt mit da koola?	What do you want with the coal?
Hinkelwoi: Feier macha.	To make fire.
Gluck: Was witt mit em feier?	What do you want with a fire?
Hinkelwoi: Kochich wasser macha.	To boil water.
Gluck: Was witt mit em kochicha wasser?	What do you want boiling water for?
Hinkelwoi: Hinkel briea.	Chicken soup.
Gluck: Fun wem seina?	From whom are you getting them?
Hinkelwoi: Fun deina!	From yours.

The hawk jumps up and the chickens all "fly away" as he tries to catch them.

12. *Hul Gul*
A guessing game. A child would place a certain number of kernels of corn in her hands, which were shut, and the others had to guess the correct number. The person holding the corn would say: *"Holli, golli, handfoll. Wie fiel?"* (Hul gul, handful. How many?)

13. *Knitting Needles (Strick-Noodla)*
Each child provides himself with a piece of wood the length of a knitting needle. One of the children, who is It, digs a hole with his stick, while the others circle around him.

One by one the children ask the one who is It: *"Woi, woi, was grawbsch-da?"* (Hawk, hawk, what are you digging?). The one digging answers, *"Strick Noodla."* Then comes the question: *"Iss des sie?"* (Is this it?).

The answer is "No" each time until the last of the participants puts the question, when the answer is "Yes." At this point the one who is It jumps up and the rest of the game is tag.

The one tagged becomes It and the game starts anew.

14. *Leapfrog (Grutte Hupse)*
Each player takes a turn kneeling, or crouching in a hands-on-knees position, while another vaults over him by placing hands on his back and pushing forward. The leaper then takes up the same position and becomes a base for others to leap over.

15. *Little Boy Game (Buuvli, Buuvli Schpiela)*
Boys and girls were seated in a row. When the game began, one said, *"Ich*

root's eerscht" (I root first). The one who was It then said to the first player, *"Buuvli, buuvli, wuu kumscht du her?"* (Little boy, little boy, where do you come from?). The child seated answered, *"Aus Six'n Sax'n wuu die gleena beesa buuva aus da hoola beem schluppa"* (From Sixon Saxon where the little angry boys come crawling out of their hollows). The one who was It then asked, *"Was iss dei handwarrick?"* (What is your job?). The first seated child answered, *"Eenich-ebbes"* (Anything). The one It said, *"Well schaff's emoll"* (Well, work once). Then the one seated, or as many as needed, got up and pantomimed a job. It was then It's duty to guess the job. If he guessed correctly, the other one became It and the game continued afresh.

16. *Little Sheep (Scheefli)*
Usually there were five of us playing. One was the Buyer. The rest were lined up, one in front of the other.

Buyer (to first in line): *"Wuu iss die mammi?"* (Where is your mother?)
Answer: *"Hinna draw"* (Behind me).
And so on to the last one, then—

Buyer: *"Wuu iss die mammi?"*
Mammi: *"Ich bin sie"* (I am it).
Buyer: *"Ich hett gern n scheefli"* (I'd like a little sheep).
Mammi: *"Du hoscht heit un geschter eens katt"* (You had one yesterday and one today).
Buyer: *"Siss in der brunna gfalla un hot blitsch-blatsch gmacht wie n alder schpiel-lumba"* (It fell in the well and went splish-splash, just like an old dishrag).
Mammi: *"Dann nemm eens, avver net s schenscht"* (Then take one, but don't take the prettiest one).

He takes the first one and murmurs to himself: *"Hunnert dausend dawler"* (Hundred thousand dollars).

Buyer (to Lamb): *"Was hoscht gessa?"* (What did you eat?)
Lamb: *"Brunna gressa"* (Watercress).
Buyer: *"Was hoscht gedrunka?"* (What did you drink?)
Lamb: *"Feier funka"* (Sparks).
Buyer: *"Gee drei mool rum unni glacht; wann'd lachscht, bisht n schoof-bock"* (Go around three times without laughing; if you laugh you are a ram).

The Buyer swung us around and usually we laughed because it was fun to be a *Schoofbock* and butt him with our heads.

17. *Long Bullet*

Long Bullet was a pastime amusement fifty years ago. My father had three or four balls weighing from a pound to two and a half (cast for artillery purposes). My brother was fond of athletic amusements, and exceeded all others I have ever seen throw them.

18. *Nipsi*

A nipsi was a piece of wood, about six inches long (usually four-sided, sometimes round) with pointed ends. On each of the four sides was cut a Roman numeral, I, II, III, IV, respectively. [In some versions, X replaced the IV, and represented an automatic "out."]

The game was played as follows: One drew a line, the base, and about 25 feet distant a circle about two feet in diameter. The object was to throw the nipsi in the circle (if it fell outside, one was out) and then with a flat bat to hit it as far away from the circle as possible. One batted the nipsi as many times as the Roman numeral which showed on the side of the nipsi in the circle facing the player. If one's opponent succeeded in catching the nipsi in the air, one was out. When the nipsi had finally been batted the full number of times, the player at bat calculated how many jumps he could safely add to his score. This number he then announced. If the opponent thought he could jump the distance from the nipsi to the circle in the number of jumps the player at bat had hit, he attempted to jump it. If successful, he added the number to his own score. If not, the player at bat had the number to add to his score.

19. *Pig Ball (Sei Balla)*

You would make a large hole in the center. Then there were small holes drilled around the outside of the center hole for all the players except one. I do not know the exact distance from the center hole, but I think around fifteen feet. Then you had a wooden ball or one made of old strings bound with leather. This ball was called the *sau* (pig).

When the game started, all players would put their sticks in the center hole and go around in a circle and sing, *"Riera, riara, loch."* As soon as the leader would call out *"Loch"* (hole), all players would run for a hole and thrust their stick in it. The fellow who was minus a hole had to drive the sau with his stick. When he got near the center hole, some player or other would try to hit it away from the hole. But if he was not quick enough to go back and claim his hole, the driver would have it. The object of the game was to get the pig into the hole and if it was hit away, then you would try to steal another fellow's hole. When the driver was successful, you would start again in the center.

20. *Piling Higher Game (Heifli greeser schpiela)*
Played by children from two to ten. They would climb on all fours and one would climb on back of the next and so on.

21. *Ring, Ring (Ringlein, Ringlein)*
They would stand in a circle each taking hold of a string that went all the way around the circle. One person would stand in the middle. On the string was a ring, and the children would slide it from one person to another. Then they would sing the following song. When the song ended, the person who had the ring had to stand in the middle and they would start over again.

Ringlein Ringlein	Ring Ring,
Du musst wandern	You must wander
Von den Einen	From one
Zu dem Andern.	To another.
Das ist freilich,	That is happy,
Das ist schön;	That is good;
Ringlein, Ringlein,	Ring, Ring,
Du musst stehen.	You must stay.

22. *Sheep, Sheep, Come Home!*
a.   One of the games played about sixty years ago was one which involved a "bear" running after the "sheep." It has a long dialogue in which someone calls out, "Sheep, sheep, come home!" "We cannot," answer the sheep. "Why not?" And they answer, "A big bear is behind the bush." "What does he eat?" "Green grass." "What does he drink?" "Pure water." And again, "Sheep, sheep, come home," is called out, whereupon they all run from their places, and the bear runs after them and tries to catch one.

b.   We formed a large circle, holding hands, and one of the group was the bear, and as he kept walking around the circle we kept reciting: *"Was dribbled and drobbled my heisley room?"* (What is walking around my home?) The bear answered: *"An grosser, schwartzer bear!"* (A great, big bear.) Then we recited: *"Nem kens fun meina shafelen"* (Take none of my sheep). And the bear answered: *"Ich du net!"* (I won't). At that instant, he took one out of the circle, which closed up again, and the same thing was said over until every sheep was "stolen."

23. *Snapping Toads (Grotta Schneppa)*

A heavy piece of wood was laid on the ground and a flat piece laid across, one end long, the other only a short extension. A stone, supposed to be a toad, was laid on the short end. The long end was hit with a sledge or club. Who can make the toad hop the longest distance?

24. *Wall Ball (Up Balla)*

One fellow threw the ball against a wall. The one that caught the ball could throw the ball the next time. To catch the ball on the first bounce was a fair catch. The game was to play the game fast and see who got the ball the oftenest. Sometimes sides were chosen to see which side could grab the ball the oftenest.

Indoor or Party Games

25. *Cat's Head (Katzakopp)*

You drew a circle, cut it in quarters and then erased the line of one of the quarters. You then had a figure that looked like this:

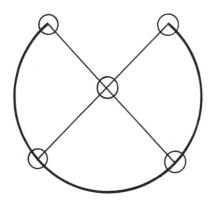

Two children, each of whom had two kernels of corn (of varying colors, of course) played the game. You began by placing your kernels one at a time [on the circles]. When the four "men" were placed you moved about [along the lines] until one player had the other in a position where he could not move any more. That was the end of the game.

26.

a. *Cow's Tail (Kie-Schwans)*

Dominoes are placed face down in the center of the table. After they have been well shuffled, each player takes five and turns them up so that he alone can see them.

The holder of the highest double lays it down in the center of the table and the playing commences, proceeding to the left of the first player. Each one in turn lays a domino with a corresponding number against that of the previous player. The doubles are played lengthwise. The domino next to the double is laid widthwise.

The player can play his domino against either of the sides of the number, thus enabling the lines to be turned instead of continuing on in a straight line. From this turning is derived the name *kie-schwans*.

If one of the players finds himself without a domino which will fit, he must draw from the "pot" until he finds one he can play. He must of course keep all he draws. If the "pot" gets empty before an appropriate domino is found, the player loses his turn. Play continues until one of the players plays the last domino in his hand. He is the winner.

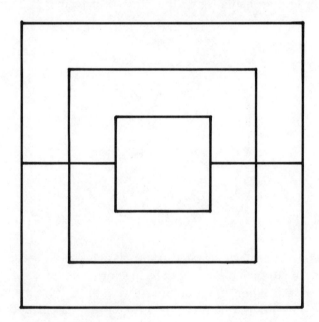

b. *Figmill (Fickmiel)*

Take any good-sized piece of cardboard and draw the figure above. There are two players. Each one gets nine checkers. The object of the game is to get three checkers in a row, whereupon you can take away one of your opponent's checkers. To begin the game, each takes a turn laying the checkers on the board one by one. You may even take away the other man's checker if you shrewdly lay down three in a row without his seeing it. At each turn you may slide a checker from one intersection of lines to the next.

When any man gets down to only three checkers, he has the privilege of jumping from any point on the board to any other point. But if his opponent gets three in a row, he takes all three of the other man's checkers in one sweep. The winner is the one with some number of checkers left.

28. *Kissing Game*

O once there was a jolly, jolly boy
Who safely came on shore.
He spent his days in many, many ways
But he shall do it no more.

As he goes round this merry, merry world,
As he goes round once more,
And if he meets a pretty, pretty maid
He may kiss her on the floor.

29. *Little Fish in the Pond (Fischlein in den Teich)*

You have a long string with a big loop in the middle of the table. And then all the kids who sit around the table have to put their finger, their index finger, in the loop. And I say, *"Fischlein in den Teich,"* and they all put their finger in, and then I say, *"Fischlein aus* [out of] *den Teich,"* and then I pull in the string, you know, when I say, "Out of the pond," hard in the string, and the one who is not fast enough gets caught with the finger, string on the finger, has to be out of the game. So you go on, play it again till everybody is out of the game. The last one who is not caught is the winner.

Handmade pegboard game from Fry family, Cumberland County, Pennsylvania, 1979. (10½" x 11) (Author's collection)

30. Pegboard (Tseppli-board)

Thirty-six holes are drilled into a board in a symmetrical cross-shape. Then a peg is placed in each hole except the center one. The object of the game is to remove all the pegs by jumping each in turn until the last peg winds up in the center hole.

31. Post Office

This was played at church socials. All forms of mail, and parcel posts, were delivered in an unlit room! The girl(s) would name the item: letter, special delivery, parcel, freight, etc., and that meant variously a swift kiss, a kiss with a tongue, a long heavy kiss, or sit on the lap and kiss. (Some guys were a long time picking up their mail.) Age limits were eight, nine, ten.

32. *Bump in the Hole (Bump ins Loch)*

On a night when the moon was shining some fellows would prepare a nest, put a fresh *kie-dreck* (cow-turd) in the nest and cover it over with straw. The fun was to get the unwitting fellow to strike with his fist with all his main into the nest. Frequently he would be covered with kie-dreck as a result.

33. *Monkey Game*

It takes an innocent person, someone who has never played the game before. Two play the game. Each gets a saucer. The innocent stays in room while the other person goes in another room and burns the bottom of the saucer black [over a candle or kerosene lamp]. Then that person returns to the room and says the other must imitate him. He rubs the bottom of his saucer with his finger and rubs it from his forehead to his chin, down the right and left cheek, across the upper lip, and across the chin. Then the innocent person is told to look in a mirror and he would see a monkey.

34. *Shoemaker (Schuu flicka)*

A kitchen chair was laid on the floor with the back in the air or up. The "shoemaker" sat on the bottom part of the chair and the other whose shoes were to be mended sat on the back of the chair. The latter raised his leg for the "shoemaker" to hammer on a sole. Then the "shoemaker" would get up and the chair, of course, toppled over and the victim fell to the floor.

35. *Snipe Hunting (Elbedritsche Fange)*

A greenhorn is asked to participate in hunting *Elbedritsche,* described as a rare animal whose pelt is very valuable. He is told to sit with an empty bag at one end of a field, usually on an extremely cold night, while the others pretend to go around the field and drive the creature into his bag. They of course go home and leave the poor dupe there holding the bag.

36. *Stars up a Coat-sleeve*

They used t' play tricks on guys that didn't know any better. They'd say, "Ya wanta see stars?" An' they'd git him t' look up a coat-sleeve, git two guys to hold up the coat-sleeve, and he'd git down to look up the coat-sleeve and they'd have a cup of water, they'd pour a cup of water down on 'im.

37. *Wiping Up the Water (Wie mer s bescht wasser uff-butzt)*
You have the person who is It sit down on the floor, with legs stretched
out. You give him a fork in each hand and pour a little water between his
legs. When he begins to defend himself, you take hold of his legs and
pull him on his rear end through the water. That cleans it up!

CHAPTER EIGHT

Customs

Customary behavior is the result of one's ethnic background, family environment, and cultural development. The manner of walking, dressing, and eating within a given community will differ slightly from the same behavior in an ethnically or culturally different group. Personal or idiosyncratic behavior will generally have meaning only to persons close to the individual in question, but culture-induced customs have significance for all members of the contiguous culture group who are able to interpret the underlying meaning of a social act or its absence. Occasionally an overt violation of the norms of social behavior becomes semiotic, in that it is symbolically expressive of the actor's attitudes or opinions.

Many of the folk customs retained by the Germans in the New World can be traced to their region of ancestral origin. Such customs, which often have a religious association, are a means of maintaining cultural ties with those left behind or with others who have migrated to the same or adjacent areas. Naturally on holidays and other special occasions, memory recalls similar past occurrences and nostalgia strives to recreate them. So it is that holiday celebrations maintain their traditional form longer than other elements of social culture. Foodways associated with those holidays are revived, and then, if ever, folk costumes are likely to be brought forth and worn.

1. *New Year's Day*
Traditional celebration of New Year's Day among Germans wherever they settled involves visiting from house to house, reciting wishes for the

New Year, and shooting guns:

> *The old custom is to meet at a certain house some time during the evening preceding the coming of the New Year, pass away their time as may seem most pleasant to them, some relating stories, some playing innocent games . . . until the last minute of the old year had passed, when all start out with guns, revolvers, pistols and ammunition, and one or more violins.*
>
> *Arriving at the house of a friend, someone calls his name, and on receiving a reply, a hymn—"Das alte Jahr vergangen ist," or "Das neugeborne Kinderlein"—is sung, after which someone designated by the party recites a long rhyme on wishing. This over, each one in succession discharges his weapon, and is then invited into the house to partake of refreshments, such as are provided.*
>
> *After an interchange of the compliments of the season, the party leaves for their next place.* [1]

Both aspects of the celebration are remembered among more recent immigrants:

> *Mrs. Schroeder remembers that they always had coffee and doughnuts on New Year's Eve and the young people went caroling. On New Year's Day the poor people went from house to house asking for food and money and said this verse:*

> Ich wünsche euch Glück zum Neujahr,
> Gebt nurs gleich segensreich,
> Lass mich nict so lange stehen,
> Dem ich muss noch weitergehen.

> *Mrs. Shroeder was not certain of the German words but she translated this verse as: "I wish you happiness in the New Year, but give me my present now. Don't let me stand too long as I have to go farther."* [2]

> *Mrs. Tangman remembers that when she was a little girl a prearranged group of men would go from house to house, carrying their guns, and at each house pick up and take with them any boys over sixteen years of age and the man of the house. They would do this collecting of men until the clock said just before midnight, then they would stay at the last person's house and shoot off their guns at the stroke of 12:00 p.m. Everyone in the community had enough food laid in that if their house was the last stop they would be prepared to feed all the men and boys a big supper.* [3]

Shooting in the New Year at midnight is still widely practiced throughout southern Pennsylvania.

2. *Groundhog Day*

February 2, Candlemas Day on the English calendar, was an important
date among the Pennsylvania Germans. Winter was half over, but still
half to come, and farmers were reminded by rhyme and proverb that they
should have half their wood and half their hay left by Candlemas Day. A
common saying was:

> *Lichtmess, Spinna vergess,*
> *Un's Fuder halwer g'fress.*[4]

Candlemas, forget spinning,
our fodder is half eaten.

—which reminded the housewife to put away her winter chores and start
preparing for spring.

By the same token, this was a date to watch for omens about the
weather for the rest of the winter. The most common was the groundhog, who, tradition said, came out on this date, and if he saw his shadow
(if it was sunny), he went back into hibernation and winter lasted six
weeks longer, as it usually did anyway.[5]

3. *Shrove Tuesday*

Shrove Tuesday, in German *Fastnacht* Day, meaning "Eve of the Fast," is
an important holiday, even among German Protestants who don't
observe Lent. On this day, everyone eats *Fastnachts,* a form of unleavened
doughnut (see the recipe, No. 18 in Chapter Nine), and the last person to
arise is called Fastnacht by his family, friends, or fellow students,
throughout the day.[6] Among more recent immigrants, the association
between day and doughnut is somewhat different:

> Kiechelle *or* Küchle *means doughnuts. It is the old German
> Catholic's way of giving children treats on the Tuesday before Ash
> Wednesday in February. Afterwards the children went on a fast from
> sweets. But this one night, they could have all they wanted.*
> *The children used to dress up in costumes, and wearing false faces, go
> from house to house calling, "Kiechelee!" Everyone along the Rhine [the
> German district of Cincinnati] gave the children the little doughnuts, or
> perhaps other goodies. "We used to have more fun, dressing up and going*

from house to house. No one knew who the other person was and every-
body tried to guess."[7]

And of course, ashes from the fires used to cook the fastnachts were sprinkled on the cattle and chickens on Ash Wednesday to rid them of lice.[8]

4. *Easter*
Easter was essentially a religious holiday, but many elements of its celebration stem from ancient tradition:

> *Mrs. Tangman remembers a tradition which had been practiced in her family for a long time. This was the making of Easter nests by using a pie pan as a pattern. Small sticks of kindling wood were laid around the center. The children went into the woods to gather the moss for the center of the nest. The children would have their egg hunt outside on Easter morning. The mothers would dye the eggs by boiling them in red onion peeling for the red color, boiling in sassafras for the quite so red [!] color and boiling in green rye water for the green color.*[9]

Pennsylvania German children set out their hats, with sometimes unexpected results:

> *We used to put our bonnets under the table for the Easter bunny to put eggs in. We'd wash them and starch them up and everything. One Easter he put rabbit pellets in Elsie's. Harry Chronister put them in. He got a lot of fun out of it.*[10]

Easter eggs were used in a variety of games, the most widespread being egg-tapping or picking. The principle is to hold a hard-boiled egg firmly and tap it against someone else's egg. Whoever breaks another's egg wins it from him, so some boys used a guinea egg, which is virtually unbreakable, and thus won all the eggs. Another trick was to use a raw egg, making sure that one tapped from above. When the egg broke, it ran over the other player's hand.[11]

A similar game played near Kassell, Germany, in the early 1900s involved throwing the eggs up into the air:

> *On Easter afternoon the boys would have an egg throwing contest. It took place on a hayfield outside of the village so that the eggs would not be broken. The eggs were boiled, of course. The trick was to see how many*

*times they could be thrown up in the air without breaking the egg. If they
came down on the point, they weren't so likely to break. Some of the boys
threw them as high as thirty feet.* [12]

The custom of decorating a tree with colored eggs is mentioned
numerous times in newspapers of the 1870s and 1880s, but it seems to be
of Pennsylvania German origin. Mention of such trees is sporadic until
the publication of a children's book, *The Egg Tree* by Katharine Milhous,
in 1950 popularized the practice. The trees are now known across the
country. [13]

5. *Ascension Day*
Ascension Day is still an important religious holiday among the Amish
and Mennonites. The day is recommended for fishing but no work is to
be done. In fact, serious consequences are believed to follow the performance of certain types of work on this day. If you sweep on this day,
you'll have ants in your house. [14] If you make beds on Ascension Day,
you'll get bed bugs. [15] Sew on Ascension Day and you will be struck by
lightning. [16] Work in the ground, and you'll be struck by lightning. [17]
Numerous stories are told of the results of working on this holy day:

> *Mother wouldn't sew on Ascension Day, but they whitewashed the fence.
> A couple of weeks later a storm came along and smashed the fence all up. I
> was only a kid.* [18]

6. *Midsummer's Day*
Though not commonly celebrated in the New World, some traditions
associated with this day were remembered by descendants of
nineteenth-century immigrants:

> *On June twenty-first, the Germans build big bonfires all around the town,
> especially a hilly one. When the fire has burned down low enough to leap
> across, each boy takes a girl by the hand and they jump across. They also
> take a big wheel and set it afire and roll it down the hill.* [19]

7. *Halloween*
Formerly Halloween was more a time for tricking than for treating. Some
of the tricks were so traditional as to be almost universal. Everyone has
heard of overturned outhouses and cows tied to the churchbell rope, but
the most widespread trick involved dismantling a wagon and
reassembling it on top of a barn or other building:

Bill Stover was hired out at Abe Lehmy's place. A bunch of fellas took the wagon up on the barn roof, and they took baskets of manure up and filled it, an' they put Britchman gears an' a saddle on the bull, an' he was watchin' an' after they were done, he come up, an' they were still talkin about it, an' he said, "Boys, I want you t' have just as much fun as ya had, gittin' it down. I've got the gun, in case ya don't know it, an' the first one that starts to leave, I'm gonna shoot him. I want you to take it all down."[20]

He had a buggy standing outside, and when Holloween time came around, well, like these young fellows like to get tricky, they took this buggy and put it on top of a shed. In a few days this old man came to the town, got in the barber shop, sat in there, soon these boys came in and they thought they were going to have fun with him, they didn't say much, and finally the old man said, "Now, boys, you were so good to put the buggy up on the roof, now go and take the buggy back again." And that's what they done, they say they never would touch this man's property any more. That's how things go.[21]

At times the tricks played have a social function, such as reminding a road supervisor of his duties or of mildly chastising neighbors who are seen as antisocial:

The kids of one woman's town always picked on the mean neighbors that didn't like the kids. "We knocked over their outhouse one year and then one year we threw smoke bombs in it. These people would hide and try to catch us doing something. So, of course their house was the big challenge for all the kids. I would try to do the worst things to them and try to get away without getting caught. My brother pulled a classic trick. He put dog crap in a brown paper bag and put it in front of these people's front door. He lit it on fire and rang the door bell, then ran. The man came out of the house and saw the fire, so he stomped and stomped on the bag. We were hiding and watching the whole scene. When he finally realized it was a joke, it was a little too late. He had dog crap all over his shoes and all over his front porch."[22]

You remember the time the boys buried old George Mentzer's buckboard on Holly Eve. They set a straw dummy on it and dug down in this mudhole till the buckboard was up to the axle. He never knew who done it. He was gonna have them arrested. They had him all dolled up and then they printed a sign and put on the back: "I'm sorry I left the road get in this bad shape."[23]

8. *Christmas*

The celebration of Christmas in German homes is more extended than among the English. It begins with the start of Advent, December 1, and continues in some areas until Epiphany, January 6, also called Twelfth Night or Old Christmas.

Now four Sundays before Christmas the advent season would start. We would get together, make an advent wreath out of fresh spruce branches and put four candles on it and then each Sunday before Christmas we would light a candle. . . . Each Sunday in the afternoon we would get together and light a candle and sit and talk and have coffee and it was a very enjoyable time and I remember it well. We also would have an advent calendar. It had twenty-four days on it and my sisters and me would share, we'd take turns in opening the windows and it was really exciting. We did it every morning before school to see what picture would appear behind the window. . . . On December 4th was another special day. That's Saint Barbara's Day. That's connected with the Catholic faith again. We would go out in the garden and cut branches off of cherry trees and we tried to pick the ones with the biggest buds on them. And we bring them in the house and my mother would put them in warm water with a pinch of salt and then naturally everyday we go see if one had bloomed yet because when they did bloom that meant good luck for the next year. I think I remember several old sayings too about Saint Barbara's day. There was one, for instance, it says if Saint Barbara walks through green grass the Christ Child will come in the snow. [24]

One date that most children looked forward to was December 6, Saint Nicholas's Day:

That is when the children hang up their stockings and receive "little gifts." This is a preview of the Christmas season and is always a source of great surprise and delight to the children. No expensive gifts are given, just little trinkets and toys. [25]

On St. Nick's Day, St. Nick comes to town, however, this is only for the younger children. The older children don't usually go to see him, but only leave their stockings out for him to fill. St. Nick carries a whip with him, so that if the children are not good he can hit them with [it]. [26]

The Christmas Tree is generally associated with the Germans, who introduced it into the New World in the nineteenth century. [27] Usually the decoration of the tree is a special part of Christmas:

We made all the children help. We made little paper ornaments or took felt-made animals, strung popcorn, cranberries, and the only thing on the tree that was not really made at the time was the string of lights, different colored ones. And we had a star at the top of the tree which wasn't hand made. So we could put a light in it. But everything we had made out of yarn, little yarn dolls when your brother wasn't around, cut them out of felt and I stitched them and stuffed them. So everybody had a part and that was done through the time before Christmas because it built up an excitement in each child and it was like an important part in making the Christmas. And then the week before Christmas, we would set up the crèche or manger scene. All of you. And we had the children, each one of you in the family had one piece of the manger scene to set up. [28]

Among the Pennsylvania Germans the crèche was part of an elaborate arrangement of miniature houses, trees and animals (often including a toy Noah's ark with the animals marching into it), called a *Putz* (decoration).[29] In some areas the tree is not decorated until Christmas Eve:

On Christmas Eve, December 24th, it is believed that old Saint Nick brings the tree and decorates it for the family. The children leave during the day, and when they return the tree is all decorated. The German people have lighted candles on their trees plus bulbs and ornaments. Also, the German people do not wrap their presents but lay them out on a table for all to see. Gabentisch is the table where they lay the gifts. Each member of the family has a certain place where they have their gifts. Thus everyone knows which are theirs. Then a table cover is placed over the gifts, called Leintuch, to cover the gifts until the special time for opening. After the presents are unwrapped [uncovered?] and everyone sings for a while, the children go to the nearest barn to hear the animals talk. It is believed that the animals will talk as the clock strikes twelve midnight on Christmas Eve. For, one time, a girl says that she was in the barn and an animal talked to her. Therefore, every year the children go to the barn to hear and talk with the animals. [30]

Everyone knows that Santa Claus brings presents, but Pennsylvania German children awaited with mixed emotions the arrival of the *Belsnickel*. The word is a corruption of *Pelz Nicholas*, a figure of Saint Nicholas dressed in furs. Dressed usually in a heavy coat and sometimes in rags, the Belsnickel had a pocketful of nuts and candies but also a whip, with which he threatened naughty children, cracking it over their heads as the scrambled for the treats thrown across the floor.[31] In later years, under influence of the European mumming tradition, Belsnicklers became masqueraders who went from house to house in the days between Christmas and New Year's, expecting treats from the householders who tried to guess their identity:

We'd all dress up in false faces and old clothes and travel from house to house and git the people to see if they could guess ya, ya know. I was at a place one night and nobody guessed me. That was right after we moved down there where Doc lives now, I fergit who we went with, but I had a cushion in here, and the women grabbed me, to see who it was, and the rest all went out, an' after they got my face off, they still didn't know me, and then they wondered who the rest was, but they'd went out already. . . . I had a cushion in here, and we went in one place and she says, "Somebody must a' turned the joke on you" *[made* you *pregnant]. We went to Harry Keck's belsnicklin', and Harry Keck, he could dance the bear dance so good, and he wanted me to dance the bear dance with him, together like this, but the cushion kep' gittin' in the road, an' he didn't have a cushion, so he could turn real easy. But it was too much for me with that cushion in there. . . . There was several of them wore hoop skirts, and they had them old time bloomers that the women used t' wear, with ruffles down around the bottom, fer pants, and he'd always set down that the hoop would fly straight up and here'd be these ruffles, you know. 'Stead of him pullin' it up in the back, he'd just set down and that would stand up in the front. . . . They use t' do this the whole week between Christmas and New Year's. . . . They'd give us apples and candy and things of that kind. . . . One time we went to Fry's. There was Diller Lehman. and Harry Lehman, an' me an' Raymond Hurley. An' Fry went down in the cellar an' got some cider, but he fixed it up a little, ya know. Well, I didn't drink any, an' Raymond didn't drink any either, but the Lehman boys did, an' we had a deal of a time gittin' them home after that.*[32]

We went up there to where Dale Barrick lives now, and we went in there, they had a couch, with a box like this, and a straw tick on there, no springs in those then. And they gave us popcorn balls. I remember John, he lifted up his mask to take a bite and his false teeth stuck in it, and he couldn't get them loose, he pulled it out and there were his teeth sticking, on top and underneath. He was afraid of breakin' them, but he did finally get the uppers loose so he could talk partly. Sometimes we'd just take a piece of cloth and put holes in it [for a mask], an' lipstick or something. And

147

then we'd go in, each one would carry the other'n's instrument, so they wouldn't know ya. We went in one place where a girl come over to me and said, "Oh, I know you." An' she set on my lap. We found out that Chronister down there was going with her, and she thought that's who I was, an when I took off my mask, she said, "Oooh."... Between Christmas an' New Year's, if the weather was nice, we'd go every night.[33]

CHAPTER NINE

Foodways

The foodways of the Pennsylvania Germans have been identified with German cooking in America, almost to the exclusion of other forms in other areas. The mere mention of German food suggests sauerkraut, noodles and dumplings, and shoofly pie. Pennsylvania German foodways, possibly as a result of tourist interest in the subject, have become one of the distinctive regional American cookeries. These culinary traditions have not always followed migration into other states, but such traditions are remembered with nostalgia by descendants of Pennsylvania German settlers.

As usual, nostalgia looks on the past with rose-colored glasses, for ordinary meals on Pennsylvania German farms tended to be monotonous—filling, but often unappetizing. Whichever vegetables were fresh were served at meals day after day as long as the season lasted, and after the November butchering, pork was served consistently, though with some variety, roasted while still fresh, then later fried, or boiled with potatoes, green beans, or sauerkraut. By winter's end, the crocks of liver pudding were the dominant food source, and in many homes fried pudding, over bread, was served at three meals a day.

The remembered abundance appeared only on special occasions, Easter, Christmas, and threshing day. The phrase, "to eat like a thresherman," reflects the quantity of food set on the table on *that* day. When the men sat down to dinner (the noonday meal), they found two and sometimes three meats, roast beef (rarely served at other times), fried ham, and sometimes chicken. At least four vegetables filled serving dishes around the table. As plate-fillers one found pickled eggs (hard-boiled in red beet juice), at least two kinds of pickles, but not the mythical seven sweets and sours, and amazingly, a few raw vegetables—celery, radishes, and carrot strips. Dessert was almost always pie but there would be two or three different kinds. Of course coffee was on the table throughout the meal. After the men had eaten and gone back to work, the women "sat up" to the second table.

Special foods befit special occasions. New Year's Day meant a meal of pork and sauerkraut, supposedly to bring good luck for the year. But unknowingly, this was a traditional means of preventing scurvy by introducing vitamin C into a diet that was almost exclusively fatty meat and starch during the winter months. Maundy Thursday (sometimes called Green Thursday) was another occasion when one deliberately sought out greens (usually dandelion) to cook and serve. Shrove Tuesday, as noted earlier, was a time for eating Fastnachts, and the Easter meal was invariably ham, even among Protestant Germans who didn't observe the strictures of Lent. By tradition, this was the day for first cutting the hams that had been smoked and stored the preceding November, a subtle way of guaranteeing that the food supply would last the winter. Summertime brought occasional picnics, with sandwiches, baked beans, and potato salad. Fall brought traditional harvest foods, gingersnaps, mince and pumpkin pies, as well as turkey, served invariably at Thanksgiving and Christmas dinners along with the same abundance found at the threshing tables.

The Germans who arrived later in the New World tended to retain the traditional foodways of the old country, and such dishes as *Hase im Topf* (rabbit stew), *Gefülte Kässepfannkuchen* (cheese-filled pancakes), and *Sauerbraten* (marinated pot roast) are popular throughout the Midwest and Midsouth. LaVern Rippley discusses the importance of these foods in Minnesota and describes a typical day's menus there. Breakfast is less heavy than the Pennsylvania German breakfast, consisting of buns with butter and marmalade and a soft-boiled egg. A *zweites Frühstück* (midmorning snack or "ten o'clock piece") consists of a sandwich and beer. *Mittagessen,* the noontime "dinner," the primary meal of the day, consists of soup, noodles or dumplings, meat and vegetables. A midafternoon snack, called *Vesperbrot,* is again a sandwich, and the evening meal, the *Abendbrot,* is a serving of cold foods, sandwiches, hard-boiled eggs, cheese and pickles (*Of German Ways,* 242–47).

Many cooks kept their recipes on scraps of paper or written on the margins or flyleaves of cookbooks. Some of these have been included here verbatim and should not be considered as complete "kitchen-tested" recipes. Since basic cooking techniques were a matter of common knowledge, these recipes are often mere lists of ingredients. A pie recipe describes only the filling, since everyone knew how to make piecrust. Rarely is there an indication of cooking time or temperature, since every type of stove and oven varied. Recipes for many common German dishes are lacking, either because their preparation was so simple that no instructions were necessary or because they were prepared so often that the procedure was easily learned and remembered. Every cook knew how to fry, boil, and bake; when in doubt about an unfamiliar foodstuff, one simply chose one of these procedures.

Since pork is such an important element in Pennsylvania German cooking, the butchering or slaughtering of hogs is (or was until recently) an essential part of their foodways. Butchering is an all-day process, requiring the help of relatives and neighbors and beginning long before the late dawn of a November or December day. Thanksgiving and Saturdays are favorite times for butchering, since more help is available those days. The process follows a fixed pattern, whether one or a half dozen hogs is involved.

1. Butchering

The hog is shot in the forehead with a 22-caliber rifle and when it collapses another man slices the large vein in the neck. Both men then clear away until the hog stops kicking. At this point the hog is transported to the wagon shed where two small chains are hooked around each of the back ankles and the hog is hoisted up in the air with a pulley and rope. The hog is lowered into a large barrel of almost-boiling water with a cup of lime mixed in. After several dippings the bristles are soft enough to be scraped off with a scraper. The scraper is a concave steel bowl with a wooden handle and a sharp edge.

After the bristles have been removed a small cut is made in each rear ankle to expose the large tendons which have a hook and tackle placed in each one. In this manner the hog is raised up and tied, hanging upside down from the rafters of the wagon shed with its rear legs spread far apart.

The teats of the hog are now removed and a slice, deep enough to cut the skin but no deeper, is made from the anus down to the neck. The anus is carefully cut out so it stays attached to the intestine, and the bladder is located and tied off with a piece of string. The guts are now removed into a tub to be discarded, except for the heart, liver, kidneys, and small intestines.

A large hook with a wooden handle is stuck through the roof of the mouth and as one person holds the head, another cuts it off the body.

The head is then taken to the back kitchen where it is cooked and cleaned. The front legs are sawed off about four inches from the tip and the hog is sawed in half lengthwise using a meat saw to cut right along the spine. Each half is then carried into the back kitchen.

Once inside the back kitchen, each half hog is carefully cut, removing the skin and lard in large pieces, leaving the leaner meat still in one piece. The lard is then cut away from the skin. The lard is cut into small pieces and boiled down in huge cast iron cauldrons over a wood fire. The boiled-down lard is then pressed in a lard press and run into crocks and taken to the basement to solidify. The piece in the bottom of the press, called cracklin's, is in a cake [form] and later will be ground in with the puddin's. The skins that have been separated from the lard are cooked and also will become part of the puddin's.

The trimmings from the shoulders and hams, and other lean scraps are used to make sausage. These are cooked, ground, and seasoned to taste with salt and pepper, then ground again. The small intestine is cleaned and scraped with a knife, and then cleaned and scraped a second time. The sausage meat is then stuffed into the cleaned intestines using the same press that was used for the lard.

The head meat, skins, liver, kidneys and heart are used to make puddin's. They are cooked in the cauldrons, and then ground, leaving the broth in the cauldron. As the meats for the puddin's are ground, the cracklin's from when the lard was pressed are ground in, a little at a time, and salt and pepper are added to taste. The puddin's are then cooked again and canned.

The broth saved from the puddin' meat is used as the base for pon-haus. This is brought to a boil, and then a mixture of corn meal, white flour, and whole wheat flour is mixed in (a ratio of two to one to one respectively). The different flours are mixed in until a proper consistency is obtained and then two to three gallons of puddin' per cauldron is mixed in and salt and pepper is added. This mixture is then cooked approximately one hour, being stirred constantly, and then is poured into bread pans and allowed to set.

Hams, bacons, and shoulders are sugar-cured and smoked. Each separate piece is set in a tub and covered with the curing mixture. The curing mixture is made from twenty pounds of salt, five pounds of dark brown sugar, and three ounces of salt peter. After each piece is covered it is laid on wooden shelves in the smokehouse and the remaining curing mixture in the tub is sprinkled over top. The meat is then smoked using hickory logs for fire, and remaining in the smokehouse until spring.

Pork chops are cut from the lean area along the backbone are sliced and frozen. Ribs are cut into small portions with a meat saw and then are also frozen. Neck roasts and leg roasts are removed and frozen also. All these parts were canned before freezing was available, a process that took an additional four to five days.

Pig's feet can be roasted or made into souse. To make souse they are cooked and salted to taste. The meat and skin is then picked off the bones. This is ground and mixed with the broth. Approximately one cup of vinegar is added for each dozen feet and the result is frozen or canned.

Breads

2. Bishop Bread
Rub together:

2 c. brown sugar	1 tsp. salt
2½ c. flour	1 tsp. cinnamon
½ c. lard	

Remove ¾ c. of crumbs for top. Add ½ tsp. soda, 1 tsp. baking powder, 1 egg, ¾ c. thick milk. Mix and put crumbs on top. Bake in moderate oven.

3. Corn Pone

1½ cups corn meal	½ cup butter or lard
1½ cups flour	1 cup sugar
1½ cups sweet milk	3 scant teaspoons baking powder

Mix and bake in iron skillet.

4. Potato Bread

1 cup mashed potatoes	1 tsp. salt
2 eggs	¾ cup shortening
1 cup sugar	2 cups warm water
1 pkg. yeast (½ cup)	

Dissolve yeast in water. Stir in remaining ingredients with about 3 lbs. flour. Mix thoroughly and knead. Cover and let rise until light. Place in greased baking pan. Rise again until double size. Bake at 350 degrees for 30 minutes.

5. Potato Pancakes
Thoroughly combine 3 eggs, 2 tab. [tbs.] flour, 1 tea. [tsp.] salt, dash of

pepper, 1 Tab. minced onion, and ⅛ tea. nutmeg. Stir in 12 ounces of diced potatoes. Fry until they are golden brown.

Cakes

6. *Funnel Cake*

1 egg	¼ tsp. salt
⅔ cup milk	¾ tsp. baking powder
1⅓ cup sifted flour	1 tsp. baking soda
2 tbs. sugar	

Beat egg and add milk. Sift together flour, salt, sugar, baking powder, and soda. Add egg and milk. Beat. Put batter in funnel and cook in hot fat. Serve with molasses.

7. *Moravian Sugarcake*

About 7 p.m. mix together 1 c. [cup] hot mashed potatoes, 2 yeast cakes dissolved in 1 c. lukewarm water, 1 c. granulated sugar, 1 c. melted butter, 2 eggs, 1 t. [tablespoon] salt and flour enough to make stiff dough. Dough should pull off spoon, leaving it almost clean. Let rise over night and in morning place in pans, spreading dough about ¾ inch thick. Let rise again, about 1½ hrs. or until it looks quite puffy. With thumb, make holes in rows, about 2 inches apart, and fill with butter, brown sugar and sprinkled cinnamon. (Use 1 lb. sugar.) Bake 20 to 15 minutes in oven heated to 400 degrees.

8. *Sponge Cake*

3 eggs—Beat 3 min.
2 cups sugar—Beat 5 min.
¾ cup warm [flour?]—Beat 1 min.
2 teaspoons Baking Pawder.

9a. *Poor Man's Cake*

2 cups sour cream	2 eggs
2 cups sugar	2 teaspoons soda
4 cups flour	2 cream of tartar

b. *Mountain Cake*

2 cups sugar	1 cup sweet milk
4 eggs	1 cup flour
1 cup butter	1 teaspoon soda

c. *Feather Cake*

1 cup sugar
1 cup buttermilk
1 egg

1 teaspoon soda
1½ cup flour
1 tablespoon butter

d. *Egles [eggless] cake*

1½ cup sugar
1 cup sour milk
½ cup butter
3 cups flour

1 cup raisins
1 teaspoon soda
½ teaspoon cinnamon
½ teaspoon nutmeg

Candy

10. *Peanut Mojhy*

1 cup firmly packed light brown
   sugar
1 cup light molasses
2 cups (about ¾ lb.) hulled
   peanuts

1 cup water

¼ cup butter

Cook sugar, molasses, and water together in a heavy saucepan to soft crack stage (280°F on candy thermometer), or till a small amount dropped into cold water separates in threads which are hard but not brittle. Just before taking from heat, add the butter and the peanuts and mix well. Pour into large well-buttered shallow pans and cool. Break into irregular pieces.

11. *Potato Candy*

Leftover mashed potatoes (cold)
About 1 box of 10-X sugar
1 tsp. vanilla and peanut butter

Take very small amount of potato and add vanilla and sugar until mixture can be rolled out like pie dough. Roll out and spread peanut butter on top. Roll from edge into a long tube and refrigerate.

12. *Walnut Taffy*

1 quart dark table syrup
2 cups granulated sugar

Boil until real hard. For this amount use 1 quart walnut goodies [nut-meats]. Spread thin on a greased pan.

Cheese

13. *Ball Cheese*
Put 1 gal. sour, thick milk into bag and drain. Salt to taste. Form into flat round balls about 3 in. in diameter and lay on china platters for three days. Then roll balls in baking soda and wrap in paper; place in glass or earthenware crock and let ripen for 2 weeks. Take out and rinse in water to remove soda, scraping balls with knife.

14a. *Schmierkase*
Pour 1 qt. sour milk, heated to lukewarm, into cheesecloth bag. Pour over this 1 qt. warm water, and allow to drain through. Repeat twice, then tie bag and let drip until whey is all gone. Mix with sweet or sour cream and season to taste.

b. *Smearcase*
Take sour milk and place it in a cloth bag to drip for a period of time. After liquid has dripped out, use solid portion as cottage cheese.

Cookies

15. *Old Fashioned Sugar Cookies*

2 c. sugar	2 t. baking powder
2 eggs	1 c. sour mllk
½ c. shortening	4 c. flour (sifted)
2 t. baking soda	

Put cream, shortening, and sugar together, add eggs. Add alternately sour milk and dry ingredients. Drop by tablespoon on greased cookie sheet. Sprinkle with sugar and place in 425° oven for 10 minutes. Makes about 4 dozen cookies.

16. *Sugar Cakes*
Three coffee cups of Sugar
five eggs and one cup of butter
beat very lite then add one nutmeg

flour enough to roll and fourth of
a cup of water and two teaspoons
of baking pawder.

Desserts

17. *Apple Dumplings*
6 medium baking apples

	Sauce:
2 cu. flour	2 cu. brown sugar
2½ tsp. baking powder	2 cu. water
½ tsp. salt	¼ cu. butter
⅔ cu. shortening	¼ tsp. cinnamon
½ cu. milk	

Peel and core apples.

Pastry—sift flour, baking powder, and salt together. Cut in shortening, until particles are about the size of a small pea.

Sprinkle milk over mixture and press together lightly, working dough only enough to hold it together.

Roll dough for pastry and cut into 6 squares, placing an apple on each.

Fill cavity in apple with sugar and cinnamon.

Pat dough around apple to cover it completely.

Fasten edges securely on top of the apple.

Place dumplings 1 inch apart in a greased baking pan.

Pour over the sauce which is made as follows:

Combine brown sugar, water and spices.
Cook for 5 minutes, remove from heat and add butter.
Bake dumplings at 375 degrees for 35–40 minutes.
Baste occasionally during baking.

Serve hot with rich milk or ice cream.

18. *Fastnachts*
Boil 3 potatoes in enough water to cover. With the potato water scald 1 pint of flour and add the potato, mashed. When cool add 1 yeast cake, dissolved in a little lukewarm water. Start this about 5:00. At bedtime mix

a pint of flour with one pint of lukewarm milk. Stir enough flour into milk to make a batter that will drop readily from the spoon. To this batter add the first mixture and let rise overnight. In the morning add 4 beaten eggs, ½ cup of melted butter, or butter and lard mixed, and 1 cup of sugar. Knead stiff enough to roll; let rise till the dough doubles its size. Now roll and cut out the dough and let rise again. When light, swim in hot fat.

19. *Kooka*

Take different fruits and onion and mix. Pour contents into pie pan lined with rich yeast dough. Fix up edges real fancy-like and bake.

20. *Plum Duck*

1¼ cup flour	1½ cup suet, chopped
2½ cups soft bread crumbs	1 cup granulated sugar
1 cup seedless raisins	1 teaspoon cinnamon
1 cup currants	½ teaspoon nutmeg
¼ cup citron, cut fine	1 teaspoon salt

Mix, add 3 eggs beaten separately, ½ glass or ¼ cup brandy or grape juice. Mix all together, turn into a thickly floured square of unbleached muslin and tie not quite tight and drop into boiling water and cook for 6 hours. To flour the muslin, wring from boiling water and put flour inside and shake well until it is coated.

Meats and Main Dishes

21. *Baked Ham*

12 lbs. tenderized ham	2 med. sized apples, quartered
36 cloves	1 orange, quartered
1 qt. water	1 c. crushed pineapple
2 c. white wine	1 lb. brown sugar or honey
1 sm. cinnamon stick	

Use skinned ham from which excess fat has been removed. Score ham with cookie cutter and in each stick a clove. Place in roaster. Add water, wine, cinnamon, apples, orange and pineapple. Bake at 300 degrees for 2 hours, basting about every 10 minutes so as to glaze ham evenly. If liquid should reduce too fast during baking, keep adding a little more hot water. When ham is cooked liquid should be reduced to a heavy syrup. Serve with sauce.

22. *Chicken or Beef Potpie*

Dough: To each cupful of flour work in a tablespoon of lard, a pinch of salt, an egg, 1 tsp. baking powder, and ½ cup milk. Mix, as for pie dough, roll as thin as possible, [slice into strips] and boil ½ hour in good broth.

Broth: Chicken or Beef broth
3 sliced potatoes
1 onion

parsley
salt and pepper to taste

23. *Hausfrauenart*

Take one or two rabbits and soak them overnight in vinegar, water and spices. Later, cook the rabbits and with the broth, make gravy. Serve with mashed potatoes, vegetables and salad.

24. *Krautflecken*

Use equal parts of cabbage and noodles. Cut the cabbage rather coarse. Boil each separately until they both are tender. Drain. Combine them and fry in bacon drippings.

25. *Mush*

Mix a cup of yellow corn meal in a quart of water and add salt, about a teaspoon full. Boil, stirring constantly. Cook until thick, "until the pot-stick stands straight up in the middle."

You can serve it hot with milk, like oatmeal, or let it cool in a pan-haus pan. When it's cool, slice it and fry it until brown. Serve with molasses.

26. *Pig's Stomach*

1 pig's stomach
1 lb. fried sausage
2–3 quarts diced raw potatoes

2 cups dried bread
1 tablespoon parsley flakes
salt and pepper

Clean pig's stomach. Mix the remaining ingredients and fill stomach. Close both ends by sewing shut with needle and cord. Bake for three hours. Keep some water in pan while roasting.

27. *Pork Ribs and Sauerkraut*

3 lbs. salted pork ribs
¼ lb. butter
6 large peeled sliced apples
¼ lb. chopped pork

1 lb. sauerkraut
½ teaspoon sugar
½ bottle white wine
¼ lb. chopped veal

| 1 egg | salt and pepper |
| 1 teaspoon butter | ¼ teaspoon minced onion |

Salt the pork for several days then cut into pieces, wash, dry and fry on both sides in hot butter. Put into a pot with sauerkraut on top. (If the sauerkraut is too sour, soak it in water and drain). Add the quarter pound of butter, apples, white wine and sugar, cover and cook slowly for 2 hours. When it gets too dry, pour in some water. For the meat dumplings chop the pork and veal; add a soaked roll of bread, the egg, 1 tablespoonful of butter and onion, mixed. Shape into dumplings and fry well done in the butter in which the fried ribs have been. Serve the sauerkraut in the middle of the platter, the ribs around it and the dumplings piled on top in a heap.

28. *Schnitz un Gnepp*

| 2 c. smoked ham | 2 tbsp. brown sugar |
| 2 c. dried sweet apples | |

Cover the dried apples with water and soak overnight. In the morning, using a kettle fairly large in diameter, almost cover the ham with cold water and cook slowly for 2 hours. Add the apples and the water in which they were soaked. Add brown sugar and cook 1 hour longer. Add gnepp last 20 min.

To make the gnepp:

2 c. flour	1 egg, beaten
4 tsp. baking powder	2 tbsp. butter
½ tsp salt	½ c. milk (scant)

Sift together flour, baking powder and salt. Stir in beaten egg and melted butter. Add enough milk to make a moderately stiff batter. Drop from spoon into boiling ham and apples. Cover kettle tightly and cook, without lifting lid, for 20 minutes.

29. *Spaetzel*

| 1 qt. flour | salt (a "pinch") |
| 3 eggs | enough milk to make a stiff batter |

Mix the ingredients. Cut this batter into boiling water. When the pieces of batter come to the top, take out. Pour cold water over them to prevent them from sticking together. Fry in bacon grease or butter until they are brown.

Pickles and Relishes

30. Chow-Chow

Take equal amounts, about a quart each, of celery, lima beans, pickles, string beans, corn, carrots and peppers, and half as much onions. [Cut into half-inch pieces.]

Then boil about 4 lb. of sugar, 1½ qts. of vinegar, 1½ quarts of water, and spices together to a syrup. Then add about 3 tbsp. of cornstarch and boil again. Add vegetables and boil. Store in sealed jars.

Spices: 1 tsp. celery seed, ½ tsp. tumeric, 2 tsp. salt, pickling spices—a good bit.

31. Cucumber Pickles

1 gal vinegar

5 cts worth saccharine

cup ground mustard

Scant cup salt.

32. Dill Pickles

Another thing that Mom would do was to make dill pickles in five-gallon crocks. She would take the longer green cucumbers from the garden, slice them lengthwise, and put them in a large crock. She would put a brine on them made of vinegar, salt water, and fresh dill. The vinegar, salt and water was heated to the boiling point and poured over the cucumbers filling almost to the top of the cucumber line. Then a layer of fresh dill was packed down among the cucumbers, some on top of them. Then grape leaves were covered over the whole top. A plate was put upside-down on them, a stone put on top and the crock allowed to stand in the dark, cool place.

Pies

33. Butter Milk Pie

5 cups of butter milk

1 cup of sugar

3 eggs

2 tablespoons of flour

Nut meg to taste.

34. Green Tomato Pie

Chop tomatoes up in pie, sprinkle salt on them and a tbsp. of flour, about ½ cup sugar, cinnamon, then put a top on it and bake it. Some people sprinkles a row of raisins in it.

35. *Lemon Sponge Pie*

1 c. granulated sugar
3 tbsp. butter
2 eggs

3 tbsp. flour
1 c. milk
juice and grated rind of 1 lemon

Mix sugar, butter, egg yolks, add flour slowly then add grated rind and lemon juice. Add milk. Fold in beaten egg whites. Put in raw pie crust and bake ¾ hour. Makes one large pie. 350°

36. *Molasses Pie*

1 cup molasses
¼ lb. butter
1 tbs. flour

sugar (to stiffen)
cinnamon (for topping)

Pour in pie shell, mix and bake.

37. *Pumpkin Pie*

1 cup cooked, pressed pumpkin
½ cup sugar
2 tablespoons molasses
3 eggs

2 cups milk
¼ teaspoon salt
½ teaspoon ginger
1 teaspoon cinnamon

Bake in pie, uncovered, or with criss-cross strips of crust across the top.

38. *Raisin Pie*

1 c. raisins
1½ c. sugar
¼ c. flour
2 c. water

1 egg, beaten
2 tbsp. grated lemon peel
3 tbsp. lemon juice
pie shell

Rinse raisins; set aside. Mix in double boiler: sugar, flour, and salt. Add the water gradually, stirring constantly. Stir in raisins. Bring to boiling over direct heat, stirring constantly, and cook about 1 min. longer. Remove from heat. Vigorously stir a small amt. of hot mixture into the egg. Stir into mixture in double boiler. Set over simmering water and cook about 5 min. Remove from water and stir in lemon. Cool. Pour into pie shell. Cover with narrow strips. Bake at 450° for 10 min. then 350° for 20 min. longer.

39. *Schnitz Pie*

1 lb. dried sour schnitz

2 c. sugar

1 qt. cold water
2 tbsp. ground cinnamon
pie shell

⅛ tsp. salt
1 orange (grated peel and juice)

Put the schnitz and the water into a saucepan and cook to a soft pulp. Add cinnamon, sugar, salt, orange juice, and orange peel, and mix together well. Set aside to cool. Line a 9-in. pie pan with pie dough and fill with schnitz. Cover top with pastry and cut several slits in crust to allow steam to escape. Bake at 450° for 10 min. Reduce the heat to 350°. Bake about 30 min. longer.

40. *Shoofly*

Bottom Part: 1 cup dark molasses
¾ cup boiling water
½ teaspoon soda

Top Part: 1½ cups flour
¼ cup shortening
½ cup brown sugar

Dissolve soda in water and add molasses. Combine sugar, flour, and shortening like crumbs. Pour in ½ liquid, then crumbs. Bake in moderate oven for ½ hour to 45 minutes.

41. *Sour Cream Pie*

1 cup of thick sour cream
½ cup seeded raisins cut in
    two
½ teaspoon of cinnamon
pinch salt

1 cup sugar
2 eggs

¼ [tsp.?] cloves

Use whites of eggs for meringue. Beat yolks of eggs well. Add sour cream. Mix cinnamon, cloves, salt and sugar. Thoroughly add to eggs and cream. Beat thoroughly with egg beater. Then add raisins. Bake slowly.

Soups

42. *Brown-Flour Potato Soup*

4 c. water
8 potatoes
4 c. milk

4 T. flour
2 T. butter
salt and pepper to taste

Cube the peeled potatoes and boil in salted water until tender. Brown the flour in melted butter at low heat and add to the soup. Blend carefully, bring to the boiling point. Season. Serves 6.

43. *Chicken Corn Soup*

1 4-pound chicken	1 tsp. chopped parsley
2 tsp. salt	⅛ tsp. pepper
2 cups fresh corn	2 chopped hard-boiled eggs
¼ tsp. saffron	

Cut up the chicken and cover with three quarts of water. Add the salt and saffron. Stew until tender. Remove chicken from stock and set aside the legs and breast for future potpie. Cut up the rest of the meat and return to stock in the kettle. Add the noodles and corn and boil for fifteen minutes longer. Add the parsley and hard-boiled eggs.

44. *Kraft Soup*
Grind dry pumpernickel bread. Sauté two tablespoons of chopped onion in two tablespoons of melted butter. Add one cup of milk. When boiling, add about one-third cup pumpernickel crumbs and thicken to a consistency of thick mush. Salt to taste. Good served with fried potatoes, made from boiled potatoes with the jackets still on them.

45. *Rivvel Soup*

2 c. unsifted flour	4 qt. of chicken broth
½ tsp. salt	2 c. of corn
1 egg, well beaten	

Combine the flour, salt and beaten egg. Mix them together with fingers until mixture is crumbly. Drop these rivvels into the broth. Add corn and simmer for 10 to 15 minutes.

Vegetables

46. *Birish Kraut*
Slice some cabbage like sour kraut. Cook [fry] and serve with mashed potatoes, and wieners, porkside or pork chops.

47. *Corn Pie*
Fill pastry-lined dish with fresh sweet corn, add:

1 or 2 chopped hard-boiled eggs
1 tbsp. butter

Season with salt and pepper
A little sugar and onion may be added, if preferred.
Add enough milk to cover this filling.

Top with strip of pastry or close with slitted pastry top. Bake and serve while hot.

48. *Corn Pudding*

6 ears (or 1 can cream-style) corn
1 tablespoon sugar
1 tablespoon cornstarch
1 teaspoon salt

3 eggs, beaten separately
4 tablespoons melted butter
1 cup milk

Combine all ingredients in the order given, except for egg whites. Fold these in last. Place in a greased 1½-quart casserole and bake 35 minutes in a 350° oven.

49. *Corn and Potato Chowder*

Combine: 2½ cups cooked corn
2 cups diced potatoes
1 tbsp. butter
¼ cup diced onion

½ tsp. salt
⅛ tsp. pepper
1 cup boiling water

Cook until potatoes are tender. Add 2 cups hot milk and thicken with 1 tbsp. flour mixed with 1 tbsp. cold water. Heat to boiling. Serve.

50. *Dandelion Salad*

Early in the spring, take dandelion leaves before the blossoms appear. Fry some bacon, chopped up. Add:

2 tbs. flour
½ cup sugar
pinch salt
Boil this in the bacon fat.

egg and beat
vinegar and water

51. *Fried Eggplant*

1 eggplant
salt & pepper
bread crumbs

1 beaten egg
1 T milk

Peel an eggplant and slice thin. Salt each [slice] and pile up. Drain for ½ hour. Dip slices in egg mixed with milk first, and then in crumbs. Fry quickly until golden brown.

52. *Grumbiere Fisil (Potato Filling)*

2 qts. cooked potatoes	½ cup butter
1 tbsp. salt	2 tbsps. parsley
1 tsp. pepper	1½ cups milk
½ cup chopped onions	2 eggs

Fry onions in butter until moist and brown. Put potatoes in mixer, add parsley, onions and bread, eggs, seasoning, butter, and milk. If the potatoes appear too dry add more milk. Put in a buttered dish and bake at 400° for ¾ hour.

53. *Redheart (Milkweed) or Dandelion Salad*

Gather redheart when about three inches in diameter in mid-spring. Cut pieces of bacon in skillet and brown. Put flour in and cook to milky brown. Fill skillet half with water and let that come to a boil, then put salad in.

Let that boil 3–4 mins., then take sugar, put that in and stir it good so it won't burn. Then taste it and if sweet enough, that's it, she's done. You can let it boil for about half an hour and cook potatoes (small ones) in salt water, then mash them up and pour your warmed salad over. We always gathered a good bread bag full to make a hell of a mess for two people. Dandelion comes up first, and we always gathered that until the red heart got big enough, then we would eat that. After that we'd eat garden lettuce, etc.

54. *Sauerkraut*

Shred cabbage and pack in brine in a stoneware crock, press down and cover with clean cabbage leaves. Place a china plate on top of the leaves, hold down with a sandstone, then cover with cloth and tie shut to keep bugs out. Let stand in a warm place so it "works" [ferments]. After six weeks, it's ready to use.

Beverages

55. *Blackberry Wine*

Put blackberries, sugar and water in a crock and mash. Let stand to ferment. Then strain to get out the seeds and store in jugs.

56. *Dandelion Wine*

Pick just the blossoms, cutting stems off close to the flower or the wine will be bitter. Put a gallon of blossoms in a kettle with a gallon of water.

Let it stand 3 days.

Add the yellow rind of 3 lemons and 3 oranges. Boil 15 minutes, then strain. When lukewarm add the juices of the lemons and oranges, 4 pounds of granulated sugar, and 1 yeast cake.

Set in a warm place for a week. Then strain and set away for 3 weeks longer. Then bottle.

Elderblossom wine is made the same way.

57. *Homemade Root Beer*

3 yeast cakes	1 bottle rootbeer extract
3 tablespoons sugar	5 gallons pure fresh water slightly lukewarm
1 pint lukewarm water	4 pounds sugar

Dissolve 3 cakes of yeast and 3 tablespoons of sugar in a pint of luke-warm water. Keep in a warm place for 12 hours, then stir well and strain through cheesecloth. Add bottle of extract, 4 pounds of sugar and 5 gallons of lukewarm water. Mix thoroughly and bottle. Keep in warm place about 48 hours. After cooling it is ready for use.

58. *Spruce Beer*
Home-made beer.

To 1 galen of water
2 tin of sugar
table spoonful of ginge[r]
1 of allspice
1 of clouvs [cloves]
1 teacup of Malas [molasses]
a little bunch of Sprus [spruce]

Boil the water, Malas, Sugar, then por over the spises. When cool put 1 cup ful of good hot eyest [yeast]. Redy to yuse in 3 days.

CHAPTER TEN

Superstition and Folk Belief

Superstitions are beliefs contrary to current scientific knowledge. Often what is fact to one generation becomes a lingering remnant of superstitious folly to the next. Bloodletting, for example, once a widely accepted medical procedure, continued in folk tradition as a veterinary practice for a time, but has now virtually disappeared. The time may come when the idea of cutting people open to cure them will be looked upon as a primitive barbarism akin to human sacrifice among the Aztecs. Each generation adds to the stock of human knowledge and reluctantly discards what is no longer useful.

Distinction might be made between beliefs involving a misunderstanding of the concept of cause and effect—that is, thinking that results in some way are foreshadowed by certain signs—and beliefs involving causal magic—thinking that results can be produced by deliberately performing an unusual action. The former involve a wide variety of good and bad luck signs: You will have good luck if you find a four-leaf clover, accidentally put an article of clothing on backwards, or see your first robin of the year sitting high in a tree. It is a sign of bad luck to break a mirror, walk under a ladder, or spill salt. Causal beliefs include hanging a dead snake on a fence to make it rain, throwing spilled salt over the left shoulder to prevent bad luck, and a whole range of practices associated with magic and witchcraft.

Most collections of superstitions are disparate listings of curious beliefs that are recalled and recorded as examples of "what the old people used to think." Some are mere lists ranging from a few items to a dozen or more:

To have the chimney cleaned, you know by a chimney sweep, means very good luck.

Walking under a ladder, breaking a mirror, and three on a match all mean bad luck.[1]

When I was a boy about 8 yrs old my Grandmother sent me on horseback to fetch an idarich *(cud) which was a piece of bread out of a family whose wife's maiden name remained the same after marriage. This bread was placed into the* boga *(cheek) of the cow's mouth. This family kept bread on hand for this purpose so they could accommodate their neighbors. While talking of cows, my grandmother warned us not to kill a toad in order to save the cows from giving bloody milk.*[2]

On New Year's Eve only, if you want to find out whether you are going to take a trip or move from the place where you are in the coming year, you must follow this procedure: Sit on the floor, take one of your shoes and place it in front of you. Turn it around several times and then throw it over your shoulder. If the shoe falls pointing outward, then you are going to travel in the next year.

When a ladybug lights on your hand, you must say, "Bzzz, Bzzz," to it until it flies away. Whichever direction he flies in will point to the direction from which your future husband or wife will come.

If you give any sort of gift which has a sharp edge (knife, scissors, sword, etc.) to someone, you will lose his friendship in the near future.

You must never give handkerchiefs as gifts, for in doing so you will be wishing great sorrow on the recipient of the gift.

If the second toe on your foot is longer than your big toe, it means that you are going to dominate your husband.

When a pregnant woman is frightened by some object, the baby will be born with a birthmark in that shape.

If the one you love sends you a "Dear John" letter, you must burn the letter with a candle. Then if you eat the ashes, your lover will come back to you. However, if the candle goes out, you cannot re-light it, and you can't eat the letter without its being burned to ashes, so you have no chance of getting your lover back if these things happen.

If someone you know has died recently, and you see and talk to them in your dreams, then you yourself will die in the near future.

If you sleep in the light of the moon, you will sleepwalk. If this occurs frequently, it is a sign that you are near death.[3]

As this last list indicates, many superstitions develop around the crucial times in human life. Such beliefs relate especially to birth, marriage, moving into a new home, and death. There are ways, the folk feel, of predicting the sex of an unborn child,[4] the number of children one will have, and even superstitious beliefs about becoming pregnant (or avoiding it). The rituals associated with these crucial times often have a basis in superstition:

If a girl was asked to be a maid of honor, she would search the village for someone who was making bread on the morning of the wedding, then ask to make the bread for them. The reason for this was so that her hands would be clean for the wedding. However, the reason for having clean hands has been lost through time.

Having clean feet for the wedding ceremony was also very important. Both the bride and her bridesmaids took part in stamping sauerkraut. The reason for having clean feet has also been lost, even though it was an integral part of the ceremony.

All women married in black dresses. This practice had economic origins. After her wedding, a girl could use her wedding gown as a formal dress.

White veils were also worn as part of the wedding costume, but the wearing of them was restricted to virgins only. The veil was a symbol of virginity, and non-virgins weren't allowed to lie.

Soon after a wedding, people would begin to watch the young bride's face very closely. The surest way to detect pregnancy was the appearance of lines at the corner of the girl's eyes.

To predict what sex the child would be, the mother's cheeks were closely inspected. Because boys were supposed to cause their mothers worry, haggard, thin cheeks foretold a male child. Girls, because they weren't as troublesome as boys, were foretold by full, round cheeks.

There were even ways to wish for the sex of a child. If the mother drank the water from the top of a well, a boy would come. Water drunk from the bottom of the well would bring a girl.

Sisters and brothers had a piece of the wishing action. A sugar cube facing west on the attic windowsill would bring a brother. How? The sugar was for the stork, who would take it and leave a boy.

Ghosts and death were a much talked about belief. One of the superstitions that was connected with death was this one: If blackbirds crowed near your home, someone will die. This originated in the winter. Blackbirds were common, and so were colds and pneumonia. Blackbirds often crowed, and people with pneumonia were sure to die, because there was no cure for it.

It was believed that if someone committed suicide, the ghost would walk in his or her home until the time for the person to die would have come naturally.

Black cats crossing one's path could bring anything from bad luck to death. It is interesting to note that this is still a very popular superstition.

My grandmother told me a very interesting story about a ghost that walked in her town. Hutten was a famous German general. He was beheaded by enemies one day as he was walking near a tree in Holzgerlingen. For years afterward, the townspeople swore that they could see the ghost of General Hutten walking near that same tree. Some claimed that he sat on the ground under the tree. My grandmother also saw him. But then, she had more of a chance to. The tree was right at the end of her family's lane. [5]

Some superstitions are remnants of ancient religious practices. Such undoubtedly are the many beliefs about the effects of the moon on plants, animals, and humans. Numerous writers from Tacitus to the twentieth century have commented on the various facets of moonlore accepted by the German people.[6] Such beliefs as these were once widespread:

A cold moon lies high in the horizon, or far north.

Good events grow better and bad ones worse if happening in the new of the moon.

A new moon happening when the sign is "in the fish" [in Pisces] indicates coming wet weather.

It is best to cut hair in the new of the moon and brush in old of the moon.

If fenceposts are set when the moon points down they will stay down, while if done when the moon points up they will back up out of the ground.

When the moon lies on her back it is a sign of dry weather.

If one butchers in the old of the moon, the meat will shrivel in the tub and frying pan.

A ring around the moon is a sure sign of foul weather.

Plant cabbage when the sign is in the head and the heads will be large and solid.

If the first snow be in the new of the moon it is a sign of a severe winter ahead.

The nearer the moon changes to midnight the fairer the weather will be for a week.

No sailor will sleep in the moonlight for fear of color blindness and no good nurse will allow the baby to sleep with the moon on its face for the same reason.

All kinds of fits come on worse with the changes of the moon and so does nosebleed.[7]

Most folk beliefs still adhered to and practiced are in the realm of folk medicine. Common ailments like colds, nosebleed, measles, mumps, hiccoughs, and warts, more inconveniences than serious illnesses, are often dealt with at home, using a remedy handed down for generations. Many such practices date from times when doctors were not readily available. Some may be facetious, as, for example, this remedy for chapped lips:

An old Amishman told me this. You take your finger and rub it around a horse's hind end, then you rub it around your lips. It works, because you don't lick your lips.[8]

Two unusual remedies were practiced in the German navy prior to and during World War II. One was for seasickness. "Tie a piece of bacon on dental floss, swallow it, and have someone pull it back out. You'll never be seasick again." The second was a remedy for cold or sore throat; "Mix one part boiling water, one part rum and a little sugar. Take on an empty stomach and go to bed." The same informant recalled a home remedy for diptheria that was recommended by a doctor: "Right after the war, penicillin was scarce in Germany. I had diphtheria, my neck swollen up all right. My mother called the doctor and he said he couldn't help, but if she took the juice [salt brine] off pickled herring and had me gargle with it, it would help."[9]

Whooping cough was a serious ailment among children, and many folk medical practices dealt with it:

A live fuzzy caterpillar is sewn in a cloth sack and hung around the neck.[10]

Steal some milk from a black cow with not even a tiny spot of white and give it to the child. It would soon stop.[11]

Put the child into the hopper [of a mill] with the grain, and let the child remain until the grain is all ground out.[12]

If kissed by a "colored" man, you wouldn't get whooping cough.[13]

Put rattles from rattlesnake into a bag and tie around child's neck for whooping cough.[14]

Place your head three times and back, through a horse collar.[15]

Whooping-cough is known as the "blue cough," from the fact that the child turns blue in the face.... Hence, apparently on the homeopathic principle of "like cures like," the child takes his drink out of a blue glass tumbler.[16]

Some remedies required the use of herbs or other materials which did undoubtedly have a beneficial effect:

> *One herb that Mrs. Hamma recalls being used was sassafras. A tea made from this was given to children who had measles. It made the spots come out and speeded recovery.*
>
> *Tincture of rhubarb was "black stuff and tasted awful." This was quite vivid to Mrs. Hamma because she said the children were given this regularly to keep them cleaned out.*
>
> *Each spring the children received a dose of sulfur and molasses. "That was to get the blood moving."*
>
> *Another tea made from powdered ginger, sugar and hot water was given for colds and pains. Sometimes one would drink it just "to warm the tummy" or follow it by going to bed to keep warm and sweat out a cold.*
>
> *If a cold was bad, red pepper was added to the ginger tea. This helped make you sweat and get rid of the cold faster.*
>
> *For coughs, onions were used. They were cooked with sugar and the sticky syrup was taken as an aid to loosen the congestion.*
>
> *Poultices were used for all sorts of pains. Onions were cooked in the oven until they were soft and used. These were placed between two cloths and placed on the body to draw soreness out.*
>
> *For hangovers, she recalled seeing Jamaica ginger being administered to some members of her family. It came in a bottle and was taken the morning after to reduce symptoms.*
>
> *Mrs. Hamma laughed and said that it took a little magic to cure warts. Rut a bean on the wart and then plant the bean. When the resulting plant dies, the warts will go away.*[17]

Sometimes an ailment requires a more serious form of magic, and then a *braucher* or *powwow* doctor is consulted. A few afflictions which modern medicine does not recognize or cannot cure, and those sicknesses attributable to spells, hexes, or other evil influence, are dealt with by these healers who combine some herbal knowledge presumably drawn from Indian sources (hence the word *powwow*), the spiritual healing power of biblical teaching, and a conglomeration of charms and prayers that undoubtedly dates from pre-Christian times in central Europe.[18] Many have been handed from one generation to the next (cross-sexually, "from a man to a woman or vice versa, so the power is not lost") in written form, and a few of these collections have been published.[19] The best known is John George Hohman's *Der Lange Verborgene Freund* (The Long-Lost Friend), published in Reading, Pennsylvania, in 1819, with many subsequent editions. Hohman included remedies for bleeding, colic, and toothache, religio-magic charms to heal wounds, prevent fire, and protect against thieves, and a variety of methods for preventing or stopping witchcraft.[20]

The simplest powwow charm is one still used by mothers to distract a child's mind from a minor hurt. While rubbing or kissing the injured area, they recite, *"Heeli heeli, hinkel dreck,/Bis marya frie is alles weck"* (Heal, heal, chicken-shit; by tomorrow everything will be all gone).[21] The concern and caring shown by the mother obviously has a better effect than the charm, and this probably explains the effectiveness of powwowing in general.

Most powwowers have the power to stop bleeding, usually by reciting a charm containing the victim's name:

Jesus Christ Dearest blood
That stoppest the blood
In this help [name]
God the Father God the Son God the Holy Ghost amen!
Help to this![22]

or by repeating Ezekiel 16:6.[23]

Many powwowers also "blow" the fire or burning sensation from burns, again reciting a religious incantation:

For the burning (if a man has been scalded or burnt)

The blessed virgin went over the land;
what does she carry in her holy hand—a fire brand;
eat not in thee, eat not farther around thee,
in the name of God, the father, the son and the holy ghost,
amen X X X.

So saying these words, stroke slowly three times with your right hand over it, bending the same downwards, for one, two or three times and blow three times, every time thrice.[24]

Âwachse (livergrown) is a mysterious but common ailment of early children, believed to be caused by taking the child over a rough road before it is a year old. Its ordinary cure involves some variant of a

174

"passing through" procedure, passing the child through a horse collar, through a raspberry bush grown tight at both ends, or around a table leg.[25] Occasionally powwow charms are recited to accompany this procedure, but usually that involves other actions:

> *Livergrown cardiaca, leave the ribs of my little child, as little Jesus left the cribs, in the name of God, the father, the son, and the holy ghost, Amen.*
>
> *Dip your thumb in grease and pass it three times over the Breast and three times over the Back until you say these Words in the morning, evening and morning, every time thrice.*[26]

Removing warts and other growths often involved looking at a new moon while rubbing the growth and reciting a charm. For corns:

> *Take the third evening of the new moon and say:*
>
> *Was ich say nemmt tsu.* (What I am looking at, increase.)
> *Was ich grife nemmt ob.* (What I am rubbing, decrease.)
> *(Three times)*
>
> *In the name of our + + +. This is a sure cure.*[27]

And for goiter:

> *My mother powwowed for a goiter with the new moon. As she rubbed the growth she said, "Vas ich seh nemmt zu; vas ich reib nemmt opp." This means, "What I am looking at, will increase; what I am rubbing, will decrease." And strangely she never developed a full goiter, just the slight lump which she had rubbed.*[28]

Some charms have relatively wide circulation. One cure for thrush, an ulceration of the mouth, has been traced from West Virginia back to the sixteenth-century *Romanusbüchlein,* and parallels to it have been found in Virginia and in Pennsylvania:

> *Job, Job gin uber Land. Er dragt ein Stablein in seiner Hand. Da vorkam ihm Gott der Herr. Gott der Herr Sprach. Job, Job, warum drauerst du so sehr. Herr warum soll ich nicht draurig sein? Es will mein Kindlein Zung und Mund verfaulen. + + + Dreimal.*

Job, Job, went across the land. He carries a wand in his hand. There came our Lord, Our Lord spoke, Job, Job, why are you so sad? Why should I not be sad? My little child has the thrash of the tongue and the mouth. + + + Three times.[29]

A common powwow charm for snakebite is:

Gott hot alles arshaffa, und alles war gut;
Als du allen Schlang, bisht ferflucht,
Ferflucht solsht du sain und dain gift. + + +

God created everything, and it was good;
Except thou alone snake art cursed,
Cursed art thou and thy poison.

The speaker then with the extended index finger, makes the sign of the cross three times over the wound, each time pronouncing the word *tsing.*[30]

Many people sought out the aid of *brauchers* when they thought their cattle or other farm animals were bewitched. The most common recommendation was that they draw a picture of the suspected witch on the barn and shoot at it with a silver bullet. The witch would be injured in the same part of the body which the bullet struck. If silver was scarce, substitutions were possible:

My daddy used t' think he was bewitched, an' somebody told him if you draw a picture an' put aluminum foil, roll up aluminum an' put in your gun an' shoot, wherever that hit, ya know, in the arm or the leg, that's where they were suppose' t' hurt. Carrie F---- was t' be the one, an' he shot, an' after that she was limpin'. An' he said, "See there, what'd I tell ya?"[31]

The story of a similar counteractant was collected in Delaware:

I was present at the time of this man's telling of stories. However, there were many stories that he told us that he refused to put on tape, because, as he said, he was afraid of the hex doctor or the hex man. This is so deep in their thoughts up in this area [Lehigh County, Pennsylvania], that they don't know just how deep the hex doctor or hex man knows of things. He did tell of a story, that, uh, he did tell of a story that a family was so-called "hexed." Their whole life was bad, they had bad fortune in their farm, their family was torn apart, and just everything was going bad, and this was a neighbor. And this hex doctor lived not too far away. The family was not on too good of terms with the family of the next farm, so the man that had had bad fortunes went to the so-called hex doctor or whatever they call him, gave him the story, and the hex doctor asked him if he thought he could do anything about it. He makes an affirmation that he, he was sure that he could. So he was told to go back to his barn, and drill a hole through the barn door from the outside, from the inside out, and get a peg that fits, not too snugly, but one that would have to be hammered in. And every day before he started his farm chores he was to push the peg in with one push of the mallet or hammer. And this he did for many days, until one day, whether the wood got, whether the wood got swollen, the man was angry at this instant and he gave it one hard push, and the peg went right through the barn door, the hole that he had drilled in the door, and the very next day, the neighbor who he was not too friendly with dropped dead. And from that time on his family had good fortune. This is a sign of the power of the hex, and what they believe in up there.[32]

Apotropaism of this type is generally performed secretly, inside the barn or other farm buildings to ward off witches. Unlike the decorative circles on the front of barns popularly called "hex signs" since the 1930s, protection against witchcraft is hidden inside, often on the lintels of the entrances. A farm in northern Dauphin County, Pennsylvania, had copies of the following charm carefully folded and tacked up over all the doors of the house, summer kitchen, barn, and other outbuildings:

Trotta Head, I forbid thee my house and premises, I forbid thee my horse and cowstable, I forbid thee my bedstead, that thou mayest not breathe upon me, breathe into some other house, until thou hast ascended every hill, until thou hast counted every fence-post, and until thou hast crossed every water. And thus dear day may come again into my house, in the name of God the Father, the Son, and the Holy Ghost. Amen.[33]

Some of the more unusual protective charms supposedly warded off fire or other threats to household security. One found in Hohman's *Long Lost Friend* also circulated in West Virginia:

To Extinguish Fire Without Water

Write the following words on each side of a plate, and throw it into the fire, and it will be extinguished forthwith:

A broadside Himmelsbrief *printed by King and Baird, Philadelphia printers.*

SATOR
AREPO
TENET
OPERA
ROTAS.[34]

Similar charms, apparently recited, were collected in Somerset County, Pennsylvania:

Father God, please place a wall of living flame around (whichever applies,
me, us, use names, our buildings, possessions, car, etc.) for protection
against danger, harm, accident, evil, illness, or fire.

And the other:

As I walked before the house of judges
Three dead men looked out the window;
One had no tongue, one had no lung,
The third blind, sick and dumb.
In the name of the Father, the Son and Holy Ghost. Amen.
Protect us (or me) (use full name).[35]

By far, the best known of these protective charms is the *Himmelsbrief*
(Letter from Heaven). The idea of a letter "Written by God Himself" dates
from the early years of the Christian era, but most of those in circulation
today purportedly date from one of several such letters found in
Germany in the eighteenth century, among them those of Holstein, 1724,
and Magdeburg, 1783. The letter generally promises protection from evil
to anyone who believes it and carries it, often specifying that no fire nor
bullet shall come near such a person. As a result, many Pennsylvania
German soldiers carried them into battle during two World Wars, and
numerous broadside copies hang in German homes to protect them from
destruction.[36]

CHAPTER ELEVEN

Folk Art

Folk art is a term generally used by museum curators and art dealers to label those objects which do not fit into the traditional categories of their field. This includes many objects not intended as art by their creators but that have an esthetic appeal or an ornamentation that sets them apart from the ordinary. Such functional, everyday items as jugs and crocks, tinware, kitchen utensils, and even furniture are often included in folk art collections because their makers chose to add a nonfunctional decoration to add a bit of pleasure to their mundane lives. The Pennsylvania German felt a need to fill the blank spaces in his life with beauty. The sides of his stoneware pottery called for a simple design, a bird or flower in cobalt blue, the only color to withstand the high temperatures of the firing process. The front of his wife's or daughter's dower chest required an elaborate display of tulips, birds, or flowers. The front of his barn had traditional symbols which some people call hex signs, because it was his pride and joy.

One significant characteristic of early Pennsylvania German folk art is the symmetrical arrangement of its elements. Whether a *Fraktur* certificate, a decorated chest, or a barn, the embellishment is usually applied in such a way that one half is a mirror image of the other. A bird facing right on one half of a *Taufschein* will confront one facing left on the other. Lilies on one end of a chest will match lilies on the other, with a different but related central element symmetrically arranged within itself.[1] On barns an outlined door at one side will require the outlining of a similar space on the opposite side, even if no door exists. And the so-called hex signs are similarly arranged so that those at opposite ends of the barn match, while one (or two) in the middle will be of a different design.[2]

Fraktur

Symmetry is particularly evident in the manuscripts known as *Fraktur*, so named because the lettering in medieval writing style appears to be broken or fractured.[3] These documents fulfilled a variety of purposes, practical rather than artistic, but the decorative compulsion filled the blank areas of the page with birds, angels, tulips, and other flowers. Many of these items were produced by schoolmasters or preachers, learned individuals who are sometimes identified by name. Others used characteristic elements that make their work recognizable, such as the "Nine Hearts Artist," who arranged a group of that number of hearts around the top and center of his pieces.[4]

The *Taufschein* (baptismal certificate) is among the oldest types of Fraktur known. It has its roots in the Palatinate and seems to have appeared in Pennsylvania with the earliest Germanic immigrants.[5] The dates of the child's birth and baptism appear on these pieces, along with the names of its parents and of the minister who performed the baptism. But the information is surrounded and almost overwhelmed by brightly colored birds, angels, flowers, or other objects. In most cases the artistry and most of the lettering was done beforehand, with blank spaces left for the names and dates to be added as the occasion arose.

Another common item was the *Vorschrift* (writing sample), which the schoolmaster produced to teach his students the technique of lettering. Besides displaying the alphabet in both capital and small letters, the typical Vorschrift contained Bible verses and usually a selection from a German hymnbook. This type too is of European, especially Swiss, origin.[6]

The most artistic pieces in this tradition are bookplates, drawn on the flyleaves of early hymnbooks, and bookmarks, often given as rewards to star pupils in the Fraktur-artist's tutelage.[7] Fraktur art, though generally found among the Pennsylvania Germans, was also produced in areas under their direct influence, the Shenandoah Valley, Ohio, and Ontario.[8]

Folk Painting

Most frequently "folk painting" is a term applied to the work of an

*Taufschein of Joseph Hey, son of Philipp Hey and Anna Maria Gilbertin,
born December 17, 1795, and baptized March 6, 1796, Berks County,
Pennsylvania. (21 x 33.5 cm.) (Pennsylvania Folklife Society)*

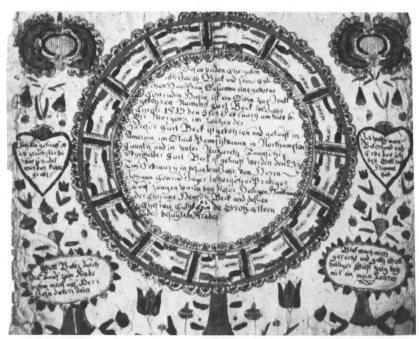

*Taufschein of Carl Beck, son of Jacob Beck and Susanna Has, born February
5, 1813, and baptized February 25, 1813, Northampton County, Pennsylvania.
(33.5 x 40.5 cm.) (Pennsylvania Folklife Society)*

Taufschein of Susanna Neidigh, December 6, 1830, Perry County, Pennsylvania. The pertinent data are filled into blank spaces on a form printed by G. S. Peters, Harrisburg, Pennsylvania. The birds, border, and angels are stenciled in red and yellow. (16 x 13½'') (Author's collection)

Taufschein of Elisabet Wilhelmina Brand, January 9, 1830, hand-drawn and -lettered by the "Path Valley" artist, Franklin County, Pennsylvania. (11¾ x 15½") (Author's collection)

untrained artist who attempts, not successfully, to imitate an academic style. Occasionally it refers to the work of someone who utilizes the medium of oil or watercolor as a way of recording an event remembered nostalgically. Less skilled in the use of words to describe the details or events in question, this artist creates a visual image of his memories. The scene is authentic, but the painter's performance is not always capable of transcribing it artistically. Many of the sketches and drawings of Lewis Miller fall into this category.

Lewis Miller was born in York, Pennsylvania, May 3, 1796, the son of Johann Ludwig Miller from Württemberg and Katharina Rothenberger of Heidelberg. During the 87 years that he lived he recorded in sketches and watercolors all the interesting and mundane events of everyday life. He depicted the great moments of American history from the death of Washington through the Civil War to the assassination of Lincoln. But he also portrayed lesser moments in the folklife of the Germans of Pennsylvania, such as butchering, making sauerkraut, fish gigging, charivaris, a Methodist camp meeting, perhaps the first picture of a

Christmas tree in America; some humorous scenes—a man urinating down a roofboard onto his brother, "the retreat of bad womans" as angry citizens drive them from their house, a wagon dismantled and reassembled on top of the market house; and examples of architectural styles of all levels, folk, vernacular and classic. During his last years, Miller made his home with a niece in Christiansburg, Virginia, where he died on September 15, 1882.[9]

Occasionally a folk artist's work is recognized outside the folk community. Such is the case with the paintings of Anna Bock, a sort of Mennonite "Grandma Moses" from northern Indiana. Born in Wakarusa, Indiana, in 1924, Bock began painting in her early twenties, depicting scenes from Mennonite life to correct misconceptions about that lifestyle. From memory and imagination she brings together stock images of farmsteads as the setting for such activities as Sunday visiting, harvesting, butchering, and preparing maple sugar. Done on standard-sized canvas boards, these scenes display the same concern with accurate detail as the genre paintings of the nineteenth century. Commissioned farmscape painting was a part of that tradition, and Schrock does much of her work on commission. Among Old Order Mennonites in Indiana such paintings are still popular, so that Bock's work is much in demand, not only among members of her own culture group but among others as well.[10]

Sometimes the style or technique of a self-trained painter falls completely outside the categories of elite art. When critics find aesthetic value in such work, they tend to label it "folk," even though it is as much outside the folk tradition as it is alien to academic art. The work of the Texas artist Eddie Arning is a case in point. The son of German immigrants who arrived in Texas in the late nineteenth century, Arning produced a series of somber crayon drawings depicting rural objects drawn from memory, "animals . . . curiously alive, even though stiff-legged and hardly distinguishable as different species."[11] The color combinations, deep blues, purples, and greens, with their geometric arrangements, are strongly suggestive of Amish quilts.[12]

Woodcarving

Some writers see folk art as a form of play. In this sense, the folk craftsman or the folk consumer may attribute a lower value to a piece of art than to a more practical artifact. Even an apparently useless decoration has value, but at the folk level such items are often viewed as a waste

"Sunday Company" (1971), by Anna Bock (12 x 16"), oil on canvas board. (Courtesy Simon J. Bronner)

"The Sugar Camp" (1973), by Anna Bock (24 x 30"), oil on canvas board. (Courtesy Simon J. Bronner)

of time. Thus much folk art is seen as the product of people who have plenty of time to waste, wandering tramps with no permanent employment, or elderly men and women retired from a lifetime job who find the creation of trivial objects to be a pleasurable experience.

One Pennsylvania German "tramp" who has achieved a high level of recognition is Wilhelm Schimmel. Born in 1817 in Germany, Schimmel arrived in the Cumberland Valley of Pennsylvania in the 1860s, fleeing military conscription, some say, or some unexplained tragedy, others say.[13] He traveled around the Cumberland Valley until the year of his death (1890), carving birds and animals from scraps of pine that he cadged from local carpenters, then trading the carvings for meals and lodging at the farms where he regularly stayed. Some were traded for whiskey at the taverns and barrooms of Carlisle. Schimmel is best known for his large, fierce-looking eagles, with notch-carved wings spreading from the dove-tailed joints where they were fitted into the bodies. His use of gesso as a base for the remnants of barn paints that he was able to scrounge for use on his carvings suggests that he possessed a certain amount of artistic training, probably gained prior to his arrival here. Like many German folk artists, Schimmel produced an occasional depiction of the Garden of Eden, with Adam and Eve behind a carefully carved picket fence, watching a snake twined around a split-shaved tree that looks more pine than apple.[14]

Aaron Mountz, a protégé of Schimmel, was born in 1873 at Possum Hill, near Carlisle, Pennsylvania. He grew up in the area frequented by Schimmel and apparently learned to carve at his side, for there is considerable similarity between their styles. The major difference is that Mountz handled his blade a bit more cautiously, and unlike the older German, did not cover his finished pieces with paint, choosing instead to leave the wood in its natural state.[15]

Another carver still active in the Schimmel tradition is Walter Gottshall, of Reinholds, Pennsylvania. Gottshall became interested in woodcarving in the early 1960s, and admiring the work of Schimmel, decided to imitate it. Eagles, parrots, and a variety of smaller birds flowed off his knife, but he left the painting to his wife June. Gottshall has also produced accurate copies of Schimmel's Garden of Eden as well as highly imaginative original pieces.[16]

This same tradition of carving small animals and other such items as toys and pleasure objects occurs in many areas where nineteenth-century German immigrants settled. Charles van Ravenswaay discusses a carver named Fritz Baurichter, who lived in Warren County, Missouri, until his death in 1937. Baurichter's wooden birds and men on horseback

Wilhelm Schimmel carved dozens of eagles which he traded for meals and lodging or for a few drinks in local bars. (Cumberland County Historical Society)

An eagle by Aaron Mountz in unpainted wood shows more carefully-detailed carving in the wing feathers and a cross-hatched style on the body. (Cumberland County Historical Society)

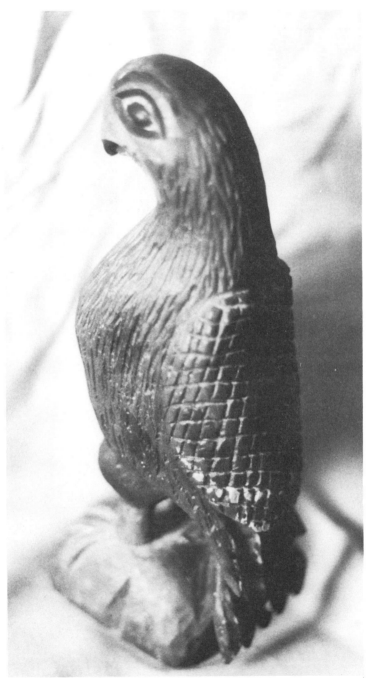

Carving by Walter Gottshall, Reinholds, Pennsylvania (1978), reveals an early influence of the style of Wilhelm Schimmel. (8¾ x 4'') (Author's collection)

Gottshall's more recent work (1985) shows a more whimsical personal style. (6 x 2⅝") (Author's collection)

"Mary's Star," by John Scholl, a fine example of the artist's free-standing creations in pine, painted red, white, and blue. (68 x 22-5/16") (New York State Historical Association, Cooperstown)

are an authentic remnant of the German folk tradition.[17]

John Scholl of Germania, Pennsylvania, produced a highly unusual, in fact unique, type of folk sculpture. Scholl was born in Württemberg in 1827 and migrated to Pennsylvania in 1853, where he worked as a carpenter and farmer until his death in 1916. His interest in wood-working and especially in the Victorian-age "gingerbread" trim used on houses at the time led him to experiment with arrangements of these elements in fantastic, free-standing creations combining traditional Pennsylvania German doves, tulips, and crosses with elaborate fretwork designs.[18] He also produced whittler's puzzles—figures linked with unbroken wooden chains[19] and elaborate toys with moving parts. In one of these, soldiers move in a circle while a star-wheel revolves below them. Another has small wooden acrobats performing on a moving wheel.[20] These objects and the magnificent decorative pieces that once cluttered Scholl's parlor are now prized possessions of folk art museums from New York to Williamsburg.

CHAPTER TWELVE

Folk Architecture

Folk architecture is that constructed by nonprofessionals with some traditional skills, following traditional concepts of form, size, and building techniques. In some cases the builder is also the person who will utilize the building. In other cases, those lacking the requisite skills enlist the aid of a skilled craftsman, tell him what they want, and usually help with the construction, under the builder's direction.

Though settlers in the New World carried with them a mental concept of traditional housing and the techniques and tools needed to reproduce that concept, their resultant structures were influenced and altered by a variety of factors. The materials available demanded new techniques. The German-Russians who settled in Kansas in 1876, for example, at first attempted a construction form familiar to them along the Volga, a mud-brick masonry that eventually yielded to more readily available stone.[1] The excess of timber in eastern areas meant that log construction often replaced a more familiar masonry concept. Differing climates meant that house forms changed to accommodate those differences. Roofing materials and gable angles adapted to varying amounts of rain or snowfall. In warmer southern climates, chimneys moved from an internal to an external position, so that the heat of cooking was more rapidly dispersed. In the northern plains, the entire kitchen was internalized to retain the heat. Then, too, the influence of contiguous buildings often changed the mental concept, especially among later migrants.

Much has been written about the tradition of log building in America and its possible European origins. Because of its importance among the

Pennsylvania Germans, the use of logs has often been ascribed to a Germanic source.[2] But log building was significant also in Scandinavia, and the earliest log houses in the New World, along the Delaware near Philadelphia, were Swedish.[3] Then too, some early log houses were built in New England, so there is a possible argument that log building grew out of the British half-timber technique.[4] Henry Glassie, among others, has noted the similarity between log buildings of the New World and those of the German-Slavic border area.[5] Terry Jordan also recognized this similarity but was unable to trace that tradition through southern Germany and Switzerland, from where the earliest German migrations took place. More recently Jordan quite logically recognized American log building styles as a synthesis of all these European influences.[6] Whatever its origin, the Germans in the New World adopted log-building with a fury, carried it into other areas they settled, from Ontario to North Carolina and westward as far as Missouri and Wisconsin,[7] and then continued to build traditional log houses as late as the 1920s.[8]

Another building technique widely used by German settlers is that called *Fachwerk*, or half-timber construction. In this technique, the framing members of the building are exposed, consisting of heavy, squared timbers mortised or pinned together, with the spaces between filled by brick or stone nogging or wattle and daub, a mixture of mud, dung, and straw or hair as a binder. This type of construction became common in western Germany when wood became scarce during the Middle Ages, but it was also found in England and elsewhere. Though few examples survive, this building manner was once relatively common among the Pennsylvania Germans.[9] Most examples of it were found in the small cities of York and Lancaster (a few half-timber buildings in Philadelphia were probably English). One interesting rural example once stood on the Shreiner farm, near the Pennsylvania Farm Museum north of Lancaster. Built in the second half of the eighteenth century by Adam Schreiner or his son Philip, the house was occupied until the construction of a new dwelling in 1808. It was photographed in 1890 by A. K. Hostetter, who recalled, "One of the interesting recollections I have of the old house is a yellow-jackets' nest which Mr. Diffenderffer and I struck while stirring about in the old house. It caused a very sudden exit on our part."[10] Considering the house an eyesore, or possibly to get rid of the yellowjackets, the owner burned it in 1900.[11]

Moravians from Pennsylvania introduced this style into North Carolina,[12] but most examples of half-timber structure in other areas are the result of later immigration. Ohio (where the building style is called *Dreckhaus*, "mud house" or "mud-filled") has a number of these struc-

The Shreiner house, a half-timbered structure that stood north of Lancaster, Pennsylvania, until 1900. (Courtesy Mrs. J. Newton Shreiner)

Balcony house-barn at Bowman's Mill, Rockingham, Virginia, before 1790. (Courtesy K. Edward Lay)

tures dating from the time of the nineteenth-century settlements.[13] Similar buildings in Wisconsin, Missouri, and Texas date from the same period.[14]

The Housebarn

European peasant housing frequently provided human living quarters and stabling for animals on different levels or at opposite ends of the same building.[15] Early migrants often duplicated this concept in the New World. The 1798 Direct Tax Lists for Pennsylvania listed three structures where the inhabitant "lives in one end of the barn."[16] The double-crib log barn once found commonly throughout the region would have lent itself well to such utilization, since it was essentially two independent struc-tures joined by a single roof.[17]

The Miller House, which once stood just south of Harrisonburg, Virginia, however, was a multi-level structure. It had a stabling area below and housing above, with a broad balcony, similar to Bavarian houses.[18]

German settlers in the central Plains also built housebarns, a dozen or so of which still survive. The best known of these is the Pelster Housebarn in Franklin County, Missouri. This structure was built about 1855 by William Pelster (1825–1908), whose parents came to the area in 1842. It exhibits features of Pelster's paternal homestead a few miles to the east, including a half-timber construction similar to that in a house built by his father, and a floor plan much like that of his father's double-crib barn. The building is a multi-level bank structure, with stables, stalls, and cellar on the lower level. Over the cellar on the south end of the building is a dwelling area for the family, with kitchen to the rear, living room, and a front room opening onto a porch. Above these are bedrooms and storage areas. The house portion of the structure is separated from the barn by a *Diele* (great hallway), entered through a double-doored wagon entrance, while the north end or barn segment has granaries and a hay chute. A hayloft extends the length of the structure on the upper level.[19]

The Continental Central-Chimney House

As the name implies, the characteristic feature of the continental central-chimney house is the location of the chimney and its large

Fort Egypt, near Luray, Virginia. (Courtesy K. Edward Lay)

cooking hearth in the center of the structure. The huge fireplace divides the floor plan into two principal areas, the *Küche* (kitchen) and the *Stube* (parlor). The Stube usually has a smaller area divided off to the rear, the *Kammer* or bedroom. In some examples, the Hans Herr house of Lancaster, for instance, the kitchen is partitioned to create a smaller room to the rear which served as a pantry. Built in 1719, the Herr House is unusual among extant central-chimney houses in having a full second story and above that an attic or loft rising into the steep gable. It does not have the opposing front and rear doors leading into the kitchen that are usually found in such houses,[20] but it does have a feature common to many early Germanic houses, particularly those built into banks with access on two levels. That is an arched cellar under one half of the house, which served as a cool storage area for fruits, dairy products, and meats. In other houses this cellar often contained a spring, which provided water and aided in cooling. Still utilized as a dwelling into the twentieth century, the house has now been restored to its original condition by the Lancaster Mennonite Conference Historical Society.[21]

Such house forms were once relatively common in Pennsylvania, but their distribution was limited to areas of direct Pennsylvania German contact, the Great Valley of Maryland and Virginia, and the North

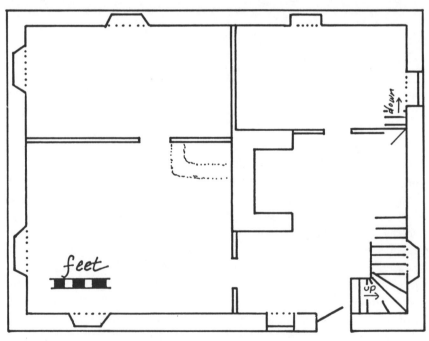

The Hans Herr house, near Lancaster, Pennsylvania, an outstanding example of a multi-level continental central-chimney house.

Carolina Piedmont settled by the Moravians.[22] Significant examples from those areas include the fieldstone structure known as Hager's Fancy, built by Jonathan Hager in 1740 at Hagerstown, Maryland;[23] Fort Egypt, built by Swiss emigrants roughly between 1725 and 1730 near Luray, Virginia;[24] and the Philip Dellinger house, near Conicville in the Shenandoah Valley, built about 1800.[25] Henry Glassie has shown a relationship between the central chimney house and the popular English subtype, the two-thirds Georgian house.[26] It also influenced a significant change in the floor-plan of Scotch-Irish log houses.

The Single-Pen Log House

A typical log house is a rectangular structure about sixteen to eighteen feet wide and twenty to twenty-four feet long, consisting of a single pen (a room enclosed within four log walls) on the first floor and a loft above.[27] Among the Scotch-Irish the tendency was to frame the floor joists of the loft at the plate that supported the rafters, while the German immigrants set these beams into the wall of the structure and raised the wall several logs above that before laying the plate, thus providing more headroom on the upper level.[28] The lower floor was used for cooking, eating, and general family activities, and in some early houses it also served as sleeping quarters. Generally, though, the loft was for sleeping and was sometimes divided by a blanket hung from the rafters or occasionally by a thin partition. In cases where the house was raised to a full two stories, the upper level was divided into two or three rooms, variously arranged.

The single-pen lower level was also occasionally partitioned into two rooms in keeping with the British hall-and-parlor tradition, or into three as a continuation of the central-chimney room arrangement, with one large room adjacent to the fireplace and two smaller rooms opposite. An interesting intermediate phase is represented by a number of houses in the New Germantown area of western Perry County, Pennsylvania, where the continental house floor plan is maintained but the chimney and fireplace are completely exteriorized.

The single-pen house became a dominant housing type in most areas where the Pennsylvania Germans eventually settled. When Ananias Hensel moved from Somerset County, Pennsylvania, to Indiana in 1852, he built a substantial log house with a large living room in the first floor's single pen. A kitchen and dining room were located in an attached wing, but the second floor of the log house was divided into two bedrooms, in typical Pennsylvania fashion.[29]

The Black-Kitchen House

Climatic factors were an important element in changes in house forms. The long, cold winters of Wisconsin forced the introduction of a Pomerania house type called the *schwarze Küche* (black kitchen). The cooking area is a windowless room in the center of the house, completely surrounded by the other rooms. Thus the heating effect of the hearth or stove achieves maximum efficiency in much the same way that the earlier central chimney house retained and circulated as much heat as possible.[30]

The Sunday House

Factors other than economic and climatic sometimes influence the development of a housing form. The Sunday houses of Fredericksburg, Texas, were built by German farmers who came to town on weekends to attend market or to go to church. Simple structures on small lots, they usually have one or two rooms on the ground floor and a sleeping area in the half story above. The unusual feature of this house is that it has no internal stairway. Access to the upper level was once gained by ladders, but now open outdoor stairways are used.[31]

The Double-Crib Barn

The double-crib barn consists of two log pens or cribs joined by a common roof that also covers the breezeway or threshing floor between them. Some of these barns developed as a natural expansion of a single-crib concept and a few may have been at one time half dwelling and half barn.

Various origins have been suggested for this barn type, since its congeners are found in England and in central and northern Europe.[32] Whether influenced by English or German tradition, the double-crib barn is found throughout the area of Pennsylvania German settlement, from Ontario to Alabama.[33] Once thought rare in Pennsylvania, the single-level double-crib barn still exists in occasional examples in the south-central counties.[34]

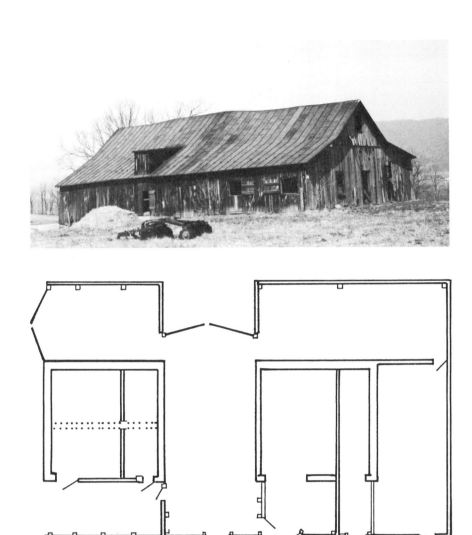

Single-level double-crib log barn near Bloserville, Cumberland County, Pennsylvania (photographed 1969).

The Pennsylvania Barn

Henry Glassie suggests an evolutionary sequence of development from the double-crib barn to the two-level Pennsylvania bank barn.[35] The suggestion is logical, considering the existence of both types of barns in the same areas of migration, but Glassie himself has traced the Pennsylvania barn to central European sources and others have supported his findings.[36]

The characteristic barn that dominates the landscape in southeastern Pennsylvania and appears frequently in areas of Pennsylvania German influence is recognizable by two dominant features (besides its size), a cantilevered forebay and a ramp in the rear providing access to the upper level. The forebay appears on a variety of building forms in the Palatinate and in Austria but it is a dominant feature on barns in northeastern Switzerland.[37] The ramp is a remnant of a tradition which built barns into banks to insulate the stables in the lower level from extreme temperatures in winter and summer. The forebay is an early solar device that allows the low-lying winter sun to heat the stables while providing shade for the cattle when the summer sun is high overhead.

The lower level was originally divided into two banks of stables, one toward the house for horses and draft animals and one at the opposite end for milk cattle. The central area was divided into entry-ways for feeding and pens where calves, sheep, and even pigs could be stabled in winter. The upper level was divided into three, four, or even five bays, those on the ends being storage mows for hay and straw and the middle bays serving as threshing floors. In earlier times, when threshing was done with flails, doors were opened at the front and rear of the barn to provide free air flow, which helped in separating the grain from the chaff. With the introduction of commercial threshing machines, the machines were pulled into the barn, sheaves of grain fed into them from one of the mows, and the straw from the process blown into another mow or into the barnyard. Some early barns had such low eaves that the blower tube could not be extended, so dormer windows were often built into the roof above the threshing floor to accommodate the blower. One such dormer can be seen in the roof of the Cumberland County double-crib barn above.

Such barns were commonly built in Pennsylvania from the late 1700s until about 1920 and only sporadically since then. Pennsylvania bank barns, or barns closely resembling them, are still found along the migration routes followed by the Pennsylvania German migrants of the late eighteenth and early nineteenth centuries, from Ontario to Tennessee[38]

Double-crib log bank barn near Bloserville, Cumberland County, Pennsylvania.

Pennsylvania German bank barn near Shippensburg, Pennsylvania.

and from New Jersey to Iowa.[39] Their influence is also noted in the southern and central parts of Wisconsin,[40] and scattered examples are seen in Missouri[41] and Texas.[42] It is not surprising that the object in which the German farmer took most pride, the structure that provided evidence of his success, should be the most lasting evidence of his presence on the landscape.

Notes

CHAPTER 1. THE GERMANS IN AMERICA

[1]Arthur Graeff, "The Colonial Melting Pot," *The Pennsylvania Germans,* ed. Ralph Wood (Princeton: Princeton University Press, 1942), 7; William Beidelman, *The Story of the Pennsylvania Germans* (Detroit: Gale Research Co., 1969), 84.

[2]Cited by Beidelman, 85–87.

[3]The story was still taught as fact in the schools of Germany in the late 1930s. However, see Jürgen Eichhoff, "The German Language in America," *America and the Germans,* ed. Frank Trommler and Joseph McVeigh (Philadelphia: University of Pennsylvania Press, 1985), vol. 1, 225.

[4]Albert Bernhardt Faust, *The German Element in the United States* (New York: Arno Press, 1969), vol. 1, 79–105.

[5]Faust, vol. 1, 230–31.

[6]Elmer Smith, John Stewart, and M. Ellsworth Kyger, *The Pennsylvania Germans in the Shenandoah Valley* (Allentown: Pennsylvania German Folklore Society, 1964), 21; Daniel Nead, *The Pennsylvania-German in the Settlement of Maryland* (Lancaster: Pennsylvania-German Society, 1914), 39–44.

[7]Jonathan Hager, its founder, arrived in Philadelphia on September 1, 1736, settled in Maryland, and laid out the town in 1762.

[8]G. M. Ludwig, "The Influence of the Pennsylvania Dutch in the Middle West," *Pennsylvania German Folklore Society* 10 (1945): 31–36, 55.

[9]Personal letter dated January 13, 1963, Los Angeles, California.

[10]Mack Walker, *Germany and the Emigration, 1816–1885* (Cambridge: Harvard University Press, 1964), 2–6, 48–49.

[11]The bibliography on that revolution is extensive: for a concise summary, see Carl J. Friedrich, "The European Background," *The Forty-Eighters,* ed. A. E. Zucker (New York: Russell & Russell, 1967), 3–25.

[12]Among A. E. Schroeder's many excellent studies of the Germans in Missouri, see "The Contexts of Continuity: Germanic Folklore in Missouri," *Kansas Quarterly* 13 (1981): 81–102. Note especially pages 90–91.

[13]Steven Rowan, *Germans for a Free Missouri* (Columbia: University of Missouri Press, 1983); Richard O'Conner, *The German-Americans* (Boston: Little, Brown, 1968), 86–94. Duden's treatise has recently been reissued in translation by the University of Missouri Press.

[14]Charles van Ravenswaay, *The Arts and Architecture of German Settlements in Missouri* (Columbia and London: University of Missouri Press, 1977), 16–17.

[15]M. Walter Dundore, "The Saga of the Pennsylvania Germans in Wisconsin," *Pennsylvania German Folklore Society* 19 (1954): 58–60.

[16]LaVern Rippley, *Of German Ways* (Minneapolis: Dillon Press, 1970), 33.

[17]*German-American Pioneers in Wisconsin and Michigan,* ed. Harry H. Anderson (Milwaukee: Milwaukee County Historical Society, 1971), 149.

[18]O'Conner, 95–97.

[19]Ibid., 86–94.

[20]Terry G. Jordan, *German Seed in Texas Soil* (Austin: University of Texas Press, 1985), 40–59.

[21]George C. Engerrand, *The So-Called Wends of Germany and Their Colonies in Texas and Australia* (Austin: University of Texas, 1934); Anne Blasig, *The Wends of Texas* (San Antonio: Naylor, 1954); George R. Nielson, "Folklore of the German-Wends in Texas," *Singers and*

Storytellers, ed. Mody C. Boatright et al., (Dallas: Southern Methodist University Press, 1961), 244–59.

[22]Faust, vol. 1, 501–2.

[23]Frederick C. Luebke, *Immigrants and Politics: The Germans of Nebraska, 1880–1900* (Lincoln: University of Nebraska Press, 1969), 19–25.

[24]Dorothy Schwieder, "A Cultural Mosaic: The Settling of Iowa," *Passing Time and Tradition,* ed. Steven Ohrn (Des Moines: Iowa Arts Council, 1984), 29–41.

[25]Faust, vol. 1, 464–65.

[26]Walker, 181–84.

CHAPTER 2. PROVERBS

1. Collected February 22, 1970, in Sacramento, California, by Roland Dickison, from a 22-year-old male. A variant, "Am Abend werden die Faulen fleissig," was collected in Sacramento by Dickison in December 1980, and in Detroit, Michigan, in 1969, from Mrs. G. Brakman. Compare: "Abends wart de Faulen flitig" (K. Wander, *Deutsches Sprichwörter-lexikon* [1867–80; reprint, Darmstadt: Wissenschaftliche Buchgesellschaft, 1964], 1:9.6).

2. Collected in 1960, in Sacramento, California, by Roland Dickison, from a female of Swabian ancestry. Jordan collected the same proverb in Mason County, Texas (*German Texana* [Austin: Eakin Press, 1980], 125). The proverb is listed by Wander (vol. 1, 106.14), and there are numerous examples in Pennsylvania German: "Der apb'l falt net wait fum shtam" (W. J. Hoffman, "Folk-Lore of the Pennsylvania Germans," *Journal of American Folklore* 2 [1889]: 198); "Der obbel folt net weit fom schtomm" (Abraham Horne, "Proverbs and Sayings of the Pennsylvania Germans," *Pennsylvania German Society Proceedings* 2 [1892]: 50); "Der Appel fallt net weit vum Stamm" (*Penn-Germania* 7 [1906]: 265); and "D'r abbel rollt net weit fum schtamm" (Edwin M. Fogel, *Proverbs of the Pennsylvania Germans* [Fogelsville: Americana Germanica Press, 1929], No. 2). See also Richard Jente, "Der Apfel fällt nicht weit von Stamm," *PMLA* 48 (1933): 26–30.

3. Fogel, No. 6. Wander lists "Wenn der Apfel reis ist, fällt er ab" (vol. 1, 107.78). The English version has been collected in Kentucky, North Carolina, and Utah. The proverb suggests that in old age, death is inevitable, but it also implies doubt that babies born less than nine months after the parents' wedding were legitimately conceived.

4. Collected in 1969 from Mrs. G. Brakman, Detroit, Michigan (Wayne State University Folklore Archive, 1969–210). Compare Wander, vol. 1, 59.20.

5. Collected by Lawrence A. Weigel, "German Proverbs from around Fort Hays, Kansas," *Western Folklore* 18 (1959), No. 2. Jordan collected this phrase in Texas along with the variant, "Arbeit macht das Leben süss, Faulheit steift die Glieder" (Laziness stiffens the limbs) (*German Texana,* 125). Wander lists several forms (vol. 5, 792:192–94).

6. Fogel, No. 75. "A young person marrying before the older sisters and brothers is said to put them on (or make them ride) the bake-oven" (E. Grumbine, "Folk-Lore of Lebanon County," *Lebanon County Historical Society Papers* 3 [1905–6]: 285). The practice was apparently widespread throughout western Europe; see Claude Lévi-Strauss, *The Raw and the Cooked,* translated by John and Doreen Weightman (New York: Harper and Row, 1969), 334–35.

7. Collected in 1969 from Mrs. G. Brakman, Detroit, Michigan (Wayne State University Folklore Archives, 1969–210). Jordan collected a similar phrase in Texas: "Der liebe Gott sorgt dafür, dass de Bäume nicht in den Himmel wachsen" (God sees to it Himself that the trees don't grow into heaven) (*German Texana,* 126).

8. Collected by Gilbert Jordan in Texas ("German Cultural Heritage," *German Culture in Texas,* ed. Glen E. Lich and Dona B. Reeves [Boston: Twayne, 1980], 182). The phrase is a smart-aleck retort to the question *Wie gehts?* (ambiguously, "How are you?" and "How do you go?"). Mark Trumbore collected an interesting variant in Montgomery County, Pennsylvania: "Uff zwae Bae, wie'n Gans, yuscht ken fedrich Schwanz" (On two legs like a goose, only without a feathery tail) (*A Superficial Collection of Pennsylvania German Erotic*

Folklore [Pennsburg, Pennsylvania: 1978], 11). Wander lists a dialectal variant: "Aff zwee Beenen wie die Gänse" (vol. 1, 301.64).

9. Horne, 53. Pennsylvania German variants appear in Hoffman (No. 44) and Fogel (No. 114). Wander lists "New besem keren wol" (vol. 1, 323.33).

10. Collected by Roland Dickison in Sacramento, California, in 1976, from a 22-year-old female who added the explanation, "Nothing's perfect." A similar message is implied in the song, "In Heaven There Is No Beer."

11. Hoffman, 198, No. 1. The complete proverb is, "Every little helps. That's what the old woman said when she pissed in the ocean" (collected from Samuel Miller, Newville, Pennsylvania, May 27, 1973). Compare Edmund I. Gordon, *Sumerian Proverbs* (Philadelphia: University of Pennsylvania Press, 1959), 222: "The fox having urinated into the sea said, 'The whole of the sea is my urine.'"

12. Collected from Hans Meurer, Shippensburg, Pennsylvania, October 2, 1972. The reference is to the flatulence produced by eating beans and peas.

13. Collected by Alfred Shoemaker from Victor C. Dieffenbach, Berks County, Pennsylvania (*Pennsylvania Dutchman* 2.5 [July, 1950]: 2). Fogel lists "Wanns brei regert hot m'r ken leffel" (22, No. 169), and Wander has "Wenn's Brei regnet, hat man keine Schüsseln (fehlt der Löffel)" (vol. 1, 458.43). William K. Ferris collected a variant in Texas: "If it was raining soup, every day at twelve o'clock raining soup, there'd be some poor son-of-a-bitch out with a fork" ("More of Ray Lum's Horse Sense," *Mid-South Folklore* 6 [1978]: 48).

14. Horne, 52. Compare Hoffman, No. 65: "Wär 'n bok shelt is ken shōf dīb."

15. Hoffman, 198, No. 4. Fogel has "'R nemmt d'r bull an de haerner" (25, No. 193).

16. Collected by Alfred Shoemaker with the explanation, "Why, the bull swam across the Schuylkill just to get a drink of water" (*Reading* [Pa.] *Eagle* [February 21, 1949]: 20).

17. John Updike, *Rabbit Is Rich* (New York: Knopf, 1981), 249. The English version is frequently cited as a "Pennsylvania Dutch proverb," as in an example collected in Chicago in 1967 (Indiana University Folklore Archives, 67–11), and as such it appears frequently on wall plaques and other tourist souvenirs. The saying does not appear in standard collections of German proverbs, so it is apparently a wisecrack now being passed off as proverbial or it may be the invention of an entrepreneur. Updike apparently got this from Phares Hertzog's *Songs, Sayings and Stories of a Pennsylvania Dutchman* (Lebanon, Pennsylvania: Applied Arts Publishers, 1966), 32.

18. Collected by Alfred Shoemaker from Norman A. Smith, Lenhartsville, Pennsylvania (*Pennsylvania Dutchman* 1.12 [1949]: 2). Similar examples are listed by Horne (51), Hoffman (199, No. 26), and Fogel (No. 284). Wander lists "Fürs Denken thut man keinen henken" (vol. 1, 573.47).

19. *Penn-Germania* 7 (1906): 265. Similarly in Hoffman (198, No. 9) and Fogel (No. 293). Wander has "Die kleinen dieb henckt man, die grossen lesst man lauffen" (vol. 1, 585.47).

20. Collected by Alfred Shoemaker from Carrie V. Bitting, Coopersburg, Pennsylvania (*Pennsylvania Dutchman* 1.25 [1950]: 3). This is also in Hoffman's collection (198, No. 13), but Fogel lists each sentence as a separate proverb (Nos. 298 and 975), the first with the note, "Usually said of a very slender and tall person; equivalent to as tall and thin as a bean pole."

21. Collected by Alfred Shoemaker from Elmer Snavely, Lititz, Pennsylvania (*Pennsylvania Dutchman* 1.7 [1949]: 2, with the explanation, "Said by sweepers"). In Horne, the phrase is "Wos grewwar is wie dreck, geht selwer aweck" (51).

22. Fogel, No. 367. Similarly in Hoffman (198, No. 2).

23. Collected from Mrs. G. Brakman, Detroit, Michigan (Wayne State University Folklore Archives, 1969–210). Variants of the proverb have been widely collected: "Egalob schtinkt" (*Penn-Germania* 7 [1906]: 265); Fogel, No. 1206; "Eeye gelobt schtinkt" (G. M. Ludwig, "The Influence of the Pennsylvania Dutch in the Middle West," *Pennsylvania German Folklore Society* 10 [1945]: 9). Jordan collected a longer form in Texas: "Eigenlob

207

stinkt; andern Lob klingt" (Self-praise stinks; others' praise clinks) (*German Texana*, 126). Compare Wander: "Eichin laub stinckt, Freunde lob hinckt" (vol. 1, 772.1).

24. "German Proverbs Collected in Los Angeles," *California Folklore Quarterly* 4 (1945), 433, No. 8. The proverb is common in Pennsylvania German: "Ee eesel brauch der anner net langawr heesa" (*Pennsylvania Dutchman* 1.25 [1950]: 3); Hoffman (199, No. 16); and Fogel (No. 452). Wander lists many examples, including the variant given here (vol. 1, 861.173).

25. Collected by Alfred Shoemaker from Carrie V. Bitting, Coopersburg, Pennsylvania (*Pennsylvania Dutchman* 1.25 [1950]: 3). Similar forms appear in Horne (52), Hoffman (201, No. 51), and Fogel (No. 456). Wander gives "Wenn man den Esel nennt, so kommt er gerennt" (vol. 1, 871.443).

26. Collected from Mrs. O. Kriegs and Mrs. G. Brakman, Detroit, Michigan (Wayne State University Folklore Archives, 1969–210). Roland Dickison collected the same proverb in Sacramento, California, February 22, 1970, and Jordan found it in Texas (*German Texana*, 128). Wander lists it as "Lange Fädchen, faule Mädchen" (vol. 1, 913). There is a Pennsylvania German folk tale in which Eileschpijjel defeats the devil in a sewing contest by giving him a long thread and using a short one himself (Thomas R. Brendle and William S. Troxell, *Pennsylvania German Folk Tales* [Norristown: Pennsylvania German Society, 1944], 154–55).

27. Collected from Mrs. O. Kriegs and Mrs. M. Brakman, Detroit, Michigan (Wayne State University Folklore Archives, 1969–210). Wander gives an East Frisian version: "Wei well fiyn siyn, mot liyn Piyn" (vol. 1, 965.12).

28. Collected by Alfred Shoemaker from William P. Shoemaker, Maple Grove, Pennsylvania (*Pennsylvania Dutchman* 1.9 [1949]: 2).

29. Collected from Mrs. Agatha Greifenberg, Detroit, Michigan (Wayne State University Folklore Archives, 1969–210).

30. Collected by Alfred Shoemaker from Elmer Snavely, Lititz, Pennsylvania (*Pennsylvania Dutchman* 1.7 [1949]: 2). Wander has the variant, "Eine Frau kann mit dem Fingerhute mehr ver schütten, als der Mann mit dem Eimer schöpfen kann" (vol. 1, 115.224). The English version has been collected in Indiana, New York, and North Carolina, as well as Pennsylvania: "A woman can throw more out the back door with a teaspoon than a man can bring in the front door with a scoop shovel" (collected from Samuel A. Miller, Newville, Pennsylvania, July 7, 1974).

31. H. M. Hays, "On the German Dialect Spoken in the Valley of Virginia," *Dialect Notes* 3 (1908): 274. Fogel lists the Pennsylvania German: "Fress od'r f'rrek" (No. 575).

32. Hoffman, 199, No. 28. Oscar Kuhns provides the German form: "Futter macht die Gäule" (*The German and Swiss Settlements of Colonial Pennsylvania* [New York: Holt, 1901], 101).

33. I. D. Rupp's notes to Benjamin Rush, *Account of the Manners of the German Inhabitants of Pennsylvania* (Philadelphia: S. P. Town, 1875), 16n. Fogel lists a similar form: "Wāēr gūt futtert dāēr gut buttert" (No. 586). Wander lists simple "Futter-butter" (vol. 1, 1309.11). Though the meaning of the proverb is obviously that well-fed animals produce better, Mildred Jordan translates it as "He who *eats* well, churns well" (*The Distelfink Country of the Pennsylvania Dutch* [New York: Crown, 1978], 14).

34. Collected by Alfred Shoemaker from John Brendel, Reinholds, Pennsylvania (*Pennsylvania Dutchman* 1.11 [1949]: 2). Variants appear in Horne (54) and Fogel (No. 610). Jordan collected the phrase in Texas: "Einem geschenkten Gaul sieht man nicht ins Maul" (*German Texana*, 127; cf. Wander, vol. 1, 1362.24). Hans Meurer, Shippensburg, Pennsylvania, adds a second phrase, "Einem geschenkten Barsch/Schaut man nicht in' Arsch" (One doesn't look a gift bass in the ass) (February 11, 1972).

35. Hoffman, 201, No. 55. Variants appear in Fogel (No. 604) and Wander (vol. 1, 1364.56, and 4, 789.33). An English variant, "Too late to shut the stable door after the horse is gone," was collected by Rosan Jordan from William Cotsakis, Chicago, Illinois, in 1967

(Indiana University Folklore Archives, 67–11).

36. Collected by Roland Dickison, Sacramento, California, September 1971. Wander lists "Mit Geduld und Spucke fängt man manche Mucke" (vol. 1, 1407.151).

37. Horne, 51. Fogel lists this (No. 730) and the longer wellerism, "Grōs gegrisch un wenich woll, hot d'r Eireschpigl gsat wi 'r di sau gschōre hot" (No. 731), which is also given as a folktale by Brendle and Troxell (169). Archer Taylor provides a bibliography of citations of the German form, "'Viel Geschrei und wenig Wolle,' sagte der Teufel und schor sein Schwein" (An Index to 'The Proverb" [Helsinki: Suomalainen Tiedeakatemia, 1934], 77–78). See also Wander, vol. 1, 1601.45.

38. Collected by Charles R. Rez from Karla Schultz, Eugene, Oregon, June 6, 1976. The same proverb has been collected in Kansas (Lawrence A. Weigel, "German Proverbs from around Fort Hayes, Kansas," Western Folklore 18 [1959]: 98) and Texas (Jordan, German Texana, 126, No. 14). Wander lists many examples (vol. 1, 1669.98).

39. Penn-Germania 7 (1906): 265. Horne lists the same proverb (50) and Jordan has a similar form: "Frisch gewagt iss halb gewonnen" (German Texana, 127, No. 20). In Kansas, however, the proverb is "Frisch begonnen ist halb gewonnen" (Weigel, 98, No. 21). Compare Fogel, No. 13: "Gūt angfange is halber gschafft."

40. Collected by Alfred Shoemaker from Elmer Snavely, Lititz, Pennsylvania (Pennsylvania Dutchman 1.7 [1949]: 2).

41. Collected from Mrs. Agatha Greifenberg, Detroit, Michigan, in 1969 (Wayne State University Folklore Archives, 1969–210). Wander has a similar form (vol. 1, 1750.462).

42. Collected by Charles R. Rez from Karla Schultz, Eugene, Oregon, June 6, 1976. Wander lists the proverb (vol. 1, 1754.551).

43. Weigel, 98, No. 19. Wander has many examples (vol. 1, 1789.47). Singer traces the phrase to medieval Latin (vol. 1, 76–77, and vol. 3, 141–42). The Pennsylvania German is "Siss net alles gold was glanst" (Pennsylvania Dutchman 1.14 [1949]: 2; Fogel, Nos. 685–86). There is a parallel variant, "Alles was glänzt ist kein Gold," collected from Mrs. O. Kriegs, Detroit, Michigan, 1969 (Wayne State University Folklore Archives, 1969–210).

44. Jacob H. Yoder, "Proverbial Lore from Hegins Valley," Pennsylvania Dutchman 3.16 (1952): 3, with the explanation that it is applied to some incident that can't be believed.

45. Horne, 54. Compare Fogel, No. 740. Wander lists "Kleine kröten haben auch gift" (vol. 2, 1640.4).

46. Collected by Alfred Shoemaker from Elmer Snavely, Lititz, Pennsylvania (Pennsylvania Dutchman 1.7 [1949]: 2). Horne (52) and Fogel (No. 741) list variants. Jordan collected a version of the proverb in Mason County, Texas: "Wer andern eine Grube gräbt, fällt selbst hinein" (German Texana, 131, No. 57; cf. Wander, vol. 2, 153.6). The phrase occurs frequently in the Old Testament (Proverbs 26:27, Psalms 7:15, Ecclesiastes 10:8, Psalms 9:15). Erasmus lists a medieval Latin form: "Incidit in foveam quam fecit" (Adagia 1, i, 52).

47. Weigel, 98, No. 13. The same form appears in Jordan (German Texana, 17, 127) and Wander (vol. 2, 298.123). The Pennsylvania German is "Ē hand wescht di anner" (Fogel, No. 797).

48. Collected by Alfred Shoemaker from Elmer Snavely, Lititz, Pennsylvania (Pennsylvania Dutchman 1.7 [1949]: 2). Fogel lists "Di aērlich hand geht daerichs land" (No. 795) and gives the English equivalent, "Honesty is the best policy." Wander has "Eine ehrliche Hand kommt durchs ganze Land und endlich durch Trogen auch" (vol. 2, 298.107).

49. Collected in Detroit, Michigan, from Mrs. G. Brakman (Wayne State University Folklore Archives, 1969–210). Also collected by Gilbert Jordan in New Braunfels, Texas (German Texana, 130, No. 48). See also Wander, vol. 2, 309–76.

50. Trumbore, 59; Fogel, No. 1986. Wander lists "Zwischen hand und mund viel zu grund" (vol. 2, 315.315).

51. Collected from Mrs. Agatha Greifenberg, Detroit, Michigan, 1969. (Wayne State

University Folklore Archives, 1969–210). Wander has a variant: "Mit Harren und Hoffen hat's mancher getroffen" (vol. 2, 364.19). Compare also No. 58, below.

52. Hoffman, 199, No. 15. Horne (54) suggests that the phrase means, "There lies the secret." However, the meaning seems to be, "That's where the difficulty lies," as suggested by Wander: "Wer weiss, wo der Hase im Pfeffer sigt" (vol. 5, 302.336) and Fogel: "Waer wes wu d'r has im peffer hokt" (No. 823). The phrase does not seem to be related to the name of the favorite German dish *Hasenpfeffer*.

53. Collected from Mrs. O. Kriegs, Detroit, Michigan, 1969 (Wayne State University Folklore Archives, 1969–210). The meaning is that old men often lose control of their senses when a young woman is involved. Wander has a variant, "Wenn ein altes Haus brennt, hilft kein Löschen" (vol. 5, 1415.735).

54. Collected by Alfred Shoemaker from Dr. Pierce E. Swope, Lebanon, Pennsylvania (*Pennsylvania Dutchman* 1.24 [1950]: 2). Also listed by Hoffman (200, No. 33), Horne (52), and Fogel (No. 895). Wander has "Kurzes Haar ist bald gebürstet" (vol. 2, 221.80).

55. Collected by Alfred Shoemaker from Dr. George Knecht, Allentown, Pennsylvania (*Pennsylvania Dutchman* 1.14 [1949]: 2). The same proverb appears in Hoffman (202, No. 66), Horne (50), and *Penn-Germania* 7 (1906): 265. The standard German form is "Wer nicht hören will, muss fühlen" ("German Proverbs Collected in Los Angeles," *California Folklore Quarterly* 4 [1945]: 434; Wander, vol. 2, 779.78).

56. Collected by Roland Dickison in Sacramento, California. LaVern Rippley records the following as a house inscription: "Eigner Herd/Ist Goldes wert,/Ist er Schon arm,/Ist er doch warm" (188). Wander lists the same form (vol. 2, 527.10).

57. Collected by Roland Dickison in Sacramento, California. Wander has the same proverb (vol. 2, 638.123).

58. Collected from Mrs. Agatha Greifenberg, Detroit, Michigan, in 1969 (Wayne State University Folklore Archive, 1969–210). Wander lists many examples (vol. 2, 718.20). Compare No. 51, above.

59. Horne, 50; *Penn-Germania* 7 (1906), 265. In Wander: "Der Hehler ist so sträflich wie der Stehler" (vol. 2, 457.7).

60. Horne, 53. Variants appear in Hoffman (202, No. 79), Fogel (No. 829), and Wander (vol. 2, 440.59). A similar concept occurs in the phrase, "I'd know his hide in a tanyard" (Conrad Richter, *The Town* [New York: Knopf, 1950], 222).

61. Collected by Alfred Shoemaker from Albert Liebenguth, Allentown, Pennsylvania (*Pennsylvania Dutchman* 1.8 [1949]: 2). There is a common variant, "Kumt mer iwwer der hund so kumt mer iwwer der schwonz," listed by Horne (49), Hoffman (200, No. 35), and Fogel (No. 926). Olive Hammond lists the English translation, "If one gets over the dog, one gets over the tail," with the explanation, "The chief difficulty mastered, others come easy" ("Social Life and Customs in Early Armstrong County, Pennsylvania," M.A. thesis, University of Pittsburgh, 1930, 76). Jordan collected the standard German form in Mason County, Texas: "Kommt man über den Hund, kommt man auch über den Schwanz" (*German Texana*, 128; Wander, vol. 2, 852.814).

62. Collected by Roland Dickison in Sacramento, California, December 19, 1980. A similar form was collected from Mrs. Agatha Greifenberg, Detroit, Michigan, in 1969. Jordan found it in Comfort, Texas (*German Texana*, 130). The Pennsylvania German is "Wu fil hund sin hot d'r has ken tschans" (Fogel, No. 925; Joanna Crawford, *Birch Interval* [New York: Dell, 1976], 117). Wander lists numerous examples (vol. 2, 860.984).

63. *Penn-Germania* 7 (1906): 265; Fogel, No. 938. Jordan collected it in Comfort, Texas (*German Texana*, 127). Wander lists several variants (vol. 2, 909.18).

64. Collected by Roland Dickison in Sacramento, California, July 23, 1969.

65. Trumbore, 11. There are many variants; see Wander, vol. 2, 930–31.

66. Collected by Charles R. Rez from Karla Schultz, Eugene, Oregon, June 6, 1976 (Northwest Folklore Archive, No. 060076073).

67. Collected from Henry Warkentin, Shippensburg, Pennsylvania, February 26, 1986,

who heard it among Low German–speaking Mennonites in Ontario, Canada.

68. Collected by Charles R. Rez from Karla Schultz, Eugene, Oregon, June 6, 1976.

69. Collected by Alfred Shoemaker from Elmer Snavely, Lititz, Pennsylvania (*Pennsylvania Dutchman* 1.7 [1949]: 2). Fogel has a similar form (No. 1016) and Wander gives the standard German, "Viel Köpff, viel Sinne" (vol. 2, 1512.324). Brendle and Troxell have this as the punchline of an Eileschpijjel tale, where the numskull upsets a basket of cabbage and watches it roll away (*Pennsylvania German Folk Tales*, 175).

70. Collected by Alfred Shoemaker from Albert Leibenguth, Allentown, Pennsylvania (*Pennsylvania Dutchman* 1.8 [1949]: 2). Variants appear in Hoffman (198, No. 10), Horne (50), *Penn-Germania* (7 [1906]: 265), and Fogel (No. 1009). Wander lists the standard German: "Kinder und Narren reden die Wahrheit" (vol. 2, 1296.570). Christopher Morley cited an abbreviated form in his novel *Thorofare* ([New York: Harcourt, Brace, 1942], 96): "Kinder sprechen immer die Wahrheit."

71. Collected by Alfred Shoemaker from George Knecht, Allentown, Pennsylvania (*Pennsylvania Dutchman* 1.15 [1949]: 2). Fogel has the same proverb (No. 1000). Wander lists the standard German: "Kleine Kinder, kleine sorgen, grosse Kinder, grosse sorgen" (vol. 2, 1299.654).

72. Collected by Roland Dickison in Sacramento, California, with the explanation, "This proverb is said just before blowing on hot soup."

73. In a letter from Milwaukee, Wisconsin, July 1854 (*German-American Pioneers in Wisconsin and Michigan*, ed. Harry Anderson (Milwaukee: Milwaukee County Historical Society, 1971], 297). Wander gives the German, "So viel Kinder, so viel Paternoster" (vol. 2, 1305.791).

74. Warren Kliewer, "Collecting Folklore Among Mennonites," *Mennonite Life* 16 (1961), 111. Collected in Minnesota.

75. Collected by Charles R. Rez from Karla Schultz, Eugene, Oregon, June 6, 1976. Wander lists many examples (vol. 2, 1377.140). The Pennsylvania German form is, "Kleeder macha Leit" (*Penn-Germania* 7 [1906], 265; Fogel, No. 667.

76. Collected in Minnesota by Warren Kliewer (*Mennonite Life* 16 [1961], 112). Jordan collected the standard German version in Texas: "Der Klügste gibt nach" (*German Texana*, 126; Wander, vol. 2, 1416.3).

77. Collected by Alfred Shoemaker from Mrs. Orin J. Farrell, Schenectady, New York (*Pennsylvania Dutchman* 1.23 [1950]: 2; Fogel, No. 1023; Horne, 50). Roland Dickison collected a variant in Sacramento, July 10, 1969: "Was ist in der Kopf nicht, mussen auf der Fusser bin." The Indiana University Folklore Archives has an English form of it from a German informant in Chicago: "What's not in your head is in your feet." Wander lists several examples (vol. 2, 1513.344).

78. Collected from Mrs. Ella Barrick, Carlisle, Pennsylvania, June 1963, and Samuel Miller, Newville, Pennsylvania, May 29, 1972. Arthur Graeff gives the Pennsylvania German version: "Zwee Kepp sin besser als aner, wann aa aner en Grautkopp iss" (*Selections from Arthur Graeff's Scholla* [Breinigsville, Pa.: Pennsylvania German Society, 1971], 147; compare Hoffman, 201, No. 50). Wander provides a variant, "Zwei Köpfe sind immer besser als einer, wäre der zweite auch nur ein Kalbskopf [calf's head]" (vol. 2, 1520.483). Conrad Richter gives still another form: "Three heads, she reckoned, were better than one, if one was a cabbage head, as Uncle Nun used to say" (*The Grandfathers* [New York: Knopf, 1964], 119).

79. Collected from Mrs. O. Kriegs, Detroit, Michigan (Wayne State University Folklore Archives, 1969–210). Variants appear in Fogel (No. 742) and Wander (vol. 2, 1641.6). See also the extensive commentary by Richard Jente (*Proverbia Communia: A Fifteenth-Century Collection of Dutch Proverbs* [Bloomington: Indiana University, 1947], 121–22).

80. Collected by Alfred Shoemaker from Norman A. Smith, Lenhartsville, Pennsylvania (*Pennsylvania Dutchman* 1.12 [1949]: 2). Fogel has two variants (Nos. 1047 and 1169).

81. Cited by I. D. Rupp in his notes to Benjamin Rush's *Account of the Manners of the*

German Inhabitants of Pennsylvania (Philadelphia, 1875), 19, and subsequently in Oscar Kuhns, *The German and Swiss Settlements of Colonial Pennsylvania* (New York: Holt, 1901), 101, and Ralph Wood, *The Pennsylvania Germans* (Princeton: Princeton University Press, 1942), 52. Wander lists a dialectal variant, "E gût Kuh sücht me im Schtoal" (vol. 2, 1669.111).

82. Collected by Alfred Shoemaker from William P. Shoemaker, Maple Grove, Pennsylvania (*Pennsylvania Dutchman* 1.9 [1949], 2). The proverb is also listed by Horne (52) and Fogel (No. 1052).

83. Collected from Mrs. M. Brakman, Detroit, Michigan (Wayne State University Folklore Archives, 1969–210). Variants appear in Hoffman (201, No. 64), Fogel (No. 34), and Wander (vol. 2, 1676.279).

84. Fogel, No. 1066. The Indiana University Folklore Archives (67–11) has the English form from a German informant in Chicago. Wander cites many examples of "Wer zuletzt lacht, lacht am besten" (vol. 2, 1746.92).

85. "German Proverbs Collected in Los Angeles," *California Folklore Quarterly* 4, (1945): 433, No. 10. Wander lists several examples (vol. 3, 32.2).

86. Hoffman, 198, No. 7. The same proverb is listed by Horne (53) and Fogel (No. 1091). The standard German is "Besser eine Laus im Kraut als gar kein Fleisch" (Wander, vol. 2, 1822.3).

87. Collected from Mrs. G. Brakman, Detroit, Michigan (Wayne State University Folklore Archives, 1969–210).

88. Collected by Charles R. Rez from Karla Schultz, Eugene, Oregon, June 6, 1976. Jordan collected the same proverb in San Antonio, Texas (*German Texana*, 128). See also Wander, vol. 3, 257.117.

89. *Penn-Germania* 7 (1906), 265. Similar forms appear in Hoffman (200, No. 38) and Fogel (No. 1892). Wander lists "Lustig gelebt und selig gestorben, heisst dem Teufel die Rechnung verdorben" (vol. 3, 293.6).

90. Collected from Mrs. G. Brakman, Detroit, Michigan (Wayne State University Folklore Archives, 1969–210). Jordan collected a similar rhyme in Mason County, Texas: "Mädchen, die pfeifen,/Und Hühner, die krähn,/Denen soll man bei Zeiten/Den Kragen (Kopf) umdrehn" (*German Texana*, 114). The Pennsylvania German is "Maid wo peifa un hinkle wo gray-a denna sut m'r all de hells rum dray-a" (E. Grumbine, "Folk-Lore of Lebanon County," *Lebanon County* [Pa.] *Historical Society Papers* 3 [1905–6]: 285), with variants in Hoffman (198, No. 12) and Horne (51). Wander list the standard German, "Mädchen die pfeifen und Hühnern die krähen, den soll man beiden die Hälse verdrehen" (vol. 3, 315.131). Fogel lists "Whistling girls and crowing hens come to a bad end" as a superstition (*Beliefs*, No. 1948). The crowing hen has widespread association with death, evil, or witchcraft (Thomas R. Forbes, *The Midwife and the Witch* [New Haven and London: Yale University Press, 1966], 1–22). Masculine behavior on the part of any female, gallinaceous or human, was proscribed. Forbes cites another German proverb, "When the hen crows before the cock and the woman speaks before the man, then the hen should be roasted and the woman beaten with a cudgel" (2).

91. Collected by Roland Dickison in Sacramento, California, July 23, 1969. Jordan collected a variant in Texas, "Wenn die Maus satt ist, schmeckt das Mēhl bitter" (*German Texana*, 131), which is similar to that listed by Wander (vol. 3, 541.177). Kliewer collected a Low German form in Minnesota: "Wann dee Mus saut es, es et koorn betta" (*Mennonite Life* 16 [1961], 112). The Pennsylvania German is, "Wan di maus sat hot is es mēl bitter" (Hoffman, 201, No. 57; Horne, 53).

92. Collected by Roland Dickison in Sacramento, California, July 23, 1969. Jordan collected a similar saying in Mason County, Texas: "Mit Messer, Gabel, Schere und Licht/Spielen kleine Kinder nicht" (*German Texana*, 132).

93. Collected by Charles R. Rez, from Karla Schultz, Eugene, Oregon, June 6, 1976. Wander lists the same form (vol. 3, 581.53).

94. *Penn-Germania* 7 (1906), 265, with the translation, "First come, first served." Fogel lists the same proverb (No. 1284), while Wander has "Wer erst zu der müle kompt, der malet erst" (vol. 3, 755–90).

95. Collected by Roland Dickison in Sacramento, California, by Charles R. Rez in Eugene, Oregon, and by Gilbert Jordan in San Antonio, Texas (*German Texana,* 129). Wander has a similar form (vol. 3, 728.23).

96. Collected by Roland Dickison in Sacramento, California, and by Charles R. Rez in Eugene, Oregon. Wander lists many examples (vol. 3, 733.4). This is one of the most widely studied of German proverbs; see the bibliography provided by Wolfgang Mieder, *International Bibliography of Explanatory Essays on Individual Proverbs and Proverbial Expressions* (Bern: Herbert Lang, 1977), 95–96. The Pennsylvania German is "Die mariya schtund hot gold im mund" (*Pennsylvania Dutchman* 1.15 [1949]: 2; variants appear in Hoffman [198, No. 11] and Horne [53]).

97. Collected by Charles R. Rez from Karla Schultz, Eugene, Oregon, June 6, 1976, and by Jordan in New Braunfels, Texas (*German Texana,* 129). See also Wander, vol. 3, 791.17, and Wood, *The Pennsylvania Germans,* 51.

98. Hoffman, 199, No. 17; Fogel, No. 1321. Wander lists several variants, including, "Ein narr macht zehen narrn" (vol. 3, 894.390).

99. Horne, 53; Fogel, No. 1328. Hoffman has a variant meaning, "Let each pull at his own nose" (200, No. 36), and Wander lists several similar forms: "Zupfe dich bei deiner Nase" (vol. 3, 964.416); "Züch dich selbs bey der nasen" (vol. 3, 952.115).

100. Collected by Roland Dickison in Sacramento, California.

101. Collected by Alfred Shoemaker from John Brendel, Reinholds, Pennsylvania (*Pennsylvania Dutchman* 1.11 [1949]: 2). Fogel lists several such phrases: "Ox mol ox is 36," "Ox mol ox is ox," etc., with the explanation that they are exclamations at seeing something stupid or foolish.

102. Prof. John G. Kunstmann of North Carolina used this phrase in a faculty meeting in Carlisle in 1968 to suggest that plans worked out in advance are easily changed. The Pennsylvania German is "Babier iss geduldich" (*Pennsylvania Dutchman* 1.12 [1949]: 2) and the standard German is "Das Papier ist geduldig" (Wander, vol. 3, 1174.4).

103. Collected by Roland Dickison in Sacramento, California, March 1977. The meaning is, "They are like two peas in a pod."

104. Collected by Roland Dickison in Sacramento, California, March 1970, from a German informant from Davenport, Iowa. There are many variant forms: "Jeder Topf hat einen Deckel" (Wayne State University Folklore Archives, 1969–210); "Doa es tjeen Groape woa nijh 'n Datjsel to pausst" (Kliewer, *Mennonite Life* 16 [1961]: 110); "Siss ken heffly so grumm os net en deckel tsu finna iss os druff bossa doot" (*Pennsylvania Dutchman* 2.5 [1950]: 2); "My mother always told me, No matter how crooked the pot is, there's always a lid for it" (collected from Samuel A. Miller, Newville, Pennsylvania, July 26, 1982); "Et is kên Pott so schêf, et find't sick (passet) ümmer en Stülp (Deckel) to" (Wander, vol. 3, 1378.9). The meaning in Pennsylvania is that everyone can find a matrimonial mate.

105. Collected by Alfred Shoemaker from A. Paul Gerhart, Telford, Pennsylvania (*Pennsylvania Dutchman* 2.11 [1950]: 2). The saying is generally listed as a weather belief or superstition (Fogel, *Beliefs,* No. 1152).

106. Collected by Roland Dickison in Sacramento, California, in March 1977; by Charles R. Rez in Eugene, Oregon, June 6, 1976; and by Gilbert Jordan in San Antonio, Texas (*German Texana,* 129). Richard Jente notes that the proverb is of Oriental origin, becoming popular in Germany after 1830 and spreading under German influence to the United States ("German Proverbs from the Orient," *PMLA* 48 [1933]: 33–37). See also Wander, vol. 3, 1559.147.

107. Mary Yoder, an Amish woman from Mechanicsville, Maryland, used the phrase in a letter dated August 3, 1979. Compare, "Es regnet, wo Gott will" (Wander, vol. 3, 1593.23).

108. Collected from Mrs. G. Brakman, Detroit, Michigan (Wayne State University Folklore Archives, 1969–210). Wander lists a variant (vol. 3, 1597.117).

109. Collected by Alfred Shoemaker from Dr. George Knecht, Allentown, Pennsylvania (*Pennsylvania Dutchman* 1.14 [1949]: 2). The same proverb is listed by Hoffman (199, No. 19), Horne (53), and Fogel (No. 1473). Wander has "Ein blindes Schwein findet auch wol eine Eichel" (vol. 4, 449.43).

110. Collected from Dr. George Knecht, Allentown, Pennsylvania, by Alfred Shoemaker (*Pennsylvania Dutchman* 1.15 [1949]: 2). Hoffman (200, No. 45) and Horne (53) have a similar proverb: "Saurkrout and bacon drive care away."

111. Collected from Samuel A. Miller, Newville, Pennsylvania, October 27, 1973. Fogel gives the Pennsylvania German, "'R is in re sēkmīl gebōre" (No. 1715). The phrase is used when someone leaves a door standing open.

112. Hoffman, 199, No. 23. Oscar Kuhns (*German and Swiss Settlements*, 101) provides the standard German, "Ein kleines Schaf ist gleich geschoren." The English equivalent is, "A short horse is soon curried."

113. Weigel, 98. The same form appears in Wander (vol. 4, 60.146). There is an interesting Pennsylvania German variant: "Geduldicha schoof geena fiel in en schtall, un ungeduldicha noch mee" (You can get many gentle sheep in a stable, but you can pack them in if they are unruly) (*Pennsylvania Dutchman* 1.8 [1949]: 2). Compare Fogel, No. 1558.

114. Trumbore, 90; Fogel, No. 2023. Wander has "Scheissen macht hunger" (vol. 4, 122.17).

115. *Penn-Germania* 7 (1906), 265; Hoffman, 202, No. 77; Horne, 54; Fogel, No. 1540. There is also a wellerism, "Wu schmoke iss aa Feier, hot der Eileschpiggel gsaat wie aer uff em Eis gschisse hot" (Where there's smoke there's fire, as Eileschpiggel said when he shat on the ice) listed by Trumbore (81) and Fogel (No. 2016). Brendle and Troxell have a similar tale which may be an expurgated version of this (*Pennsylvania German Folk Tales*, 168).

116. Horne, 54; Hoffman, 201, No. 48. Fogel lists this as two separate proverbs (Nos. 1505, 1586). Wander gives "Zu scharf schneidd nödd, zu spötz stichd nödd" (vol. 4, 103.8).

117. Horne, 54; Hoffman, 200, No. 43. Wander has many examples of "Mit Speck fängt man Mäusse" (vol. 4, 674.37).

118. Weigel, No. 8. Fogel lists the same form (No. 1701). Jordan collected the proverb in Fredericksburg, Texas (*German Texana*, 125).

119. Collected from Mrs. M. Brakman, Detroit, Michigan (Wayne State University Folklore Archives, 1969–210).

120. Collected by Charles R. Rez from Karla Schultz, Eugene, Oregon, June 6, 1976. Jordan collected a similar proverb in Mason County, Texas: "Ein Spatz [sparrow] in der Hand ist besser als die Taube auf dem Dach" (*German Texana*, 126). Wander lists numerous variants (vol. 4, 687–88).

121. Collected from Clair Slaybaugh, Idaville, Pennsylvania, in 1968. Fogel gives the Pennsylvania German, "Ich schmeiss d'r a mol en schtē in d'r Garte," with the explanation that it means "I'll do you a favor some time" (No. 1617). The medieval Latin is similar: "Iecit lapidem in horto eius" (Singer, *Sprichworter* 2, 148). The cited phrase, however, was used in the sense of a tease, meaning, "You weren't home, so I played a little trick on you to show I was there." A former generation of rural Pennsylvanians often stacked the porch furniture against the door when the folks they went to visit were not at home.

122. Collected by Alfred Shoemaker from Dr. George Knecht, Allentown, Pennsylvania (*Pennsylvania Dutchman* 1.15 [1949]: 2). Fogel has two variants (Nos. 29 and 1735). See also Wander, vol. 4, 954.38.

123. Collected by Alfred Shoemaker from Mrs. Orin J. Farrell, Schenectady, New York (*Pennsylvania Dutchman* 1.23 [1950]: 2).

124. Collected by Charles R. Rez from Karla Schultz, Eugene, Oregon, June 6, 1976. Jordan collected a similar proverb in Texas (*German Texana,* 128) and Wander lists it (vol. 4, 1008.375). Fogel provides several Pennsylvania German variants (Nos. 230, 238). Archer Taylor has made an extended study of this proverb ("In the Evening Praise the Day," *Modern Language Notes* 36 [1921]: 115–18).

125. "German Proverbs Collected in Los Angeles," 434.

126. Collected from Mrs. G. Brakman, Detroit, Michigan (Wayne State University Folklore Archives, 1969–210). Wander lists "Jedes Thierchen hat sein Pläsirchen" (vol. 4, 1154.1).

127. Collected by Charles R. Rez from Karla Schultz, Eugene, Oregon, June 6, 1976. Jordan collected the same proverb in San Antonio, Texas (*German Texana,* 129). Compare also Wander, vol. 4, 1402.14.

128. Collected by Charles R. Rez from Karla Schultz, Eugene, Oregon, June 6, 1976. Wander lists the same proverb (vol. 4, 1441.85).

129. Collected by Roland Dickison in Sacramento, California.

130. Collected from Mrs. G. Brakman, Detroit, Michigan (Wayne State University Archives, 1969–210). Wander lists the same proverb (vol. 4, 1634.40).

131. Collected from Mrs. O. Kriegs, Detroit, Michigan (Wayne State University Archives, 1969–210). Jordan collected a variant in Comfort, Texas: "Ein'n Vogel, der morgens singt, holt abends die Katz" (*German Texana,* 127).

132. *Penn-Germania* 7 (1906), 265. Hoffman (201, No. 63), and Horne (50) have a shorter form, "Wer lauert an der wand, haert sei egne schant." Wander lists several variants, including a Jewish saying from Warsaw: "Steh nit hinter der Wand, west dü nit hören dein eigen Schand" (vol. 4, 1777.32).

133. This is a Low German proverb collected by Kliewer in Minnesota (*Mennonite Life* 16 [1961]: 110). The Pennsylvania German is "Wanns net f'r des wann waer" (Fogel, No. 1782). Compare also Wander, vol. 4, 1781.

134. Collected in Chicago from a German informant (Indiana University Folklore Archives, 67–11). The Pennsylvania German is "Schtill wasser laft gaern dīf" (Fogel, No. 1787). Wander has "Stille Wasser haben tiefe Gründe" (vol. 4, 1813.316).

135. Collected from Mrs. Agatha Greifenberg, Detroit, Michigan (Wayne State University Archives, 1969–210). Jordan collected the same proverb in Mason County, Texas (*German Texana,* 130). The Pennsylvania German is "Was mer net wees, macht em net hees," collected by Alfred Shoemaker from Ida V. Hollenbach, Saegerville, Pennsylvania (*Pennsylvania Dutchman* 2.1 [1950]: 2; *Penn-Germania* 7 [1906]: 265; Hoffman, 202, No. 69).

136. Horne, 51. Similar forms appear in Hoffman (199, No. 30) and Fogel (No. 1825). Kuhns gives the standard German, "Gut gewetzt ist halb gemäht" (*German and Swiss Settlements,* 101). The whetstone was carried in a *wetzkumpf,* a carved and reshaped cowhorn that hung from the mower's waist. In earlier days, when the scythe blade was of wrought iron rather than steel, a new edge was hammered into it against a *dengelschtock,* a small, portable anvil that could be driven into a stump or fencepost.

CHAPTER 3. RIDDLES

[1] See for example Donn V. Hart, *Riddles in Filipino Folklore* (Syracuse: Syracuse University Press, 1964), 47–52, and Kenneth S. Goldstein, "Riddling Traditions in Northeastern Scotland," *Journal of American Folklore* 76 (1963): 330–36.

[2] Sigmund Freud, *Jokes and Their Relation to the Unconscious,* translated by James Strachey (New York: Norton, 1963), 153n.

[3] John Baer Stoudt, *Folklore of the Pennsylvania Germans* (Philadelphia: William J. Campbell, 1916), 79. The word *Ent* means both "duck" and "end," so the riddle in English is, "How can one make an end [duck] of a goose? By eating it."

[4] Collected from Hans D. Meurer, Shippensburg, Pennsylvania, June 16, 1986. "Persil

bleibt Persil" is a well-known advertising slogan for a German detergent. The English meaning is, "What is the difference between a virgin and Persil? Persil remains Persil."

[5]Mrs. Bertha Gutshall, cited in Mac E. Barrick, "Riddles from Cumberland County (Pa.)," *Keystone Folklore Quarterly* 8 (1963): 59.

[6]Edna M. Stump, Reading, Pennsylvania; cited in *Pennsylvania Dutchman* 1.14 (1949): 2.

[7]Such jokes were being told all over Europe within days of the accident; see Robert Gillette, "Poles Seeking Solace in Humor and Drink," *Philadelphia Inquirer* (May 4, 1986): 8.

[8]F. J. Norton, "Prisoner Who Saved His Neck with a Riddle," *Folk-Lore* 53 (1942): 27–57.

[9]Baer, *Folklore*, 62.

[10]Collected by Alfred Shoemaker from Albert Leibenguth, Allentown, Pennsylvania (*Pennsylvania Dutchman* 1.9 [1949]: 2). Baer publishes a similar text with the traditional explanation (*Folklore*, 62).

[11]Taylor, *English Riddles from Oral Tradition* (Berkeley and Los Angeles: University of California Press, 1951); Taylor, "Riddles," *Frank C. Brown Collection of North Carolina Folklore* (Durham: Duke University Press, 1952), vol. 1, 283–328. Taylor's classification system owes a great deal to the work of Robert Lehmann-Nitsche, "Zur Volkskunde Argentiniens," *Zeitschrift des Vereins für Volkskunde* 24 (1914): 240–55.

[12]Stoudt, *Folklore*, 60–85; Jordan, *German Texana*, 136–39.

1. Collected by Alfred Shoemaker from William P. Shoemaker, Maple Grove, Pennsylvania (*Pennsylvania Dutchman* 1.1 [1949]: 2). John Baer Stoudt lists a similar form in *Folklore of the Pennsylvania Germans* (Philadelphia: Campbell, 1916), 77. Taylor cites Flemish, German, and Swiss examples (693, No. 32b).
2. Collected by Alfred Shoemaker from Mae S. Heisler, Tamaqua, Pennsylvania (*Pennsylvania Dutchman* 1.16 [1949]: 2). Stoudt has a similar form (77).
3. Stoudt, 77.
4. Collected by Alfred Shoemaker from William P. Shoemaker, Maple Grove, Pennsylvania (*Pennsylvania Dutchman* 1.3 [1949]: 2). This is a variant of a German riddle, "What has six legs and walks on only four?" (see Taylor, 695, No. 49).
5. Collected by Alfred Shoemaker from John B. Brendel, Reinholds, Pennsylvania (*Pennsylvania Dutchman* 1.12 [1949]: 2).
6. Collected from Mrs. Elsie Snyder, Carlisle, Pennsylvania, April 1, 1969. Compare Taylor, No. 75d.
7. Stoudt, 71. The answer in Germany is usually "a mill," but American riddles with this description are usually of a clock. Gilbert Jordan collected one such in Texas: "What is the thing there on the wall?/It strikes and has no fists at all,/It hangs, but still goes on and on,/It goes, but still is never gone. A wall clock," (*German Texana*, 139).
8. Collected from Mrs. Elsie Snyder, Carlisle, Pennsylvania, April 1, 1969. Stoudt lists a German version: "Was geht ums Haus rum un macht just een Spuhr? (En Schubkarrich)" (*Folklore*, 80). Taylor cites Flemish, Frisian, and German examples (704, No. 174).
9. Collected by Alfred Shoemaker from William P. Shoemaker, Maple Grove, Pennsylvania (*Pennsylvania Dutchman* 1.3 [1949]: 2). Stoudt has a similar riddle (72). This resembles the riddle found in most European languages, "What goes through the water without getting wet? The sun" (see Taylor, 59, 64).
10. Collected by Alfred Shoemaker from George C. Kerchner, Berne, Pennsylvania (*Pennsylvania Dutchman* 1.23 [1950]: 2). Compare Taylor, No. 186.
11. Collected from Mrs. Elsie Snyder, Carlisle, Pennsylvania, April 1, 1969. A longer Pennsylvania German variant is cited by Stoudt (75): "Was is das? fern armer Drop, Muss die Steg uf un ab geh uf em Kop? (Shuhnagel.)" Taylor traces this riddle to medieval sources (66–67, No. 188).
12. Collected from Mrs. Elsie Snyder, Carlisle, Pennsylvania, April 1, 1969. See the

bibliography listed by Taylor (707, No. 203a). Compare also riddle No. 23.
13. Stoudt, 80. Taylor cites an English example (76, No. 213) but found no parallels in continental European collections.
14. Collected from Mrs. Elsie Snyder, Carlisle, Pennsylvania, April 1, 1969. Taylor cites numerous European examples (712–13, No. 247).
15. Collected by Alfred Shoemaker from William P. Shoemaker, Maple Grove, Pennsylvania (*Pennsylvania Dutchman* 1.17 [1949]: 2). Taylor traces this riddle to fourteenth-century Latin and cites numerous examples from Europe (88).
16. Collected by Alfred Shoemaker from William P. Shoemaker, Maple Grove, Pennsylvania (*Pennsylvania Dutchman* 1.1 [1949]: 2).
17. Collected by Alfred Shoemaker from George C. Kershner, Berne, Pennsylvania (*Pennsylvania Dutchman* 1.22 [1950]: 2). Taylor lists several English variants (94–95, No. 277). Jordan collected this same riddle in Texas: "Was hat ein Auge und kann doch nicht sehen?" with the answer, "Eine Nähnadel" (a sewing needle) (*German Texana*, 138, No. 8; cf. Taylor, No. 282).
18. Collected from Mrs. Elsie Snyder, Carlisle, Pennsylvania, April 1, 1969. Taylor lists this with the answer, "A river" (95, No. 288).
19. Collected by Alfred Shoemaker from Mae S. Heisler, Tamaqua, Pennsylvania (*Pennsylvania Dutchman* 1.16 [1949]: 2). See Taylor, 114.
20. Collected by Alfred Shoemaker in Palmyra, Pennsylvania (*Pennsylvania Dutchman* 1.24 [1950]: 2). Taylor cites several German examples (148).
21. Collected by Alfred Shoemaker from William P. Shoemaker, Maple Grove, Pennsylvania (*Pennsylvania Dutchman* 1.11 [1949]: 2).
22. Collected by Alfred Shoemaker from William P. Shoemaker, Maple Grove, Pennsylvania (*Pennsylvania Dutchman* 1.5 [1949]: 2).
23. Collected by Alfred Shoemaker from Helen J. Moser, Bally, Pennsylvania (*Pennsylvania Dutchman* 3.22 [1952]: 1). Stoudt provides a variant form: "En eisner Gaul, un en flächse Schwäntzel. Wie de stärken das des Gäuliche springt, we kürtzer das sei Schwäntzel werd. (Nodle un Fadem)," with the answer, "Needle and thread" (*Folklore*, 69). As Taylor notes (733), a needle and thread are often compared to an animal with a flaxen tail in European folklore.
24. John Baer Stoudt, "Some Palatine Riddles," *Olde Ulster* 9 (1913): 286. The riddle is left incomplete in his *Folklore of the Pennsylvania Germans* (74). Jordan collected a similar riddle in Mason County, Texas: "Was wächst im Garten, hat grüne Röhrlein, hat viele Häute, beisst alle Leute? (Eine Zwiebel.) What grows in the garden, has tubular stems, has many peelings, hurts people's feelings? (An onion)" (*German Texana*, 139). In European riddles the onion is frequently described as having many skins or patches (Taylor, 844).
25. Stoudt, *Folklore*, 72.
26. Eugene Laatz, "German Games and Plays," *Bucks County* [Pa.] *Historical Society Papers* 4 (1917): 33. This is similar to the English riddle "Dick Red-Cap," where the answer is usually "a cherry" (see Taylor, 224–30). Comparisons of a mushroom to a man standing on one leg are virtually universal (Taylor, 469–70).
27. Trumbore, 7. Stoudt includes the text of this riddle in his collection but, not surprisingly, omits the answer (*Folklore*, 66).
28. Stoudt, *Folklore*, 72.
29. Collected by Alfred Shoemaker from Victor Dieffenbach, Bethel, Pennsylvania (*Pennsylvania Dutchman* 1.7 [1949]: 2). Taylor cites numerous European examples of this riddle (402–3, 791–92).
30. Collected from J. Russell Barrick, Carlisle, Pennsylvania, 1963. A Pennsylvania German variant appears in the *Pennsylvania Dutchman* (1.4 [1949]: 2): "Was waxt s menscht unnerschich? N eis-tsappa." The riddle is common in Europe; see Taylor, 801.
31. Collected by Alfred Shoemaker from John B. Brendel, Reinholds, Pennsylvania (*Pennsylvania Dutchman* 1.4 [1949]: 2). See Taylor, 802, No. 1056.

32. Stoudt, "Some Palatine Riddles," 286; reprinted in *Folklore,* 69. For European comparisons of the egg to a flower, see Taylor, 816.

33. Collected by Stoudt in Philadelphia (*Folklore,* 70). This is almost identical to another rhymed variant collected by Jordan in Texas (*German Texana,* 137). Taylor cites numerous examples (815).

34. Collected by Alfred Shoemaker from Edna M. Stump, Reading, Pennsylvania (*Pennsylvania Dutchman* 1.14 [1949]: 2). Stoudt includes a variant form (*Folklore,* 68). Compare Taylor, 494–95.

35. Collected by Alfred Shoemaker from Edna M. Stump, Reading, Pennsylvania (*Pennsylvania Dutchman* 1.14 [1949]: 2). Stoudt has a variant (*Folklore,* 69). Comparing the egg to a barrel without hoops is a common riddle in Europe (Taylor, 497, 820).

36. Collected by Alfred Shoemaker in Palmyra, Pennsylvania (*Pennsylvania Dutchman* 1.24 [1950]: 2). Norman Smith of Berks County contributed the same riddle with the answer "Mush" (*Pennsylvania Dutchman* 1.2 [1949]: 2).

37. Stoudt, *Folklore,* 73.

38. Collected from Albert Gutshall, Cumberland County, Pennsylvania, 1963. Stoudt has a similar riddle with the solution, "Chestnut": "So hoch ass en Haus,/So nidder ass en Maus,/So rauh ass en Riegel,/So glatt ass en Spiegel,/So bitter ass Gall,/Un is gut fer uns all. (Kescht.)" (Stoudt, *Folklore,* 70). As Taylor notes, this riddle is widely disseminated (536–37, 832).

39. Collected by Alfred Shoemaker from Mrs. Hattie M. Berks, New Ringgold, Pennsylvania (*Pennsylvania Dutchman* 1.9 [1949]: 2).

40. Ibid. Obviously the first line is missing from the German text. This is similar to riddles cited by Taylor (582–83).

41. Collected by Alfred Shoemaker from William P. Shoemaker, Maple Grove, Pennsylvania (*Pennsylvania Dutchman* 1.3 [1949]: 2). Stoudt has a variant: "Fleesh hinne, Fleesh forne, Eise und Holtz in der mitt" (*Folklore,* 75). Taylor notes the popularity of this riddle form in Europe (580, 832).

42. Collected by Alfred Shoemaker from Edna M. Stump, Reading, Pennsylvania (*Pennsylvania Dutchman* 1.14 [1949]: 2).

43. Collected by Alfred Shoemaker from Helen Moser, Bally, Pennsylvania (*Pennsylvania Dutchman* 1.13 [1949]: 2). Jordan collected a variant of the same riddle in Fredericksburg, Texas: "Loch an Loch, und hält doch. Antwort: Eine Kette oder ein Netz" (*German Texana,* 138).

44. Collected by Roland Dickison in California. This is apparently related to the catch used in Pennsylvania and elsewhere of handing someone a mirror and saying, "Look at the monkey in there."

45. Collected by Jordan in Mason County, Texas (*German Texana,* 136), the riddle is identical to one collected by Stoudt in Philadelphia (*Folklore,* 68). The Pennsylvania German version is "Was is so weiss wie schnee, so grie as graws, so root wie bluut un so schwatz wie'n huut? (En schwatzkasch [A black cherry])" (*Pennsylvania Dutchman* 1.3 [1949]: 2; Stoudt, 67). See also Taylor, 238–39.

46. Collected by Alfred Shoemaker from William P. Shoemaker, Maple Grove, Pennsylvania (*Pennsylvania Dutchman* 1.5 [1949]: 2). The riddle is a form of catch in which the victim is misled into giving an embarrassing answer. Taylor seems unaware of the erotic nature of the riddle-description (see his discussion of such riddles, 600–602).

47. Collected by Hans Meurer, Shippensburg, Pennsylvania, from a Ukrainian informant, September 24, 1981. The guitar, because of its form, figures prominently in sexual symbolism.

48. Collected from Albert Gutshall, Cumberland County, Pennsylvania, 1963. Taylor cites several European examples (648–49, 858–59).

49. Collected by Alfred Shoemaker from William P. Shoemaker, Maple Grove, Pennsylvania (*Pennsylvania Dutchman* 1.11 [1949]: 2), but the translation he provides

should read "you take an inch away. . . ." There are many European parallels; see Taylor, 673–76, 863–64).

50. Collected by Roland Dickison in Sacramento, California, with the explanation, "The informant's mother made up this riddle while shelling and eating walnuts" (in Germany in 1954).

51. Collected by Alfred Shoemaker from L. G. Kriebel, Barto, Pennsylvania (*Pennsylvania Dutchman* 1.23 [1950]: 2). Stoudt provides a variant form (*Folklore*, 74). Taylor cites several European parallels (684, 867). A similar description occurs in a riddle about a coffin.

52. Collected by Alfred Shoemaker from William P. Shoemaker, Maple Grove, Pennsylvania (*Pennsylvania Dutchman* 1.5 [1949]: 2). Several nonsense rhymes and traditional sayings include these same concepts. Henry Glassie collected one in Ireland: "I see, said the blind man, You're a liar, says the dummy, Give him a kick in the arse, says the cripple" (*Passing the Time in Ballymenone* [Philadelphia: University of Pennsylvania Press, 1982], 276).

53. Collected by Alfred Shoemaker from L. G. Kriebel, Barto, Pennsylvania (*Pennsylvania Dutchman* 1.23 [1950]: 2).

54. Collected by Alfred Shoemaker from William P. Shoemaker, Maple Grove, Pennsylvania (*Pennsylvania Dutchman* 1.10 [1949]: 2).

55. Collected by Alfred Shoemaker from William P. Shoemaker, Maple Grove, Pennsylvania (*Pennsylvania Dutchman* 1.5 [1949]: 2). Stoudt lists a variant with seven corners, seven sacks, seven cats, and seven kittens (*Folklore*, 71).

56. Collected by Alfred Shoemaker in Snyder County, Pennsylvania (*Pennsylvania Dutchman* 1.20 [1949]: 2). Stoudt also lists this riddle (*Folklore*, 85).

57. Collected by Alfred Shoemaker from Albert Leibenguth, Allentown, Pennsylvania (*Pennsylvania Dutchman* 1.8 [1949]: 2). Stoudt has the same riddle (*Folklore*, 78).

58. Stoudt, *Folklore*, 82. Gilbert Jordan collected a version in Fredericksburg, Texas, in which "Es sassen zehn Sperlinge auf dem Dach" and a hunter shot four of them. How many are left? "Keine. Die andern sind fortgeflogen" (*German Texana*, 138).

59. Collected from Mrs. Elsie Snyder, Carlisle, Pennsylvania, April 1, 1969.

60. Collected by Alfred Shoemaker from Helen Moser, Bally, Pennsylvania (*Pennsylvania Dutchman* 1.13 [1949]: 2).

61. Stoudt, *Folklore*, 81.

62. Collected by Alfred Shoemaker from William P. Shoemaker, Maple Grove, Pennsylvania (*Pennsylvania Dutchman* 1.10 [1949]: 2).

63. Stoudt, *Folklore*, 76.

64. Collected by Alfred Shoemaker in Snyder County, Pennsylvania (*Pennsylvania Dutchman* 1.20 [1949]: 2). The riddle is found in such medieval Latin question books as the *Joca Monachorum* (see Mathilde Hain, *Rätsel* [Stuttgart: Metzlersche, 1966], 9).

65. Collected by Alfred Shoemaker from L. G. Kriebel, Barto, Pennsylvania (*Pennsylvania Dutchman* 1.23 [1950]: 2). Stoudt has the same riddle (*Folklore*, 76).

66. Collected by Alfred Shoemaker from John B. Brendel, Reinholds, Pennsylvania. (*Pennsylvania Dutchman* 1.4 [1949]: 2). In Stoudt the question is, "Wu hat der *Adam* der ersht Nagel hie gschlage?" [emphasis added] (*Folklore*, 80). Peter and Iona Opie see this and the next riddle as part of a medieval tradition ridiculing the quibbles of theologians (*The Lore and Language of Schoolchildren* [Oxford: Oxford University Press, 1959], 85).

67. Collected by Alfred Shoemaker, from Helen Moser, Bally, Pennsylvania (*Pennsylvania Dutchman* 1 No. 13 [1949]: 2). Sarah Lawson sees the riddle as a parody of the biblical quizzes used in fundamentalist churches ("'Where Was Moses When the Lights Went Out?'," *Journal of American Folklore* 85 [1972]: 183–84). Eric Partridge published the suggestion that it was coined during the Zeppelin raids of 1915–16 (*A Dictionary of Catch Phrases* [New York: Stein and Day, 1977], 249), but it is much older. Mark Twain used it in *Huckleberry Finn* (Chapter 17), and it has been dated to at least 1821 (Opie, 85). There are longer forms, suggesting that the present form may be an expurga-

tion: "Where was Moses when the lights went out? Down in the cellar eating sauerkraut" (*Pennsylvania Dutchman* 1.8 [1949]: 2); "Know whar Moses was when the light went out? Sitting in the corner with his shirttail hanging out" (F. Roy Johnson, *Oral Folk Humor from the Carolina and Virginia Flatlands* [Murfreesboro, North Carolina: Johnson, 1980], 122); "Where was Moses when the lights went out? Under the table with his peter out" (collected in Newville, Pennsylvania, November 1974). The latter is probably the version mentioned by Tennessee Williams in *The Glass Menagerie* (Act 1, Scene 8). Partridge also hints at an erotic version.

68. Collected from Albert Gutshall, Cumberland County, Pennsylvania, 1963. The Pennsylvania German is "Wie iss der buchweetza ivver der see kumm? (Drei-eckich)" (*Pennsylvania Dutchman* 1.8 [1949]: 2; Stoudt, *Folklore*, 77).

69. Collected by Alfred Shoemaker from Victor Dieffenbach, Bethel, Pennsylvania (*Pennsylvania Dutchman* 1.7 [1949]: 2).

70. Collected by Alfred Shoemaker from Daniel C. Keller (*Pennsylvania Dutchman* 1.9 [1949]: 2).

71. Collected by Alfred Shoemaker from William P. Shoemaker, Maple Grove, Pennsylvania (*Pennsylvania Dutchman* 1.1 [1949]: 2). Stoudt has a similar riddle (*Folklore*, 81).

72. Collected by Alfred Shoemaker from Mae S. Heisler, Tamaqua, Pennsylvania (*Pennsylvania Dutchman* 1.16 [1949]: 2).

73. Collected by Alfred Shoemaker from Helen Moser, Bally, Pennsylvania (*Pennsylvania Dutchman* 1.13 [1949]: 2).

74. Collected by Alfred Shoemaker from H. L. Knecht, Allentown, Pennsylvania (*Pennsylvania Dutchman* 1.15 [1949]: 2).

75. Collected by Alfred Shoemaker from Daniel C. Keller (*Pennsylvania Dutchman* 1.9 [1949]: 2).

76. Collected by Alfred Shoemaker from Mrs. Henry Adair, Lititz, Pennsylvania (*Pennsylvania Dutchman* 1.9 [1949]: 2).

77. Collected by Alfred Shoemaker from Mrs. Orin J. Farrell, Schenectady, New York (*Pennsylvania Dutchman* 1.19 [1949]: 2). Stoudt has a similar riddle about a wagon-wheel and a lawyer (*Folklore*, 83).

78. Collected by Roland Dickison in Sacramento, California, June 1973.

79. Collected from Charles C. Miller, Newville, Pennsylvania, May 11, 1986. The Pennsylvania German is "Was far beem waxa es menscht im busch? (Runda)" (*Pennsylvania Dutchman* 1.8 [1949]: 2; Stoudt, *Folklore*, 81).

80. Collected by Alfred Shoemaker from Albert Leibenguth, Allentown, Pennsylvania (*Pennsylvania Dutchman* 1.8 [1949]: 2). Stoudt lists the same riddle (*Folklore*, 76)

81. Stoudt, *Folklore*, 80.

82. Collected by Alfred Shoemaker from John B. Brendel, Reinholds, Pennsylvania (*Pennsylvania Dutchman* 1.12 [1949]: 2). There is a similar riddle in Stoudt, *Folklore*, 84.

83. Collected by Alfred Shoemaker from William P. Shoemaker, Maple Grove, Pennsylvania (*Pennsylvania Dutchman* 1.10 [1949]: 2; cf. Stoudt, *Folklore*, 79). Jordan collected the standard German version in Texas: "Welche Fische haben die Augen am nächsten zusammen? (Die kleinsten)" (*German Texana*, 139).

84. Collected by Alfred Shoemaker from George C. Kershner, Berne, Pennsylvania (*Pennsylvania Dutchman* 1.22 [1950]: 2).

85. Collected from Albert Gutshall, Cumberland County, Pennsylvania, in 1963. The Pennsylvania German is "Was is älter ass sei Mutter? (Essig)" (Stoudt, *Folklore*, 75).

86. Stoudt, *Folklore*, 84. Compare Jordan, *German Texana*, 138.

87. Collected by Alfred Shoemaker from George C. Kershner, Berne, Pennsylvania (*Pennsylvania Dutchman* 1.22 [1950]: 2).

88. Collected by Gilbert Jordan in Texas (*German Texana*, 138), with the explanation, "This riddle was often used to tease little boys by older friends and brothers." The riddle is also

known in Pennsylvania.

89. Collected by Trumbore in Montgomery County, Pennsylvania (27).

90. Trumbore, 11.

91. Collected by Alfred Shoemaker in Snyder County, Pennsylvania (*Pennsylvania Dutchman* 1.20 [1949]: 2). Stoudt has the same riddle (*Folklore,* 76).

92. Stoudt, *Folklore,* 84.

93. Trumbore, 22.

94. Collected by Alfred Shoemaker from William P. Shoemaker, Maple Grove, Pennsylvania (*Pennsylvania Dutchman* 1.11 [1949]: 2).

95. Trumbore, 82.

96. Collected by Alfred Shoemaker from George C. Kershner, Berne, Pennsylvania (*Pennsylvania Dutchman* 1.22 [1950]: 2).

97. Collected by Alfred Shoemaker from William P. Shoemaker, Maple Grove, Pennsylvania (*Pennsylvania Dutchman* 1.1 [1949]: 2).

98. Collected by Alfred Shoemaker from William P. Shoemaker, Maple Grove, Pennsylvania (*Pennsylvania Dutchman* 1.11 [1949]: 2).

99. Collected from Mrs. Ella Barrick, Carlisle, Pennsylvania, May 31, 1963. Stoudt gives the Pennsylvania German version: "Was is schwartzer ass en Kräpp? (Die Feddre)" (*Folklore,* 77).

100. Collected by Alfred Shoemaker in Snyder County, Pennsylvania (*Pennsylvania Dutchman* 1.20 [1949]: 2). Stoudt has the same riddle (*Folklore,* 81).

101. Collected by Alfred Shoemaker from F. Wayne Gruber, Reading, Pennsylvania (*Pennsylvania Dutchman* 1.6 [1949]: 2).

102. Collected by Alfred Shoemaker from Victor Dieffenbach, Bethel, Pennsylvania (*Pennsylvania Dutchman* 1.7 [1949]: 2).

103. Stoudt, *Folklore,* 79.

104. Collected by Alfred Shoemaker from William P. Shoemaker, Maple Grove, Pennsylvania (*Pennsylvania Dutchman* 1.11 [1949]: 2).

105. Trumbore, 16. There is a common popular comparison, "Useless as tits on a boar hog" (Barrick, "Popular Comparisons and Similes," *Keystone Folklore Quarterly* 10 [1965]: 32).

106. Stoudt, *Folklore,* 78.

107. Trumbore, 74. This type of riddle commonly has an erotic or obscene connotation; see Alan Dundes and Robert A. Georges, "Some Minor Genres of Obscene Folklore," *Journal of American Folklore* 75 (1962): 223.

108. Collected by Alfred Shoemaker from B. Franklin Reber, Reading, Pennsylvania (*Pennsylvania Dutchman* 1.24 [1950]: 2). Stoudt has a similar riddle about a rabbit (*Folklore,* 84). Compare also, "Wann hockt der fux uff'm schtumba? (Wann der bawm umkackt is.) When does a fox sit on a stump? (When the tree is felled.)" (*Pennsylvania Dutchman* 1.2 [1949]: 2).

109. Collected by Alfred Shoemaker from William P. Shoemaker, Maple Grove, Pennsylvania (*Pennsylvania Dutchman* 1.17 [1949]: 2). Stoudt lists the same riddle (*Folklore,* 79.)

110. Collected by Alfred Shoemaker from William P. Shoemaker, Maple Grove, Pennsylvania (*Pennsylvania Dutchman* 1.11 [1949]: 2). Often cited as a classic example of an old joke, this riddle is known to be popular by the number of parodies on its punchline.

111. Trumbore, 25.

112. Collected by Alfred Shoemaker from H. Wayne Gruber, Reading, Pennsylvania (*Pennsylvania Dutchman* 1.6 [1949]: 2). Stoudt has a similar riddle (*Folklore,* 78).

113. Collected by Gilbert Jordan in Fredericksburg, Texas (*German Texana,* 138). The Pennsylvania German version is, "Welle Schoof fresse es mensht, die schwartze odder die weise? (Die weise, weil es mehr hat wie Schwertze)" (Stoudt, *Folklore,* 81).

114. Collected by Alfred Shoemaker from Norman A. Smith, Lenhartsville, Pennsylvania (*Pennsylvania Dutchman* 1.2 [1949]: 2). A variant appears in Stoudt's *Folklore of the Pennsylvania Germans,* 79.

115. Collected by Alfred Shoemaker from William P. Shoemaker, Maple Grove, Pennsylvania (*Pennsylvania Dutchman* 1.5 [1949]: 2). Stoudt has the same riddle (*Folklore,* 81).

116. Collected by Alfred Shoemaker from John B. Brendel, Reinholds, Pennsylvania (*Pennsylvania Dutchman* 1.12 [1949]: 2). Stoudt also has this riddle (*Folklore,* 82).

117. Collected from Mrs. Bertha Gutshall, Cumberland County, Pennsylvania, 1963.

118. Collected by Alfred Shoemaker from William P. Shoemaker, Maple Grove, Pennsylvania (*Pennsylvania Dutchman* 1.11 [1949]: 2). See also Stoudt, *Folklore,* 75.

119. Collected from Mrs. Ella Barrick, Carlisle, Pennsylvania, May 1963. The Pennsylvania German is "Fer was schmokt der Schornstee? (Veil er net jawe kann)" (Stoudt, *Folklore,* 80; *Pennsylvania Dutchman* 1.2 [1949]: 2).

120. Collected by Alfred Shoemaker from H. L. Knecht, Allentown, Pennsylvania (*Pennsylvania Dutchman* 1.15 [1949]: 2). Stoudt has a variant with the answer, "Fer uf zuduh (To wear)" (*Folklore,* 79).

121. Collected by Alfred Shoemaker from Mae S. Heisler, Tamaqua, Pennsylvania (*Pennsylvania Dutchman* 1.16 [1949]: 2). There is a variant with a fox instead of a rooster (*Pennsylvania Dutchman* 1.15 [1949]: 2).

122. Collected by Alfred Shoemaker from Helen Moser, Bally, Pennsylvania (*Pennsylvania Dutchman* 1.13 [1949]: 2).

123. Collected from Hans Meurer, Shippensburg, Pennsylvania, January 12, 1979. This riddle became a popular joke on television during 1980 with Baptists as the subject. There was even a graffiti of it in California (Marina Haan and Richard Hammerstrom, *Graffiti in the Pac Ten* [New York: Warner, 1981]: 110).

124. Collected by Alfred Shoemaker from H. Wayne Gruber, Reading, Pennsylvania (*Pennsylvania Dutchman* 1.6 [1949]: 2).

125. Collected by Alfred Shoemaker from William P. Shoemaker, Maple Grove, Pennsylvania (*Pennsylvania Dutchman* 1.3 [1949]: 2).

126. Stoudt, *Folklore,* 79.

127. Collected by Alfred Shoemaker from William P. Shoemaker, Maple Grove, Pennsylvania (*Pennsylvania Dutchman* 1.3 [1949]: 2).

128. Collected from Hans Meurer, Shippensburg, Pennsylvania, September 29, 1972. Rose Marie Nitribitt was a promiscuous chorus girl, upon whose death numerous jokes were coined about her being a friend of birds (*Vögelen,* also slang for sexual intercourse) and the similarity between her name and nitrate, a meat preservative.

129. Collected by Alfred Shoemaker from H. L. Knecht, Allentown, Pennsylvania (*Pennsylvania Dutchman* 1.15 [1949]: 2).

130. Collected by Alfred Shoemaker from John B. Brendel, Reinholds, Pennsylvania (*Pennsylvania Dutchman* 1.12 [1949]: 2). Stoudt has a variant (*Folklore,* 83).

131. Collected by Alfred Shoemaker from Jacob Weik, Kleinfeltersville, Pennsylvania (*Pennsylvania Dutchman* 1.19 [1949]: 2).

132. Collected by Alfred Shoemaker from William P. Shoemaker, Maple Grove, Pennsylvania (*Pennsylvania Dutchman* 1.17 [1949]: 2). Stoudt lists the same riddle (*Folklore,* 76).

133. Collected by Alfred Shoemaker from Norman A. Smith, Lenhartsville, Pennsylvania (*Pennsylvania Dutchman* 1.2 [1949]: 2). Stoudt gives only the answer "hornet" (*Folklore,* 78). Another possible answer is "brenneesel" (nettle) (*Pennsylvania Dutchman* 1.7 [1949]: 2).

134. Collected by Alfred Shoemaker from H. L. Knecht, Allentown, Pennsylvania (*Pennsylvania Dutchman* 1.15 [1949]: 2). The same riddle appears in Stoudt, *Folklore,* 78.

135. Collected by Alfred Shoemaker from Helen J. Moser, Bally, Pennsylvania (*Pennsylvania Dutchman* 3.22 [1952]: 1). See the recipe for panhaus in Chapter 9.

136. Collected by Alfred Shoemaker from William P. Shoemaker, Maple Grove, Pennsylvania (*Pennsylvania Dutchman* 1.1 [1949]: 2). In Pennsylvania German, *leeb* means both "lion" and "loaf."

137. Collected from Henry Barrick, Newville, Pennsylvania, November 22, 1975.

138. Collected by Alfred Shoemaker from William P. Shoemaker, Maple Grove, Pennsylvania (*Pennsylvania Dutchman* 1.1 [1949]: 2).

139. Collected from Hans Meurer, Shippensburg, Pennsylvania, January 1982. The riddle was told in Germany in the 1940s, when Hermann Goering was a field marshall and Nazi party leader.

140. Collected by Alfred Shoemaker from John B. Brendel, Reinholds, Pennsylvania (*Pennsylvania Dutchman* 1.12 [1949]: 2). Stoudt has the same riddle (*Folklore,* 81).

141. Trumbore, 67. The pun is on the pronunciation of the word *Geographie.*

142. Stoudt, *Folklore,* 77.

143. Collected by Alfred Shoemaker from John B. Brendel, Reinholds, Pennsylvania (*Pennsylvania Dutchman* 1.12 [1949]: 2). Stoudt has a variant (*Folklore,* 76).

144. Collected by Alfred Shoemaker from Mrs. Henry Mease, Lititz, Pennsylvania (*Pennsylvania Dutchman* 1.7 [1949]: 2). There are other riddles based on the dual meaning of the word "smell": "How do you keep a fish from smelling? Cut off his nose"; "How would a goat smell without a nose? Just as bad."

145. Collected by Alfred Shoemaker from Albert Leibenguth, Allentown, Pennsylvania (*Pennsylvania Dutchman* 1.8 [1949]: 2). Stoudt has the same riddle (*Folklore,* 78).

146. Collected by Alfred Shoemaker from William P. Shoemaker, Maple Grove, Pennsylvania (*Pennsylvania Dutchman* 1.10 [1949]: 2).

147. Collected by Alfred Shoemaker from William P. Shoemaker, Maple Grove, Pennsylvania (*Pennsylvania Dutchman* 1.11 [1949]: 2).

148. Stoudt, *Folklore,* 67.

149. Collected by Alfred Shoemaker in Palmyra, Pennsylvania (*Pennsylvania Dutchman* 1.24 [1950]: 2). Stoudt has a similar riddle where the dog's name is Also (*Folklore,* 66–67).

150. Fogel, *Proverbs,* No. 465. Mark Trumbore explains that someone hearing the first statement would exclaim, "The Bible doesn't mention tobacco," whereon he was told, "I didn't say tobacco is mentioned in the Bible; I said *that* is in the Bible" (*A Superficial Collection,* 6).

151. Collected from Samuel Miller, Newville, Pennsylvania, August 17, 1982. The catch lies in the belief that one is being asked to name the crupper, the piece of harness that goes under a horse's tail.

152. Trumbore, 17.

153. David P. Lick and Thomas R. Brendle, "Plant Names and Plant Lore among the Pennsylvania Germans," *Pennsylvania-German Society Proceedings* 33 (1922): 51. Frequently used to tease small children.

154. Collected from J. Russell Barrick, Carlisle, Pennsylvania, September 22, 1967.

155. John Baer's *Pennsylvanischer Calender,* 1843, fol. B 5ʳᵒ. Such rhymed riddles are literary rather than folk, but they have attracted the attention of writers and scholars since the sixteenth century. Literary riddles flourished in Renaissance Germany (Archer Taylor, "The Riddle," *California Folklore Quarterly* 2 [1943]: 143–44; see also Hain, *Rätsel,* 23 ff.).

CHAPTER 4. RHYMES

1. Collected April 1963, from J. Russell Barrick, Carlisle, Pennsylvania, who first heard it about 1900. His wife recalled a version beginning "Head-bumper, Eye-winker . . ." There are similar rhymes in the *Frank C. Brown Collection of North Carolina Folklore* (Durham: Duke University Press, 1952), vol. 1, 189.

2. Collected by Alfred Shoemaker from Aaron Zook, a Church Amish from Intercourse,

Pennsylvania, October 19, 1954.

3. Collected by Alfred Shoemaker in Palmyra, Pennsylvania (*Pennsylvania Dutchman* 1.23 [1959]: 2). More a game than a rhyme, it has characteristics of other tickling rhymes, since it is done by adults to small children.

4. Collected by Alfred Shoemaker from Mrs. Charles H. Butzer, Manheim, Pennsylvania (*Pennsylvania Dutchman* 2.8 [1950]: 2).

5. Collected by Alfred Shoemaker from George Hartman, Hamburg, Pennsylvania (*Pennsylvania Dutchman* 1.1 [1949]: 2). Shoemaker reprints this in his *Traditional Rhymes and Jingles of the Pennsylvania Dutch* (Lancaster: Dutch Folklore Center, 1951), 4. Gilbert Jordan collected a similar rhyme in Texas (*German Texana*, 15).

6. Collected in Minnesota by Warren Kliewer (*Mennonite Life* 16 [1961]: 110), this Low German rhyme ends logically with the thumb as "louse-cracker."

7. Stoudt, *Folklore of the Pennsylvania Germans*, 32. Here the index finger is the "louse-cracker" and the thumb is the "oats-sticker," because the thumb is used to tuck in the band when tying oats sheaves.

8. The first version was collected from Hans D. Meurer, Shippensburg, Pennsylvania, February 26, 1979. Similar verses have been collected in Comfort, Texas (Jordan, *German Texana*, 14) and Dubois County, Indiana (Mary Jo Meuser, *German Rhymes and Songs* [1978], 2). The second version was collected by Carol Seelig from Arthur Seelig, Highland Park, Illinois, November 27, 1960. The third, a Pennsylvania German variant, was collected by Alfred Shoemaker (*Pennsylvania Dutchman* 1.1 [1949]: 2). Other variants appear in Stoudt, *Folklore*, 32–33, and in David E. Lick and Thomas R. Brendle, *Plant Names and Plant Lore among the Pennsylvania Germans* [Lancaster: Pennsvlvania-German Society, 1923], 240). The rhymes are similar in function to the English toe-tickling rhyme beginning, "This little pig went to market . . ."

9. The first version was collected by Alfred Shoemaker from Mrs. Edith Rumbaugh in Reading, Pennsylvania (*Pennsylvania Dutchman* 1.1 [1949]: 2). A variant was collected by Albert Buffington in Somerset County, Pennsylvania (*Ebbes fer Alle-Ebber, Ebbes fer Dich* [Breinigsville, Pa.: Pennsylvania German Society, 1980], 24). The second example is a standard German version collected by Curt Nash, from Mrs. Mills-Price in Eugene, Oregon, March 28, 1974 (Northwest Folklore Archive), by Meuser in Indiana (11) and by Jordan in Texas (with the final line, "Schieb in den Ofen 'nein'" [Shove it through the oven door]) (*German Texana*, 15–16). The third version was collected by Alfred Shoemaker from Marian Long, Robesonia, Pennsylvania (*Pennsylvania Dutchman* 1.23 [1950]: 2). The fourth version was collected by Alfred Shoemaker from Helen Moser, Bally, Pennsylvania, April 5, 1954. Variants of most of these verses appear in Stoudt, *Folklore*, 30–32. These are, of course, the German equivalent of English "patty cake" rhymes.

10. Collected by Alfred Shoemaker from Mazie Newcomer, Lancaster, Pennsylvania (*Pennsylvania Dutchman* 1.3 [1949]: 2). Shoemaker collected another version in Saegersville, Pennsylvania: "Mammy bakes cakes, she bakes them too hard. She locks me in the cellar and lets me go hungry. She gives me some crumbs to call the chicks: 'Come chickie, come chickie, and eat my crumbs.' If she does this to me again, I'll take my bundle and say, 'Good Night.'" (*Pennsylvania Dutchman* 1.15 [1949]: 2). Other variants appear in Stoudt, *Folklore*, 30–32.

11. Collected by Alfred Shoemaker (*Pennsylvania Dutchman* 1.2 [1949]: 2) who expresses puzzlement at its meaning. Perhaps there is a relationship with the proverb, "There are more ways to kill a cat than choking it with butter."

12. The first version was collected by Alfred Shoemaker from Mrs. Samuel F. Bomberger, Lebanon, Pennsylvania (*Pennsylvania Dutchman* 1.10 [1949]: 2). The second was from H. Wayne Gruber, Reading, Pennsylvania (*Pennsylvania Dutchman* 1.2 [1949]: 2) and the third from a group of Amish children at Mill Creek School, Pennsylvania (*Pennsylvania Dutchman* 1.12 [1949]: 2). Phares Hertzog includes the latter in *Songs, Sayings and Stories of a Pennsylvania Dutchman* (Lebanon: Applied Arts, 1966), 18. The fourth version was

collected by Shoemaker from Claude Miller, of Johnstown, Pennsylvania (*Pennsylvania Dutchman* 1.25 [1950]: 4). There are many variants of the rhyme (see Stoudt, *Folklore,* 25–30; Elmer Smith, *The Pennsylvania Germans of the Shenandoah Valley* [Allentown: Pennsylvania German Folklore Society, 1964], 277), but most who remember it say it was recited while bouncing the child, horsey-style, on the foot or knee. Albert F. Buffington (*Pennsylvania German Secular Folksongs* [Breinigsville, Pa.: Pennsylvania German Society, 1974], 70–73) collected numerous sung versions of this rhyme.

13. Collected by Lawrence Templin from Frieda Warkentin, Bloomington, Indiana, October 1957. Jordan collected a similar rhyme in New Braunfels, Texas (*German Texana,* 16). Stoudt has the same rhyme under the category *Steckereite* (Riding a hobby horse); see *Folklore,* 29.

14. Collected by Marilyn Walter, in Bayside, New York, November 1961. The last line suggests that the child is gently dumped on the floor at the end of the ride. A similar suggestion occurs in a rhyme collected in Dubois County, Indiana: "Horse rider, horse/The rider sits on the horse./He wears a little red cap./He sits astride so gently/And Thump, there he lies" (Meuser, 9).

15. Collected by Albert Buffington in Somerset County, Pennsylvania (*Ebbes fer Alle-Ebber,* 21). There is nothing to indicate whether these were the names of actual participants or just part of the rhyme.

16. Collected by Henry C. Mercer in Bucks County, Pennsylvania ("Folk Lore, Notes Taken at Random," *Bucks County Historical Society Papers* 2 [1909]: 409). Stoudt lists this as the beginning of a longer rhyme (*Folklore,* 50–51). Compare Jordan, *German Texana,* 29.

17. Mercer, 409. This is a meaningless rhyme, except for the last line, which is "You lie out, you are out." Stoudt lists this rhyme (*Folklore,* 50) on the basis of Mercer's citation.

18. Collected by Dr. Ezra Grumbine ("Folk-Lore of Lebanon County," *Lebanon County* [Pa.] *Historical Society Papers* 3 [1905–6]: 292). The rhyme is, as he indicates, "a jingle of unmeaning terms."

19. Collected by Alfred Shoemaker from Mr. Grant of Reamstown, Pennsylvania, November 20, 1955. Grumbine lists this slightly differently: "Inty, minty, unicorn;/Apple-seeds and briar-thorn;/Briar, briar, limber-lock;/Ten geese in a flock/With a rotten dish-cloth—O, U, T, out" ("Folk-Lore of Lebanon County," 294). The mishearing of "seeds" as the German *siess* (sweet) and the change from ten geese to the magic number three illustrates how such verses change in oral transmission.

20. Collected by Alfred Shoemaker from Esthyr Daly of Virginville, Pennsylvania (*Pennsylvania Dutchman* 2.8 [1950]: 2). Stoudt lists a similar rhyme (*Folklore,* 52).

21. Mercer, 409.

22. Collected by Alfred Shoemaker from Mrs. Bertha M. Steiner, Sunbury, Pennsylvania (*Pennsylvania Dutchman* 1.5 [1949]: 2; reprinted in Shoemaker, *Traditional Rhymes and Jingles,* 14). Grumbine has the same verse, without the last line ("Folk-Lore of Lebanon County," 292). Children at butcherings, eating salted liver from the cooking pot, were warned not to get salt in the lard, because then it wouldn't render properly. Buffington collected a fragment of this rhyme in Somerset County, Pennsylvania: "Eens, zwee, drei,/Budder uff em Brei" (*Ebbes fer Alle-Ebber,* 21).

23. Eugene Laatz, "German Games and Plays," *Bucks County Historical Society Papers* 4 (1917): 34.

24. Collected by Alfred Shoemaker from Prof. Walter Oswald, Goshen, Indiana (*Pennsylvania Dutchman* 1.13 [1949]: 2).

25. The first rhyme was collected from Mrs. Elsie Snyder, Carlisle, Pennsylvania, April 1963. Stoudt has, "Eins, zwei, drei,/Mother caught a fly,/The fly died,/mother cried,/Eins, zwei, drei" (*Folklore,* 48). There is a similar rhyme in Roger D. Abrahams and Lois Rankin, *Counting-Out Rhymes* (Austin: University of Texas Press, 1980), No. 429. The second rhyme was collected from J. Russell Barrick, Carlisle, Pennsylvania, December 1963, and is also listed in the *Brown Collection of North Carolina Folklore* vol. 1, 166n.

26. Collected by Alfred Shoemaker from Amish children at the Mill Creek School (*Pennsylvania Dutchman* 1.12 [1949]: 2; reprinted in his *Traditional Rhymes and Jingles,* 5–6). The same form was collected in Dubois County, Indiana, in 1978 (Meuser, 1). Stoudt has several variants of the first part only (*Folklore,* 23–24). Albert Buffington collected a similar rhyme in Somerset County, Pennsylvania, with the last stanza: "Wann der Dreck, weggeht,/Noh tschumpt sie uff der Schtumbe/Mit em Aarsch voll Lumbe" (When the dirt goes away, then she jumps on the stump with her arse full of rags) (*Ebbes fer Alle-Ebber,* 22). Elmer Smith collected a variant in Shenandoah County, Virginia, that ends, "She jumped on the stump with her mouth full of rags; she goes in the barn with her mouth full of fire" (*The Pennsylvania Germans of the Shenandoah Valley,* 277). Gilbert Jordan collected still another version in Texas: "The cat ran in the snow; and when she came out again, she had a white toe" (*German Texana,* 31).

27. Collected by Margaret R. Sheviak from Walter Gemming, Bloomington, Indiana, November 8, 1957. The same rhyme appears in Laatz (*Bucks County Historical Society Papers* 4 [1917]: 34) and in Jordan (*German Texana,* 30). Stoudt lists several variants (*Folklore,* 49–50).

28. The first version was collected by Alfred Shoemaker from Richard E. Adams, Fleetwood, Pennsylvania (*Pennsylvania Dutchman* 1.10 [1949]: 2). The second was collected in Sugar Grove, West Virginia, by Elmer L. Smith (*Pennsylvania Germans of the Shenandoah Valley,* 276). The first line is flawed and should end in *Fingerhut* (thimble) to maintain the sense and the rhyme. Stoudt lists several variants (*Folklore,* 49). Albert Buffington collected an interesting version in Somerset County, Pennsylvania: "Peter, Peter, thimble! An old man is sitting in the garden. He wants to wait for an old woman. I or you are the one" (22).

29. Collected by Alfred Shoemaker from Carl Trexler, Topton, Pennsylvania, in a letter dated February 17, 1948.

30. Collected by Alfred Shoemaker from Lester Bashore, Robesonia, Pennsylvania (*Pennsylvania Dutchman* 2.8 [1950]: 2).

31. Collected from Mrs. Elnora Schaffer, Schnecksville, Pennsylvania, in 1935, and cited by Alfred L. Shoemaker in "Tongue Twisters," *Pennsylvania Dutchman* 5.9 (1954), 4. A similar version where Mommy makes mush with Mahlen Moyer's milk appeared in Stoudt's *Folklore of the Pennsylvania Germans,* 54. There is also a variant from Akron, Ohio, in *Pennsylvania-German* 10 (1909): 358.

32. Collected by Alfred Shoemaker from Lester Bashore of Robesonia in 1948 ("Tongue Twisters," 4). Stoudt has a variant (*Folklore,* 54). The following version was collected in Philippsburg, New Jersey: "Hinnich Hennesley Honnesley haus/Hucka hunnert hawsa haus./Hunnert hawsa hucka haus/Hinnich Hennesley Honnesley haus."

33. Collected by Alfred Shoemaker from Lester Bashore of Robesonia, Pennsylvania ("Tongue Twisters," 4).

34. Collected by Alfred Shoemaker from Esther Moser of Bally, Pennsylvania ("Tongue Twisters," 4).

35. Collected by Gilbert Jordan in Texas (*German Texana,* 122). The same rhyme appears in Alvin Schwartz, *A Twister of Twists, A Tangler of Tongues* (Philadelphia: J. B. Lippincott, 1972), 101.

36. Collected from Hans D. Meurer, Shippensburg, Pennsylvania, November 2, 1981. The word *Dampfer* (steamboat) repeated rapidly sounds like *verdam* (Damn it!).

37. Collected by Alfred Shoemaker from Weda Wolfinger, Kutztown, Pennsylvania, December 10, 1955. Said rapidly, "Meis im eckel" (mice in the corner) sounds like "mei seckel" (my scrotum).

38. Collected by Alfred Shoemaker from Weda Wolfinger, Kutztown, Pennsylvania, December 10, 1955. Said rapidly, "Fuftsich bulla, fuftsich kie" (Fifty bulls, fifty cows), explains what the bulls do to the cows.

39. Collected by Alfred Shoemaker from Sam Yoder, Goshen, Indiana (*Pennsylvania*

Dutchman 1.13 [1949]: 2). The trick here is that the reciter promises to tell another's fortune by reading his palm. In saying the last line, the teller spits in the hand, so the fortune comes true.

40. Collected by Alfred Shoemaker from Miriam Himelberger, Bernville, Pennsylvania (*Pennsylvania Dutchman* 1.20 [1949]: 2). Stoudt has the same catch (*Folklore,* 85). Stoudt also notes that German children readily adopted the English catch, "I one it, I two it . . . I ate it."

41. Collected by Alfred Shoemaker from Miriam Himelberger, Bernville, Pennsylvania (*Pennsylvania Dutchman* 1.20 [1949]: 2). The fifth step was omitted, possibly in error. The catch is common in many languages; see William W. Newell, *Games and Songs of American Children* (New York: Harper, 1883), 141.

42. Collected from Mrs. Ella Stover Barrick, Carlisle, Pennsylvania, April 27, 1963.

43. Collected from Charles K. Snyder, Carlisle, Pennsylvania, 1945. Iona and Peter Opie (43) cite its use in Illinois and elsewhere.

44. Collected by Alfred Shoemaker from Ida V. Hollenbach, Saegersville, Pennsylvania (*Pennsylvania Dutchman* 2.2 [1950]: 2; reprinted in Shoemaker, *Traditional Rhymes and Jingles,* 12).

45. Collected by Alfred Shoemaker from Ida V. Hollenbach, Saegersville, Pennsylvania (*Pennsylvania Dutchman* 2.2 [1950]: 2). A similar verse ending, "Du bist ein alter Nasweis" (You are an old nosy person) was collected in Eugene, Oregon, by Curt Nash from Mrs. Mills-Price in 1974.

46. Collected from Charles K. Snyder, Carlisle, Pennsylvania, in 1945.

47. Collected from Mrs. Bertha Gutshall, Cumberland County, Pennsylvania, June 1963.

48. Collected in Newville, Pennsylvania, January 28, 1981.

49. Collected by Alfred Shoemaker from John Z. Harner, Boyertown, Pennsylvania (*Pennsylvania Dutchman* 1.21 [1949]: 2).

50. Collected by Marilyn Walter from Ingrid Werkgartner, Bloomington, Indiana, October 1961.

51. Collected by Albert Buffington in Somerset County, Pennsylvania (*Ebbes fer Alle-Ebber,* 24). The rhyme has a strong similarity to No. 54, below.

52. Collected by Nancy Ryan from Mary Magdalen Ryan, Saint Louis, Missouri, July 1959. Jordan collected a similar rhyme in Texas (*German Texana,* 111).

53. Collected by Alfred Shoemaker from Mrs. Ida L. Krick, Sinking Spring, Pennsylvania (*Pennsylvania Dutchman* 1.5 [1949]: 2).

54. Collected by Alfred Shoemaker from Henry K. Deisher, Kutztown, Pennsylvania (*Pennsylvania Dutchman* 1.18 [1949]: 2; reprinted in his *Traditional Rhymes and Jingles,* 8). Compare Stoudt, *Folklore,* 95.

55. Collected by Alfred Shoemaker from Daniel W. Hamm, Allentown, Pennsylvania (*Pennsylvania Dutchman* 1.18 [1949]: 2; reprinted in *Traditional Rhymes and Jingles,* 8).

56. Collected by Don Yoder in Williamstown, Pennsylvania, August 1948.

57. Collected by Alfred Shoemaker from Amish children at Mill Creek School (*Pennsylvania Dutchman* 1.12 [1949]: 2).

58. Collected by Alfred Shoemaker from Mrs. M. H. Dotterer of Reading, Pennsylvania (*Pennsylvania Dutchman* 2.7 [1950]: 2; reprinted in *Traditional Rhymes and Jingles,* 16).

59. Mercer, "Folk Lore," 409. Stoudt has numerous variants (*Folklore,* 39–40) and others have appeared often in the *Pennsylvania Dutchman* (1.3, 2; 1.11, 2; 1.16, 2).

60. Collected by Alfred Shoemaker from Brenda Schiedt (*Pennsylvania Dutchman* 1.6 [1949]: 2; reprinted in his *Traditional Rhymes and Jingles,* 13).

61. W. J. Hoffman ("Folk-Lore of the Pennsylvania Germans," *Journal of American Folklore* 2 [1889]: 196–97) identifies Peter Kutz as a scavenger in upper Lehigh County, Pennsylvania, about whom the children were wont to cry these verses because of his loathsome profession. Stoudt has a similar rhyme (*Folklore,* 98), but says the man was from Kutztown, Berks County.

62. Collected by Alfred Shoemaker from Elsie M. Smith, Lenhartsville, Pennsylvania (*Pennsylvania Dutchman* 1.7 [1949]: 2). Compare "Des bucklich Mennli," in Chapter 5.

63. Mercer, "Folk Lore," 409. Alfred Shoemaker collected a similar rhyme from Edward Bergstresser, Walnutport, Pennsylvania (*Pennsylvania Dutchman* 2.2 [1950]: 2).

64. Collected by Alfred Shoemaker from Mrs. M. H. Dotterer, Reading, Pennsylvania (*Pennsylvania Dutchman* 1.24 [1950]: 2).

65. Collected by Roland Dickison in Sacramento, California, November 28, 1974. This is the translation; the informant, an 81-year-old farm housewife, was unwilling to write out the German.

66. Collected by Alfred Shoemaker from William P. Shoemaker, Maple Grove, Pennsylvania (*Pennsylvania Dutchman* 1.8 [1949]: 2; reprinted in *Traditional Rhymes and Jingles,* 14). Jordan collected a similar rhyme in Fredericksburg, Texas: "Methodist, der du bist,/Der die grossen Brocken frisst,/Und die kleinen liegen lässt" (*German Texana,* 122). Such parodies as this rhyme and the next are quite common, even among deeply religious peoples; see Mary and Herbert Knapp, *One Potato, Two Potato: The Folklore of American Children* (New York: W. W. Norton, 1976), 170–72.

67. Collected by Alfred Shoemaker from E. R. Smith, Dallastown, Pennsylvania (*Pennsylvania Dutchman* 2.7 [1950]: 2).

68. Collected from Ella (Stover) Barrick, Carlisle, Pennsylvania, July 6, 1962. With slight variation, this is a verse in the folksong "Rye Whiskey."

69. Collected by Roland Dickison, in Sacramento, California, from an informant who said he read it in *Playboy* magazine. The rhyme does appear in the *Pennsylvania Dutchman* (1.24 [1950]: 2), and in Shoemaker's *Traditional Rhymes and Jingles,* 10.

70. Collected from Glenn Knisely, Perry County, Pennsylvania, March 27, 1982. A variant form appears in *A Book of Vulgar Verse* (Toronto, 1981), 123.

71. Collected by George L. Moore, Palmyra, Pennsylvania (*Pennsylvania Dutchman* 2.11 [1950]: 2). Many such rhymes appear in German and English almanacs of the nineteenth and twentieth centuries.

72. Ibid.

73. Ibid.

74. Ibid.

75. Collected by Alfred Shoemaker from Mrs. Grace M. Shank, Philadelphia, Pennsylvania (*Pennsylvania Dutchman* 2.3 [1950]: 2). Stoudt has the rhyme in his *Folklore of the Pennsylvania Germans* (34), and Elmer Smith collected several variants in Virginia (*The Pennsylvania Germans of the Shenandoah Valley,* 4–5). The rhyme is still known, but fragmentarily in many cases. The following was collected by Michael J. Rock in Franklin County, Pennsylvania, March 1986: "Da fish dey schawm/Da schtay buck schprung/Da washama geesch/Da schish a ma schees." The rhyme of course refers to the symbols which surround the Man of the Signs in German (and English) almanacs (see Shoemaker, *Traditional Rhymes and Jingles,* 6–7) and may have been a mnemonic device for remembering their order.

76. The rhyme is on the tombstone of Christian Hebel, Somerset, Pennsylvania, who died April 12, 1813 (Shoemaker, "German Epitaphs in the Dutch Country," *Pennsylvania Dutchman* 2.1 [1950]: 2). A similar epitaph appearing in the old Lutheran burial ground, York, Pennsylvania, is illustrated in a drawing by Lewis Miller, *Sketches and Chronicles* (York: Historical Society of York County, 1966), 11.

77. Collected by Alfred Shoemaker from Melville B. Schmoyer, who found it in an Allentown, Pennsylvania, cemetery (*Pennsylvania Dutchman* 1.5 [1949]: 2). The same verse was occasionally written into autograph and friendship albums.

78. Collected by Don Yoder in August 1948 from Albert Strasser, Shamokin, Pennsylvania. He used to tell of a man who had such a bad wife that he had this verse carved on her stone. Alfred Shoemaker once collected a variant of this rhyme from Helen Moser, Bally, Pennsylvania.

79. P.C.C., "Quaint and Humorous Epitaphs," *The Pennsylvania-German* 1.4 (1900): 33. The verse presumably appears on the tombstone of a child named Ochs (Ox) in the Swamp Churchyard of Lancaster County, an area settled by Swabians. A variant of the verse appears in some editions of *Till Eulenspiegel.*

80. This is one of the most widely recorded epitaphs, adapted to German on the tombstone of Magdalena Bleyler (1786–1813) in Ziegel's church cemetery, Lehigh County, Pennsylvania: "Sehet das an und thut das lesen,/Was ihr seyd bin ich gewesen." The epitaph had inspired a migratory legend almost as widespread as the verse itself: A passerby reading the inscription adds, "To follow you I'm not content/Till I find out which way you went" (see, for example, Elmer Smith, *The Pennsylvania Germans of the Shenandoah Valley,* 237).

81. On the tombstone of Samuel Hodge (died March 17, 1783), in the Round Hill cemetery near Hampton, Pennsylvania. Because of the phrase "the strongest man," numerous strong man motifs have been attracted to the Hodge legend: "This here fellow was supposed to be the strongest man in the world. He used to lift a barrel of whiskey up on one arm an' drink from the bung" (Eugene Utech, Carlisle, Pennsylvania, May 20, 1969). Alfred Shoemaker notes several other incidents ("The Strongest Man That Ever Lived on Earth," *Pennsylvania Dutchman* 2.2 [1950]: 2).

82. Written on a men's room wall at the University of Pennsylvania, Philadelphia, August 1967.

83. Collected from Hans D. Meurer, Shippensburg, Pennsylvania, December 1979, who saw it in the Hamburg (Germany) railway station.

84. Dickinson College, Carlisle, Pennsylvania, May 1978. Kurt Vonnegut attributes the same lines, respectively, to Socrates, Jean-Paul Sartre, and Frank Sinatra (*Deadeye Dick* [New York: Delacorte, 1982], 224).

85. Collected from Hans D. Meurer, Shippensburg, Pennsylvania.

86. Ibid.

87. F. L. Wells, "Frau Wirtin and Associates," *American Imago* 8 (1951): 93, reprinted by Gershon Legman in *The Limerick* (New York: Brandywine Press, 1970), 468.

88. Collected by Gregory Zatirka from Dr. E. Dabringhaus (Wayne State University Folklore Archives, 1979–102). Dr. Dabringhaus heard the rhymes while serving in the American army in Germany during World War 2.

89. Ibid.

90. Collected by Alfred Shoemaker from Mrs. Laurence Viering, Temple, Pennsylvania (*Pennsylvania Dutchman* 2.7 [1950]: 2; reprinted in his *Traditional Rhymes and Jingles,* 11).

91. Collected by Alfred Shoemaker from Ed Marburger, Rehrersburg, Pennsylvania, September 11, 1955.

92. Collected by Alfred Shoemaker in Lancaster County, Pennsylvania (*Pennsylvania Dutchman* 1.20 [1949]: 2). The rhyme was recited by a tramp in that area about 1875.

93. Laatz, *Bucks County Historical Society Papers* 4 (1917), 34.

94. Collected by Warren Kliewer in Minnesota (*Mennonite Life* 16.3 [1961]: 111).

95. Collected by Alfred Shoemaker from Mary A. Sunday, Hamburg, Pennsylvania (*Pennsylvania Dutchman* 1.2 [1949]: 2).

96. Collected by Marilyn Walter from Joan Corell, Bloomington, Indiana, October 1961.

97. Collected by Alfred Shoemaker from Amish children at Mill Creek School (*Pennsylvania Dutchman* 1.12 [1949]: 2; reprinted in his *Traditional Rhymes and Jingles,* 6).

CHAPTER 5. SONGS

1. This universally-known lullaby has almost as many variants as informants who remember it. John Joseph Stoudt collected 27 versions of it ("Pennsylvania German Folklore," *Pennsylvania German Folklore Society* 16 [1951]: 167), and it has been found from Canada to Texas. The first version here was collected in the Shenandoah Valley of

Virginia by Elmer Smith (*The Pennsylvania Germans of the Shenandoah Valley,* 5). Similar versions appear in Stoudt (*Folklore,* 20), Boyer (*Songs,* 31), Buffington (*Secular Folksongs,* 82) and Jordan (*German Texana,* 19). The second text was collected by Arthur Graeff from a small child near Maples, Ontario (*The Pennsylvania Germans in Ontario, Canada,* 61), though Boyer has a variant (*Songs,* 31). The third verse was collected by Alfred Shoemaker in Ephrata, Pennsylvania (*Pennsylvania Dutchman* 1.11 [1949]: 2). Buffington has two examples of it (*Secular Folksongs,* 79–80). Buffington also collected the fourth text, in Somerset County, Pennsylvania (*Ebbes fer Alle-Ebber,* 24), though Elmer Smith found a form almost identical to it in Sugar Grove, West Virginia (*Shenandoah Valley,* 276). The fifth verse was collected from A. George Stahl, Allentown, Pennsylvania, in a letter to Alfred Shoemaker, February 18, 1950. Despite its unusual content, Jordan collected the same text in standard German in Fredericksburg, Texas (*German Texana,* 20). Alfred Shoemaker collected the sixth text from Alice Sechrist, Sheridan, Pennsylvania (*Pennsylvania Dutchman* 1.7 [1949]: 2). Variants involving red cows and white cows are found in Stoudt (20), Boyer (32), and Buffington, (*Folksongs,* 82). The next verse is from Ephrata (*Pennsylvania Dutchman* 1.11 [1949]: 2) and contains the unusual word *glebberyacht,* "gab-fest" or "serenade." In these songs it is usually the mother who is off on a *Blauderyacht* (gossip spree); see Boyer (31) and Buffington (79–80). The last example was collected in Detroit, Michigan (Wayne State University Folklore Archives, 1979–99). Jordan collected the same verse in Texas (*German Texana,* 19), and Pennsylvania German variants appear in Stoudt (*Folklore,* 20) and Buffington (80).

2. Transcribed by J. William Frey, as he remembered it from York County, Pennsylvania (*Pennsylvania Dutchman* 1.22 [1950]: 8). A text virtually identical to this was collected from Mrs. Eva Roth in Lehigh County, Pennsylvania, in 1937 (Thomas R. Brendle and William S. Troxell, "Pennsylvania German Songs," *Pennsylvania Songs and Legends,* ed. George Korson [Baltimore: Johns Hopkins Press, 1949], 91–92). Elmer Smith collected a similar text (*The Pennsylvania Germans of the Shenandoah Valley,* 277–78) and the song has also been found in Ontario, Canada (Graeff, 59). Other variants appear in Stoudt (*Folklore,* 135–37) and Buffington (*Folksongs,* 112–14). Once thought to relate to a Palatine house sprite or *kobold,* the song has been traced by Ralph Wood to a popular Austrian source ("Das bucklige Männlein," *American-German Review* 8 [August 1942]: 27–30).

3. Collected by Cindy Gentry April 13, 1985, in West Chester, Pennsylvania, from 74-year-old Eli Stoltzfus, a native of Lancaster, the song has an apparent relationship with "Des bucklich Mannlei."

4. Collected by Marilyn Walter from Joan Corell, Bloomington, Indiana, October 1961. Pennsylvania German variants appear in the *Pennsylvania Dutchman* (1.23 [1950]: 2) and Buffington (*Folksongs,* 68, a much longer version).

5. Collected by Edith Ferber from Vernon Bruger, Bloomington, Indiana, November 1, 1960. Gilbert Jordan collected the same version in Mason County, Texas (*German Texana,* 81–82). A shorter form was found in Dubois County, Indiana (Meuser, *German Rhymes and Songs,* 14). Buffington has two Pennsylvania German variants, one collected in Durham, New Hampshire (*Folksongs,* 21).

6. Collected by Elinor Aumann, from Emma Genner, Leberwaring, Michigan (Wayne State University Folklore Archives, 1939–2). A shorter version was collected by Ronald Bosecker in Mt. Carmel, Illinois, in 1967. As Gershon Legman notes, "Donderbeck's Machine" is a "modern comedy song," which perhaps draws inspiration from Wilhelm Busch's *Max und Moritz,* where naughty children are stuffed into a grinding machine (*Rationale of the Dirty Joke,* vol. 2, 558).

7. Collected by Craig Bemesderfer from his grandfather in Lancaster County, Pennsylvania, April 1986.

8. Collected in Detroit, Michigan, March 9, 1976 (Wayne State University Folklore Archives, 1979–99).

9. Sung by Keith and Karlene Brintzenhoff, at Kutztown, Pennsylvania, June 30, 1986.

The same song appears in Boyer (*Songs,* 66–70), with additional verses about shoemakers and carpenters. Variants appear in Stoudt (*Folklore,* 137–39) and Buffington (*Folksongs,* 59–63), and in such popularized collections as Ruth L. Hausman's *Sing and Dance with the Pennsylvania Dutch* (New York: Edward B. Marks Music Co., 1953), 57–58. It has even been recorded in the Afrikaans dialect of South Africa (see Graeff, *The Pennsylvania Germans in Ontario,* 60). Though similar songs exist in German collections, the original has not yet been discovered (Albert F. Buffington, "Maidel wilscht du heirathen—A Hybrid Poem," *American-German Review* 12 [June 1946]: 30–32).

10. Collected in Detroit, Michigan, March 9, 1976 (Wayne State University Folklore Archives 1979–99). The collector or the informant neglected to include the repeated phrases in brackets, which are essential to the way the song is usually sung. The song is quite popular among nineteenth-century immigrants and has frequently been collected (Jordan, *German Texana,* 85–86; Francis Abernethy, "*Deutschtum* in Texas: A Look at Texas-German Folklore," *German Culture in Texas,* ed. Glen Lich and Dona Reeves [Boston: Twayne, 1980], 218–19). William Owens noted that Germans who sailed from Bremen to the tune of "Muss I Denn" were greeted with the same song when they arrived in Galveston (*Texas Folk Songs* [Austin: Texas Folklore Society, 1950], 157).

11. Collected by Alfred Shoemaker from Charles R. Miller, Tower City, April 20, 1957. Both versions of the song, sung to the tune of "My Sweetheart's the Man in the Moon," have been collected by George Korson (*Minstrels of the Mine Patch* [Hatboro: Folklore Associates, 1964]: 122–23; "My Sweetheart's the Mule in the Mines," *Two Penny Ballads and Four Dollar Whiskey,* ed. Kenneth Goldstein and Robert Byington [Hatboro: Folklore Associates, 1966], 1–14).

12. Collected by J. William Frey from Miss Amy Herr, New Holland, Pennsylvania (*Pennsylvania Dutchman* 3.5 [1951]: 8). The song has been extensively collected; variants appear in Stoudt (*Folklore,* 131–35), Brendle and Troxell ("Pennsylvania German Songs," 85–87), Boyer (*Songs,* 60–66), Buffington (*Folksongs,* 83–91), and Frey ("The Dutch in Word and Song," *Pennsylvania Dutchman* 2.9 [1950]: 8). It has also been found in Ontario, Canada (Graeff, *Pennsylvania Germans in Ontario,* 60). In some versions, the daughter is offered a husband, and then suddenly her hand (or finger) is no longer sore (Paul K. Cressman, "Pennsylvania German Secular Songs," *Pennsylvania Dutchman* 3.9 [1951]: 7).

13. Collected by Craig Bemesderfer from his grandfather in Lancaster County, Pennsylvania, April 1986. W. K. McNeil suggests that the source of this item is a popular song of the 1920s and 1930s about a "consumptive Sara Jane."

14. Collected from A. G. Stahl, Allentown, Pennsylvania (*Pennsylvania Dutchman* 1.24 [1950]: 8). The song was collected by A.E. Schroeder in Rhineland, Missouri, July 12, 1974 ("Traditional Song Current in the Midwest," *Proceedings of the International Centenary Conference of the Folklore Society,* ed. Venetia Newall [London, 1981]: 388), by students in Dubois County, Indiana, in 1978 (Meuser, *German Rhymes and Songs,* 15) and by Gilbert Jordan in Texas (*German Texana,* 96). Pennsylvania German variants appear in Boyer (*Songs,* 137–38) and Buffington (*Folksongs,* 55–58).

15. Collected by Harold Sherman in Birmingham, Michigan, from Joachim Matthesius, January 1956 (Wayne State University Folklore Archives, 1969–105).

CHAPTER 6. FOLK NARRATIVE

1. Collected by Juan Rodríguez from Anny Sixt, Bloomington, Indiana. The Lorelei is a large rock on the Rhine River near Burg Katz castle, West Germany. The "legend" of the beautiful maiden who sits on the rock singing to lure sailors to their death is the creation of Klemens Brentano in the ballad *Die Lore Lay* (1802).

2. Collected by William J. Buck from "Mrs. Jacob Fulmer of Springfield [Pennsylvania], who died in 1839 at the advanced age of eighty-five. She had often heard it related when a girl; the circumstances occurred in Bedminster" ("Local Superstitions," *Collections of the*

Historical Society of Pennsylvania 1 [1853]: 380–81). The story was recorded in Philadelphia in 1749 by Peter Kalm (*Travels in North America* [New York: Wilson-Erickson, 1937], vol. 1, 317) and has been widely reported among the Pennsylvania Germans: W. J. Hoffman, "Popular Superstitions," *Pennsylvania German Society Proceedings* 5 (1894): 76; Thomas R. Brendle and William S. Troxell, *Pennsylvania German Folk Tales* (Norristown, Pa.: Pennsylvania German Society, 1944), 185–86; Phares Hertzog, "Pennsylvania German Snakelore," *Pennsylvania Folklife* 17.4 (1968): 18. Conrad Richter uses the story in his novel *The Fields* (New York: Knopf, 1946), 194–95. The story of the snake drinking from the child's bottle is No. 105 in the Grimms' collection, and Ernest Baughman lists fifteen occurrences from non-Germanic sources (*Type and Motif Index of the Folktales of England and North America* [The Hague: Mouton, 1956], 5, Type 285: "The child and the snake").

3. Collected by Roxann Miller, February 9, 1984, Shippensburg, Pennsylvania, from her grandmother, who noted that the story had been passed down for generations. Stith Thompson (*Motif-Index of Folk Literature* [Bloomington: Indiana University Press, 1955]) lists two motifs that are pertinent: A2378, "Origin and nature of animal's tail," and D136, "Transformation: man to swine," but this particular version does not appear.

4. Collected from J. Russell Barrick, Carlisle, Pennsylvania, May 17, 1963. Harry Kramer was a German peddler in Cumberland County about 1920; see Mac E. Barrick, "The Image of the Jew in South-Central Pennsylvania," *Pennsylvania Folklife* 34 (1985): 133–34. This is Motif A2471.1, "Why dogs look at one another under tail."

5. Collected by Alfred Shoemaker from William P. Shoemaker, Maple Grove, Pennsylvania (*Pennsylvania Dutchman* 1.19 [1949]: 2); translation by Alfred Shoemaker. The story has been widely told and collected; see Baughman, *Type and Motif Index,* 160, Motif E345.1(a), "Ghost walks boundary line, carrying stone, asking: 'Where shall I put it?'" Variants appear in Madeleine Vinton Dahlgren, *South-Mountain Magic* (Boston: Osgood, 1882), 96–99 (Maryland); Joseph W. Yoder, *Rosanna of the Amish* (Huntingdon, Pennsylvania: Yoder Publishing Co., 1940), 202–4; Nevin Moyer, "Moyerettes" (unpublished typescript history of Linglestown, Pennsylvania, 1915–40), 87; Isaac Shirk Simons, "Haunted Places and Tales of Black Magic," *Pennsylvania Dutchman* 2.11 (1950): 2; Ray F. Smith, "Pennsylvania German Folklore—Introducing a Few Snyder County Ghosts," *Snyder County Historical Society Bulletin* 2 (1972): 915; Henry Snyder Gehman, "An Octogenarian's Reminiscences of Ghost Stories in Lancaster County," *Historic Schaefferstown Record* 9.1 (1975): 41; Errol Vincent Coy, *Cracker Barrel Tales* (Shippensburg: News-Chronicle, 1977), 5. Brendle and Troxell list eight versions (*Folk Tales,* 122–27).

6. Collected by Lillian J. Klahn from Fred Klahn, Hobart, Indiana, October 17, 1965. The folk motif here is D1385.4, "Silver bullet protects against giants, ghosts and witches." Charlie Miller recalled that landlords in Cumberland County, Pennsylvania, would at times fasten a chain to a turtle's shell and release the turtle in the attic of a house they wanted the tenants to vacate (June 28, 1978). For similar stories in Kentucky, see William Lynwood Montell, *Ghosts along the Cumberland* (Knoxville: University of Tennessee Press, 1975), Nos. 426, 447.

7. The first variant was collected from J. Russell Barrick, Carlisle, Pennsylvania, January 5, 1973; in earlier tellings the people were described as "colored guys." The second was collected in Hobart, Indiana, by Lillian J. Klahn from Fred Klahn, October 17, 1965. The story has an almost infinite number of variants; see Baughman, 47, Type No. 1791, to which add a Pennsylvania German version told by William P. Shoemaker, "Two Folktales," *Pennsylvania Dutchman* 1.19 (1949): 2. Hazel Harrod traces the story to a Latin tale of the late sixth century ("A Tale of Two Thieves," *The Sky is My Tipi,* ed. Mody C. Boatright [Austin: Texas Folklore Society, 1949], 207–14).

8. Collected by Gary L. Stone from Vicco von Stralendorff, Bloomington, Indiana, July 25, 1961. The tale appears in the Grimms' collection as No. 69 and is listed by Antti Aarne and Stith Thompson, *The Types of the Folktale* (Helsinki: Suomalainen Tiedeakatemia Academia Scientiarum Fennica, 1964) as Type No. 405.

9. Collected by Gary L. Stone from Vicco von Stralendorff, Bloomington, Indiana, July 6, 1961. This is Type No. 480, "The spinning-women by the spring. The kind and the unkind girls," and No. 24 in the Grimms' collection.

10. Collected by Nancy Griffith from Anita Birutschenko, Bloomington, Indiana, May 12, 1966. Cinderella has been extensively studied and discussed; see the bibliography provided by Aarne and Thompson (*Types,* 176–77) and more recently, Alan Dundes, *Cinderella, a Casebook* (New York: Wildman Press, 1983). The central motifs of the variant presented here are H36.1, "Slipper test," and K1911.3.3.1, "False bride's mutilated feet."

11. Collected by M. Mayo from a Mrs. Salzman, Detroit, Michigan, in December 1973. This is apparently a fragment of Type 85, "The mouse, the bird, and the sausage," found in the Grimms' collection as No. 23. Kurt Ranke includes in *Folktales of Germany* (Chicago: University of Chicago Press, 1966), No. 6, a cumulative tale of which this is the first part. The tale first appears in Hans Moscherosch's *Gesichte Philanders von Sittewald* in 1650.

12. Collected by Nancy Griffith from Anita Birutschenko, May 1, 1966, in Bloomington, Indiana. The tale appears in the Grimms' collection (No. 83) and in the Aarne and Thompson type index as No. 1415.

13. Collected in Bloomington, Indiana, by Sally Brock from Rose Marie Bank. Baughman lists the story as Motif J1649*(f), citing a seventeenth-century jestbook, but it occurs earlier in Melchor de Santa Cruz's *Floresta española de apotegmas* (1574), translated into English in 1595.

14. Collected by Alfred Shoemaker from Merlin Bennetch (*Pennsylvania Dutchman* 1.24 [1950]: 2). Gershon Legman provides a variant where the "billiard" drinker is served urine and retorts, "If I weren't an experienced billiard-drinker from away back, I'd swear that was piss" (*Rationale of the Dirty Joke* [New York: Breaking Point, 1975], vol. 2, 856).

15. Baer's *Agricultural Almanac for the Year 1870* (Lancaster: John Baer's Sons). fol. A 16[vo]. The joke is widely told, for example, by J. Russell Barrick, Carlisle, Pennsylvania, November 15, 1964, and in Mildred Jordan, *The Distelfink Country of the Pennsylvania Dutch* (New York: Crown, 1978), 20.

16. Collected from Charlie Miller, Cumberland County, Pennsylvania, April 12, 1981; see also Mac E. Barrick, "Numskull Tales in Cumberland County," *Pennsylvania Folklife* 16.4 (1967), 52. The closest applicable motif listed by Stith Thompson is J1772.9.1, "Excrement thought to be berries." Compare Legman, *Rationale* vol. 2, 934.

17. Collected by Sally Brock from Rose Marie Bank, Bloomington, Indiana, January 1963.

18. Collected by Nancy Griffith from Anita Birutschenko, Bloomington, Indiana, May 12, 1966. The story is widely told in Europe; see Type 1245, "Sunlight carried in a bag into the windowless house." Peter Brueghel's painting *Netherlandish Proverbs* depicts a man carrying daylight in a basket. Baughman cites eleven American examples (*Type and Motif Index,* 28–29), to which add Roger Welsch, "Molbo Tales," *Folkways,* No. 3 (1964): 21 (from Nebraska). Stories of Swabians as numskulls are common among the Pennsylvania Germans; see Brendle and Troxell, *Pennsylvania German Folk Tales,* 109–20, and Albert Buffington, "Schwoweschtories," *Folkways,* No. 3 (1964): 22–24.

19. Collected by Nancy Griffith in Bloomington, Indiana, from Anita Birutschenko. Baughman lists this as Motif J1811.5*(c). "Simpletons interpret frog cries as, 'Knee deep! Knee deep! Chicken waded! Chicken waded!' They walk into the waters, drown." People in Cumberland County, Pennsylvania, in the 1940s insisted that bullfrogs were saying, "Knee deep."

20. Collected by Alfred Shoemaker from William P. Shoemaker, Maple Grove, Pennsylvania (*Pennsylvania Dutchman* 1.2 [1949]: 2). European versions of the story usually involve a magpie; see Type 237, "Magpie tells why sow is muddy." American joking versions have a parrot punished by having his feathers pulled out; he later accuses a bald-headed man of the same misconduct, see Gershon Legman, *Rationale of the Dirty Joke* (New York: Grove, 1968), vol. 2, 201.

21. Collected in Carlisle, Pennsylvania, March 17, 1966. A variant functioning as a Neck Riddle appears in Brendle and Troxell (171). The same collection has several variants of Eileschpijjel's sewing contest with the devil. Tailors and millers were often the butt of popular humor in the Middle Ages; see Alexander H. Krappe, *The Science of Folklore* (New York: Norton, 1964), 54.

22. Collected by Alfred Shoemaker from Mrs. Harvey Rothenberger (*Pennsylvania Dutchman* 5.10 [1954]: 3).

23. Collected from Samuel Miller, Newville, Pennsylvania, March 11, 1973. Brendle and Troxell attribute the story to Eileschpijjel (*Folk Tales,* 169–70). The bibliography on this tale is extensive; see Type 1319, Motif J1772.1, "Pumpkin sold as an ass's egg." It is currently told as a "dirty joke" about a man sitting on what he thinks is an elephant's egg; his wife, feeling underneath, says, "It's hatching; I can feel its trunk" (Legman, *Rationale of the Dirty Joke* 1, 600–1).

24. Daniel C. Keller, "Dialect Jests," *Pennsylvania Dutchman* 1.12 (1949): 2. Baughman lists this as Motif J1155.1.1*(b). The story appears frequently in jokebooks.

25. Collected by Alfred Shoemaker from N. H. Groff, Bareville, Pennsylvania (*Pennsylvania Dutchman* 2.3 (1950): 2. Baughman lists this as Motif X1651.3.1*, "Fish swim in fog." Mildred Jordan reported hearing the same story in Oley, Pennsylvania (*Distelfink Country,* 247).

26. Collected from Charlie Miller, Cumberland County, Pennsylvania, November 21, 1976. Usually this is the second part of a longer tale, where a man bragging about a large fish in the first part offers to take twenty pounds off his fish if the other will "blow out the lantern" (Type 1920H*). Roy Chandler attributes the tale to one Heinz Orwan (*Tales of Perry County* [Deer Lake, Pennsylvania: Bacon and Freeman, 1973], 106).

27. Collected from Paul Fanus, Brandtsville, Pennsylvania, November 16, 1974. Variants appear in William Ryman, *The Early Settlement of Dallas Township, Luzerne County, Pennsylvania* (Wilkes-Barre, 1901), 92–93, and in Brendle and Troxell (*Folk Tales,* 192–93). The tale is Type 1920B, Motif X905.4, "The one says, 'I have not time to lie,' and yet lies."

28. Collected by Lisa Bohn from her mother-in-law, Sally Bohn, Allentown, Pennsylvania, March 3, 1986. The word in question may be a corruption of *Rotznase* (snot-nose), which is sometimes applied to children who are too nosy.

29. Collected from Bill Ryall, Bloomington, Indiana, by Martha Ryall, July 24, 1966. Similar stories are listed as Type 1700, Motif J2496.

30. Collected by Cathy George, Shippensburg, Pennsylvania, February 1983, from a neighbor. By implication, the man in the buggy was Amish.

31. Collected by Alfred Shoemaker from David W. Quickel, Dover, Pennsylvania. Quickel also remembered a story of how Mr. Bull used his name to gain free admission to the York Fair.

32. Collected by Alfred Shoemaker from Mrs. Henry Mease, Lititz, Pennsylvania (*Pennsylvania Dutchman* 1.6 [1949]: 2. Mark Trumbore has a similar story in *A Superficial Collection of Pennsylvania German Erotic Folklore* (28), with the punchline: "Wann du net kumme waerscht, hett des Biebli sei Memm noch" (If you hadn't come, this baby would still have its tit).

33. H. Wayne Gruber, "Dialect Jests," *Pennsylvania Dutchman* 1.23 (1950): 2.

34. Collected by Alfred Shoemaker from H. Wayne Gruber, Reading, Pennsylvania, February 4, 1949. The same story is told about numerous preachers since the eighteenth century; see Mac E. Barrick, "Pulpit Humor in Central Pennsylvania," *Pennsylvania Folklore* 19.1 (1969): 28–29. Alfred Shoemaker collected a version of it related to Rev. Benjamin Dunkelberger Zweizig ("Old Berks Folklore, Legends and History," *Reading* [Pa.] *Eagle,* [March 11, 1949]: 9). It is told about the York County preacher, Yost Henry Fries (Jacob G. Shively, "Tales of Old Pastor Fries," *Pennsylvania Dutchman* 3.13 [1951]: 6). Another variant appears in Brendle and Troxell, *Folk Tales,* 188. And Conrad Richter incorporated it into his novel *A Simple Honorable Man* (New York: Knopf, 1962), 28–29.

35. Collected by Nevin Moyer from Adeline Moyer, Linglestown, Pennsylvania ("Moyerettes," 72). William Woys Weaver notes that in the 1850s potatoes were served three times a day in German homes, particularly in poorer households. His version of the rhyme is: "Marjets Grumbiere in aller Frieh,/Middaags Grumbiere in geeli Brieh,/Owets Grumbiere un alle Zeit,/Grumbiere bis in Ewichkeit!" (*Sauerkraut Yankees* [Philadelphia: University of Pennsylvania Press, 1983], 112). Compare a similar verse about dumplings recorded by George Korson (*Black Rock: Mining Folklore of the Pennsylvania Dutch* [Baltimore: Johns Hopkins Press, 1960], 200–201). Such tales are a special narrative form called *cante fable* and are listed in Thompson's *Motif Index* as Nos. J1341.11 and J1341.12. See the extensive bibliography provided by Herbert Halpert in "The Humorous Grace Cante Fable," *Mid-South Folklore* 3 (1975): 71–82. Several other Pennsylvania German examples appear in Mac E. Barrick, "The Competitive Element in the Cante Fable," *Southern Folklore Quarterly* 45 (1981): 126–27.

36. Harvey H. Hartman, "Jests and Legends from Upper Bucks [County]," *Pennsylvania Dutchman* 2.7 (1950): 2. Moses Dissinger was the subject of numerous jokes, anecdotes, and memorates; see Brendle and Troxell, *Folk Tales*, 215–24.

37. Collected November 8, 1960, by Edith Ferber from Vernon Bruger, Bloomington, Indiana. The anecdote is attributed to Mark Twain in *Woman's World* (April 1, 1986): 3.

38. Maurice Mook in a letter dated November 21, 1969, said he heard this in Saegertown, Pennsylvania, between 1910 and 1920. The story has been popular in jokebooks since the 1920s: Irvin S. Cobb, *Many Laughs for Many Days* (New York: Garden City, 1925), No. 364; Samuel Roth, *Anecdota Americana* (New York: Nesor, 1934), No. 12; Larry Wilde, *The Last Official Italian Joke Book* (Los Angeles: Pinnácle, 1978), 82–83.

39. Collected by Alfred Shoemaker from Allen E. Snyder, Elizabethville, Pennsylvania, August 10, 1959. Gershon Legman cites a pseudo-German example of this joke from 1928 and notes that a similar poem appeared about 1620 in England (*The Limerick* [New York; Brandywine Press, 1970]: 408). It is, of course, another example of the cante fable mentioned in note 35 above.

40. Collected from Jesse Kurtz, Carlisle, Pennsylvania, March 24, 1971. Numerous other examples occur in contemporary jokebooks. Usually the punchline is, more ironically, "I do own that building; which one do you own?"

41. Collected by Mary Weeg from Les Vohs, LaSalle, Illinois, December, 1960.

42. Collected by Debbie Hershey from Peter Guren, Cleveland, Ohio, May 9, 1971.

43. Collected by Alfred Shoemaker from Allen E. Snyder, Elizabethville, Pennsylvania, August 10, 1959.

44. Collected by Alfred Shoemaker from H. Wayne Gruber, Reading, Pennsylvania, February 27, 1951. Gershon Legman collected this joke in England in 1954 (*Rationale* vol. 2, 173), though it often appears in print; for example, Bennett Cerf's *Good for a Laugh* (Garden City: Doubleday, 1952), 128.

45. Collected by Alfred Shoemaker (date and place not indicated). The same story was collected in Cumberland County, Pennsylvania, June 28, 1973. Legman provides a variant from Idaho Falls, 1946 (*Rationale* vol. 1, 640).

46. Collected from Harold Weigel, Shippensburg, Pennsylvania, April 19, 1974. The punchline is the traditional sentry's challenge, which in English is "Halt or I fire!"

47. Collected from Lester Brown, Carlisle, Pennsylvania, June 19, 1966. In joke books and other popular publications, the response is, "That's the farmer."

48. Collected by Linda Wong from Danny Kurbursky, Indianapolis, Indiana, December 24, 1970. Actually a riddle, but told here as a joke, this is similar to other jokes about Poles and blacks or Poles and Italians; see Willlam M. Clements, *The Types of the Polack Joke*, Folklore Forum Bibliographic and Special Series No. 3 (1969), 4–44.

49. Collected from Hans D. Meurer, Shippensburg, Pennsylvania, who recalled hearing it in Germany about 1945. Numerous jokes at the time played on Winston Churchill's initials' being W.C., the abbreviation for "watercloset." Baughman indexes this joke as

Motif X691.5.1*, "Men of three nationalities out walking come to skunk hole. One man goes in, cannot stand the odor, comes out. The second goes in, soon comes out. Finally Englishman goes in. Pretty soon the skunk comes out."
50. Collected from Henry Warkentin, Shippensburg, Pennsylvania, September 15, 1986. The humor lies in the pun on the word Schwein, which usually means "pig," but in the phrase *Schwein haben* means "to have luck."

CHAPTER 7. GAMES

1. Collected from Bertha Gutshall, Ella Barrick, and other residents of Cumberland County, Pennsylvania, in 1963. The game there is often called "Tick-Tickle-e-Over," though in other areas it is called "Anthony Over, Ballie Over, or Haley Over." Around Shippensburg, Pennsylvania, the game is called "Cooney Over." The game has been widely collected and described; see William W. Newell, *Games and Songs of American Children* (New York: Harper, 1883), 181–82; ("Haley-Over"); *Brown Collection of North Carolina Folklore* vol. 1, 36 ("Anthony Over"); Paul R. Wieand, *Outdoor Games of the Pennsylvania Germans* (Plymouth Meeting: Mrs. C. Naaman Keyser, 1950), 17–18 ("Balley-Over"); J. Lewis Schanbacher, *Boy of Appalachia* (Elmira, 1973), 55 ("Andy Over"). In a scrapbook printed serially in the *Reading* (Pa.) *Evening World* in 1895, Morton L. Montgomery described the game as similarly played there. Calvin Stump of Maxatawny, Pennsylvania, in a letter to Alfred Shoemaker, February 16, 1948, provided a slightly different version: "The ball was thrown over the schoolhouse, one side to throw, the other side to catch the ball, to see which side caught the most balls."
2. Collected by Paul R. Wieand in Lehigh County, Pennsylvania (*Pennsylvania Dutchman* 1.2 [1949]: 2). Newell describes a similar game called "Weighing" (*Games,* 212–13).
3. Collected by B. Franklin Reber in Kempton, Pennsylvania (*Pennsylvania Dutchman* 5.12 [1954]: 15), this seems to be an imperfectly remembered version of "Blummsack," the next game below.
4. Collected by Henry A. Showalter in Lancaster, Pennsylvania (*Pennsylvania Dutchman* 1.9 [1949]: 2). Phebe Gibbons noted that the game was played at Amish weddings (*Pennsylvania Dutch and Other Essays* [Philadelphia: Lippincott, 1882], 29).
5. Collected by Morton L. Montgomery in Reading, Pennsylvania. Montgomery's scrapbook notes were frequently reprinted, for example, as "Boyhood Sports in Reading in the Fifties," *Historical Review of Berks County* 9 (1943): 17–21, and "Games a Century Ago," *Pennsylvania Dutchman* 5.12 (1954): 12–13. The game is similarly described by Newell (*Games,* 184–85), Wieand (*Outdoor Games,* 22), and J. R. Johns ("Outdoor Sports Around 1800," *Pennsylvania Dutchman* 1.18 [1949]: 3). John J. Cornwell noted that the game was played in West Virginia when he taught school there (*A Mountain Trail* [Philadelphia: Dorrance, 1939], 31).
6. Collected by Morton L. Montgomery ("Games of Reading in Last Century," *Pennsylvania Dutchman* 1.17 [1949]: 2; *Historical Review of Berks County* 9 [1943]: 19). Wieand also lists the game (*Outdoor Games,* 23).
7. Collected by Alfred Shoemaker from Dr. Melvin Gingerich, who heard it in Iowa (*Pennsylvania Dutchman* 1.13 [1949]: 2). Newell includes a version from Cincinnati, Ohio, noting that it is a translation from German (*Games,* 151–52). An almost identical version was collected in North Carolina from 1926 to 1928 (*Brown Collection* 1, 63).
8. Collected by Alfred Shoemaker in an unsigned letter that notes the game was played near Easton, Pennsylvania, from 1921 to 1929. This is similar to a game called "Duck on a Rock" described by Evelyn Gardner (*Folklore from the Schoharie Hills, New York* [Ann Arbor: University of Michigan Press, 1937], 246–47), and by Wieand (*Outdoor Games,* 19–20).
9. Collected by Evelyn A. Benson in Rohrerstown, Pennsylvania, 1947–49 (*Pennsylvania Dutchman* 3.3 [1951]: 2). Newell has a similar game called "Old Mother Cripsycrops" (*Games,* 217–18).

10. Newell found this game among the Pennsylvania Germans (*Games*, 183; cf. Wieand, *Outdoor Games*, 12). It was also played in German communities of south-central Illinois (Gilbert C. Kettelkamp, "Country-School Games of the Past," *MidAmerica Folklore* 8 [1981]: 118).

11. Collected by Don Yoder in Hegins, Pennsylvania, August 1948 (*Pennsylvania Dutchman* 1.14 [1949]: 2). Newell includes a version from Schleswig-Holstein (*Games*, 156). A similar game was played in Fredericksburg, Texas, with the title "Kluck mit Huenkel" (Hen with Chicks), where the chicks clung to the hen's waist, swinging around behind her (Estill, "Children's Games," 235). Note also its similarity to "Knitting Needles" (No. 13, below).

12. Collected by Alfred Shoemaker from Mrs. David Wolf, Reamstown, Pennsylvania, December 6, 1955. English versions appear in Newell (*Games*, 147–48) and the *Brown Collection of North Carolina Folklore* (vol. 1, 59–60).

13. Collected by Alfred Shoemaker, learned ultimately from his great-grandmother (*Pennsylvania Dutchman* 1.5 [1949]: 2). Newell has a text where the mother has lost "eine silberne Nodel" (a silver needle) (*Games*, 157).

14. The game has been widely played and collected: Wieand, *Outdoor Games*, 11; Montgomery, *Pennsylvania Dutchman* 5.12 (1954): 12; H. L. Mencken, *Happy Days, 1880–1892* (New York: Knopf, 1940), 143, 160. The game dates to at least the sixteenth century; Brueghel shows boys playing leapfrog in his painting of children's games. In Germany the game is called "Hammelsprung" when the player stands at right angles to the leaper and "Bocksprung" when they are parallel (Franz Böhme, *Deutsches Kinderlied und Kinderspiel* [Leipzig: Breitkopf und Härtel, 1897], 591).

15. Collected by Alfred Shoemaker from Mrs. Susan Edwards, Hopeland, Pennsylvania, March 12, 1954.

16. Collected by Alfred Shoemaker in Palmyra, Pennsylvania (*Pennsylvania Dutchman* 1.20 [1949]: 2).

17. Described in a letter to *Notes and Queries, Historical, Biographical and Genealogical*, ed. William Egle (1894; Baltimore: Genealogical Publishing Co., 1970), vol. 1, 25. The German folk artist Lewis Miller has a drawing of boys playing "Long Bullet" in 1806 (Lewis Miller, *Sketches and Chronicles* [York: Historical Society of York County, 1966], 34).

18. Collected by Alfred Shoemaker ("Let's All Play Nipsi," *Pennsylvania Dutchman* 1.3 [1949]: 2). The game has an ancient lineage and is widely played; see Erwin Mehl, "Baseball in the Stone Age," *Western Folklore* 7 (1948): 147, and Denis Mercier and others, "'Nipsy': The Ethnography of a Traditional Game of Pennsylvania's Anthracite Region," *Pennsylvania Folklife* 23.4 (1974): 12–21.

19. Collected by Alfred Shoemaker from Carl L. Trexler, Topton, Pennsylvania (*Pennsylvania Dutchman* 1.1 [1949]: 2). Compare Wieand, *Outdoor Games*, 20. In Illinois the game was called "Sowhole" (Kettelkamp, *MidAmerica Folklore* 8 [1981]: 118–20).

20. Collected by Alfred Shoemaker from Viola Miller, January 6, 1958.

21. Collected by Sally Brock from Rose Marie Bank, Bloomington, Indiana, January 1963, who notes that it was a kindergarten-type game played every Sunday in a German church.

22. The first version was collected by Don Yoder from Mrs. Mary J. Faust, Hegins, Pennsylvania (*Pennsylvania Dutchman* 2.6 [1950]: 5) and the second by Alfred Shoemaker from Mrs. Arta Bortner, Wilmington, Delaware (*Pennsylvania Dutchman* 3.5 [1951]: 1).

23. Collected by Alfred Shoemaker from Henry K. Deisher, Kutztown, Pennsylvania.

24. Described by Calvin Stump, Maxatawny, Pennsylvania, in a letter to Alfred Shoemaker dated February 16, 1948. Wieand lists the same game (*Outdoor Games*, 14); Montgomery calls it "House Ball" (*Pennsylvania Dutchman* 5.12 [1954]: 13).

25. Collected by Alfred Shoemaker in Lancaster County, Pennsylvania (*Pennsylvania Dutchman* 1.16 [1949]: 2). There is an identical Japanese game, "Ko-no" (Iris Vinton, *The Folkways Omnibus of Children's Games* [Harrisburg: Stackpole, 1970]: 265–66).

26. Collected by Richard Druckenbrod in Reinholds, Pennsylvania (*Pennsylvania Dutchman* 1.6 [1949]: 2).

27. Collected by J. William Frey in York County, Pennsylvania (*Pennsylvania Dutchman* 1.15 [1949]: 2). Fickmiel is still a popular game among Mennonites in Iowa (*Pennsylvania Dutchman* 1.13 [1949]: 2).

28. Collected by Elinor Aumann, from Emma Genner, Leberwaring, Michigan (Wayne State University Folklore archives, 1939–2). The musical transcription as provided by the collector was defective, nor was a description made of the game itself.

29. Collected by Patricia Shanks in Detroit, Michigan, February 24, 1975 (Wayne State University Folklore Archives, 1979–101).

30. Collected by Alfred Shoemaker from Phares Hauck, Denver, Pennsylvania, November 11, 1955. In Lebanon County the game was called *Tzeppa Rubbar* (George L. Moore, "My Childhood Games," *Pennsylvania Folklife* 13.4 [1964]: 57). For further discussion of the game and its solution, see Mac E. Barrick, "Folk Toys," *Pennsylvania Folklife* 29 (1979): 31–32.

31. Described by L. O. Ramer, Berkeley, Michigan, in a letter dated March 30, 1969. Mr. Ramer remembered the game being played in Mifflin County, Pennsylvania, before 1920.

32. Collected by Alfred Shoemaker from Ira Marsh, a retired schoolmaster from Danielsville, Pennsylvania.

33. Collected by Alfred Shoemaker from William Reinert, Fredericksville, Pennsylvania, March 1, 1953. Mrs. Ella Barrick, Carlisle, Pennsylvania, played the game in the early 1940s. Of course it is the saucer of the 'innocent' that is blackened, not the other player's, and this is done surreptitiously before the game begins.

34. Collected by Alfred Shoemaker, November 30, 1955, from an "old-timer" in Kleinfeltersville, Pennsylvania.

35. The game has been extensively collected and described: "Hunting 'Elbetritches,'" *Pennsylvania-German* 7 (1906): 35–37; George A. Shuman, "Apple Kretchers," *Pennsylvania Dutchman* 2.20 (1951): 1; Theodore K. Long, *Forty Letters to Carson Long* (New Bloomfield, 1931), 40–41; James Glimm, *Flatlanders and Ridgerunners* (Pittsburgh: University of Pittsburgh Press, 1983), 12–13. Elmer E. S. Johnson reported this as a New Year's trick in Germany ("More About 'Elbetritches,'" *Pennsylvania-German* 7 [1906]: 122–23), suggesting that the word derives from *elbe* ("nightmare"), related to the English word *elf.* In fact, in the earliest references to the game in the New World it is described as chasing "elfen" (William J. Buck, "Local Superstitions," *Collections of the Historical Society of Pennsylvania* 1 [1853]: 381; H. L. Fisher, *Olden Times* [York: Fisher Bros., 1888], 172–74). The game has been reported in Maryland (Annie Whitney and Caroline Bullock, *Folk-Lore from Maryland* [New York: American Folklore Society, 1925], 181) and Texas (Gilbert J. Jordan, *Yesterday in the Texas Hill Country* [College Station and London: Texas A&M University Press, 1979], 134. See also Baughman, *Type and Motif Index,* No. J2349.6*.

36. Collected from Samuel A. Miller, Newville, Pennsylvania, March 18, 1973. Mrs. Ella Barrick played this as a party game in the 1940s. Usually when the victim complained, "I'm getting wet," he was told, "Well, you can't see stars when it's raining." However, one victim ended the game very quickly when he said, "Hey, somebody pissed on me."

37. Collected by Alfred Shoemaker from William Reinert, Fredericksville, Pennsylvania, March 1, 1953.

CHAPTER 8. CUSTOMS

[1]An account from Bechtelsville, Pennsylvania, published in the *Reading Weekly Eagle,* January 7, 1882; reprinted in *Pennsylvania Dutchman* 2.15 (1951): 1.

[2]Collected by Sarah McMillan from Mrs. Conrad Schroeder, Shelbyville, Indiana, November 1960. Mrs. Schroeder recalled this as the way New Year's Day was celebrated in Kassell, Germany, in the early 1900s. Many *Wünsche* (Wishes) verses were collected by

John Baer Stoudt (*Folklore*, 102–17) and others appear scattered throughout early issues of the *Pennsylvania Dutchman.* Walter E. Boyer studied such verses appearing in newspapers and broadsides ("The New Year Wish of the Pennsylvania Dutch Broadside," *Pennsylvania Folklife* 10.2 [1959]: 45–49). The custom was still remembered in Virginia and West Virginia in the 1960s; see Elmer L. Smith et al., *The Pennsylvania Germans of the Shenandoah Valley,* 101–6. Walter L. Robbins describes the custom in North and South Carolina ("Wishing in and Shooting in the New Year among the Germans in the Carolinas," *American Folklife,* ed. Don Yoder [Austin and London: University of Texas Press, 1976], 257–79).

³Collected by Sarah McMillan from Mrs. Louise Tangman, Bargersville, Indiana, October 1960. Shooting in the New Year was once so common and annoying that the Pennsylvania legislature passed an act against it in 1774 (*Pennsylvania Dutchman* 3.15 [1952]: 1). Robbins finds the first mention of it among the Moravians of Winston-Salem, North Carolina, in that same year. The practice also occurred in Virginia (Smith, 101–3), and Missouri (A. E. Schroeder, "The Contexts of Continuity: Germanic Folklore in Missouri," *Kansas Quarterly* 13 [1981]: 96). In Texas, dynamite is set off to celebrate the New Year (Jordan, *German Texana,* 42). In primitive societies, noise is called for when two paired terms (sky and earth, a potential married couple, an old year and a new) are in a state of disjunction (Lévi-Strauss, 295).

⁴John Baer Stoudt, "Weather-Prognostications and Superstitions among the Pennsylvania Germans," *Pennsylvania-German* 7 (1906): 243.

⁵The bibliography on Groundhog Day is too extensive to cite. The earliest reference is in James L. Morris's diary for February 4, 1841, cited by Alfred Shoemaker ("February Lore," *Pennsylvania Dutchman* 5.11 [1954]: 11): "According to the Germans, the Groundhog peeps out of his winter quarters and if he sees his shadow he pops back for another six weeks nap, but if the day be cloudy he remains out, as the weather is to be moderate."

⁶Alfred L. Shoemaker, "The First Week of Lent in Pennsylvania Dutch Lore," *Pennsylvania Dutchman* 1.23 (1950): 3; see also Shoemaker, *Eastertide in Pennsylvania* (Kutztown: Pennsylvania Folklife Society, 1960), 7–11.

⁷Collected by Eleanor M. Peterson from Mrs. Tom Emmert, Cincinnati, Ohio, November 29, 1958. Charles van Ravenswaay describes the same practice in Missouri (*The Arts and Architecture of German Settlements in Missouri* [Columbia and London: University of Missouri Press, 1977], 53).

⁸Collected from Charles C. Miller, Cumberland County, Pennsylvania, December 22, 1976. The same belief is listed by Edwin M. Fogel, *Beliefs and Superstitions of the Pennsylvania Germans* (Philadelphia: Americana Germanica, 1915), No. 1322.

⁹Collected by Sarah E. McMillan from Mrs. Louise Tangman, Bargersville, Indiana, October 1960.

¹⁰Collected from Mrs. Ella Barrick, Carlisle, Pennsylvania, May 1963.

¹¹Shoemaker, *Eastertide,* 35–37. The game is also reported from Virginia (Smith, *Pennsylvania Germans of the Shenandoah Valley,* 113–14) and Missouri (Shroeder, *Kansas Quarterly* 13 [1981]: 98).

¹²Collected by Sarah E. McMillan from Conrad Shroeder, Shelbyville, Indiana, November 1960.

¹³Shoemaker, *Eastertide,* 63–69; Olive G. Zehner, "The Egg Tree Recognized as Pa. Dutch Custom as Far as Seattle, Washington," *Pennsylvania Dutchman* 3.21 [1952]: 3), citing references from Ohio, Illinois, and Minnesota.

¹⁴Collected from Elmer Piper, Shippensburg, Pennsylvania, March 1979. Cited by Amos Long, Jr., *The Pennsylvania German Family Farm* (Breinigsville, Pa.: Pennsylvania German Society, 1972): 104.

¹⁵Collected in Mercersburg, Pennsylvania, March 1979.

¹⁶Collected from Paul C. Hoffman, White Hall, Pennsylvania, April 1975. The belief is widespread among the Pennsylvania Germans: Ezra Grumbine, "Folk-Lore and Supersti-

tious Beliefs of Lebanon County,"*Lebanon County Historical Society Papers* 3 (1905–6): 259; Fogel, *Beliefs,* No. 1285; Isaac Simmons, "Dutch Folk-Beliefs [1915]," *Pennsylvania Dutchman* 5.14 (1954): 3; E. L. Knohr, "Customs and Beliefs in South-Eastern Pennsylvania Concerning the Holidays of the Year," *Pennsylvania Dutchman* 2.20 (1951): 5.

[17]Collected from Mabel Shoemaker, Fayetteville, Pennsylvania, May 1979.

[18]Collected from J. Russell Barrick, Carlisle, Pennsylvania, May 10, 1963. Brendle and Troxell include a story of a man walking along a country road who is struck by lightning. His shoes had been resoled on Ascension Day and the lightning tore the soles from his shoes (*Folk Tales,* 83–84).

[19]Collected by Cynthia Thompson from Sharon Miller, Bloomington, Indiana, July 11, 1959.

[20]Collected from J. Russell Barrick, Carlisle, Pennsylvania, October 6, 1970. Lewis Miller depicted a similar incident in York, Pennsylvania, in 1804, where "one night some young men and boys had some sport, the putting a wagon on top of the market house. The[y] got it up after takeing it apart, piece by piece" (*Sketches and Chronicles,* 19). Hans Meurer of Shippensburg, Pennsylvania, once recalled that students in Germany dismantled a teacher's car and reassembled it on the second floor of a dormitory.

[21]Collected by Debbie Orlando from Norman Kline, Lehigh County, Pennsylvania, in 1973. The implication here is that the victim, a powwow doctor, used magic to determine who put the buggy on the roof.

[22]Collected by Christine Gollie from a 43-year-old Lehigh County woman in April 1985.

[23]Collected from J. Russell Barrick, Carlisle, Pennsylvania, May 26, 1963.

[24]Collected by Sandy Wood from her mother, Elisabeth Schmid Wood, Petersburg, Indiana, November 6, 1977. LaVern Rippley describes the *Adventskranz* (Advent wreath) as prepared in Germany and Wisconsin (*Of German Ways,* 194).

[25]Collected by Eleanor Peterson from Mrs. Tom Emmert, Cincinnati, Ohio, November 29, 1958. The custom is also observed in Fredericksburg, Texas (Julia Estill, "Customs among the German Descendants of Gillespie County," *Coffee in the Gourd,* ed. J. Frank Dobie [Austin: Texas Folklore Society, 1923], 71).

[26]Collected by Lynn Heiser from a Mrs. Ozaeta, Bloomington, Indiana, December 21, 1966. Formerly, Saint Nicholas was accompanied by a sinister character called Knecht Ruprecht, who carried a whip to punish naughty children (see Tristram P. Coffin, *The Illustrated Book of Christmas Folklore* [New York: Seabury Press, 1973], 66–67). A similar figure called Black Peter sometimes appears in Missouri (Shroeder, *Kansas Quarterly* 13 [1981]: 98).

[27]See Rudolf Hommel, "On the Trail of the First Christmas Tree," *Pennsylvania Dutchman* 1.21 (1949): 1; Alfred Shoemaker, *Christmas in Pennsylvania* (Kutztown: Pennsylvania Folk[life] Society, 1959), 52–60.

[28]Collected by Nancy Curtis from her mother, Aline Curtis, Nashville, Indiana, April 12, 1978.

[29]George P. Nitzsche, "The Christmas Putz of the Pennsylvania Germans," *Pennsylvania German Folklore Society* 6 (1941): 3–28; Shoemaker, *Christmas in Pennsylvania,* 110–11.

[30]Collected by Pat Piatek from Mary English, Gary, Indiana, in 1952. The belief that animals talk on Christmas Eve is widespread; see Fogel, *Beliefs,* No. 1284; Newbell Puckett collected it among Amish, Germans, and Dutch in Ohio (*Popular Beliefs and Superstitions,* ed. Wayland Hand et al. [Boston: G. K. Hall, 1981], Nos. 29909–11); and Anthon S. Cannon found it in Utah (*Popular Beliefs and Superstitions from Utah* [Salt Lake City: University of Utah Press, 1904], Nos. 11897 ff.).

[31]Andrew S. Berkey, "Christmas Customs of the Perkiomen Valley," *Pennsylvania Dutchman* 4.8 (1952): 3. Alfred Shoemaker has amassed a considerable number of

references to the custom (*Christmas in Pennsylvania*, 73–85).

[32]Collected from J. Russell Barrick, Carlisle, Pennsylvania, December 30, 1969. The custom shows the cross-influence of a Scotch-Irish mumming tradition. Compare a similar practice called "sernatin'" in Georgia: Max E. White, "Sernatin': A Traditional Christmas Custom in Northeast Georgia," *Southern Folklore Quarterly* 45 (1981): 89–99.

[33]Collected from Charlie Miller, Cumberland County, Pennsylvania, March 9, 1977. The use of musical instruments is in keeping with European tradition, where mummers entertained the families they visited in exchange for treats of food or money (Shoemaker, *Christmas,* 73; Henry Glassie, *All Silver and No Brass: An Irish Christmas Mumming* [Bloomington and London: Indiana University Press, 1975], 23–24).

CHAPTER 9. FOODWAYS

1. Described by Stephen Goodyear, April 30, 1982, after observing the process used by the Heberlig family, Cumberland County, Pennsylvania. Germans in east-central Missouri follow essentially the same method of butchering; see Howard Wight Marshall, "Meat Preservation on the Farm in Missouri's 'Little Dixie,'" *Journal of American Folklore* 92 (1979): 400–17, esp. 407–11. Compare a similar procedure in Tennessee described by Wendell Stephens ("Hog-Killing Time in Middle Tennessee," *Tennessee Folklore Society Bulletin* 36.3 [1970]: 83–91). Some Germans saved the blood for Blutwurst and puddings.

2. Collected by Vicki Latsha from her grandmother, Steena Hepner Latsha in Harrisburg, Pennsylvania, April 19, 1981. Mrs. Latsha was originally from Malta, Northumberland County, Pennsylvania.

3. Collected from Mrs. Sarah Felmy Shaffer (1897–1984) by Patricia A. Shaffer. The recipe came from Mrs. Shaffer's mother, Mrs. Anna Felmy, of Snyder County, Pennsylvania. Variations of this appear in the *Pennsylvania Dutch Cook Book* (Reading: Culinary Arts Press, 1936), 28, and in Edna Eby Heller's *The Art of Pennsylvania Dutch Cooking* (Garden City: Doubleday, 1968), 126.

4. Collected by Lori Zeigler from Mrs. Erma May Gettle, Franklin County, Pennsylvania.

5. Collected by Chris L. Hottinger from his aunt, Mary Bibler, in Muncie, Indiana, October 8, 1977. The recipe was his grandmother's and is almost identical to one still used in Germany today ("Cooking German on Christmas Day," *Better Homes and Gardens* 53 (December 1975): 74.

6. Collected by Vicki Latsha from her grandmother, Mrs. Steena Hepner Latsha, Harrisburg, Pennsylvania, April 19, 1981. Of course the batter is dribbled from the funnel into the hot fat. Recipes for funnel cake are listed in Heller (*Art of Pennsylvania Dutch Cooking,* 117–18). Funnel cake is especially popular at fairs, festivals, and other public gatherings.

7. Collected by Karen Hart, Shippensburg, Pennsylvania, April 1979. A recipe in Heller's *Art of Pennsylvania Dutch Cooking* (16–17) requires less lead time.

8. Written in the margin of a copy of the *Martha Washington Cook Book* (New York: F. Tennyson Neely, 1897), by Annie Stover (1874–1945), with the note, "Spunge cake Marry Thumey," meaning Mary Thumma, who died about 1925. Annie Stover was a lifelong resident of Cumberland County, Pennsylvania. Such recipes as this William Woys Weaver calls "mere outlines for dishes a cook could elaborate upon according to her talent and means" (*Sauerkraut Yankees* [Philadelphia: University of Pennsylvania Press, 1983], xviii).

9. These four recipes were written in a general store ledger from Mifflinburg, Pennsylvania, and were transcribed by Patricia A. Shafer in May 1985. Dates on the ledger range from 1884 to 1899. A "milkless, eggless, butterless" cake requiring brown sugar, lard, and cloves is listed by Heller (*Art of Pennsylvania Dutch Cooking,* 179–80).

10. Collected by Annette Fuhrman in Lancaster County, Pennsylvania, April 1982. This recipe appears in the *Pennsylvania Dutch Cook Book* (47). *Moschi,* the popular Pennsylvania German candy (also spelled *mosie, moshey,* etc.), is usually made with black walnuts (Heller, *Art,* 212–13), though Weaver lists a form with chopped almonds (144–45). The

word, Weaver says, derives from a corruption of *muscovado* (unrefined) sugar. See also Shoemaker, *Christmas in Pennsylvania,* 36–37.

11. Collected by Cindy Painter from her mother, Mrs. Betty Painter, Birdsboro, Pennsylvania. Heller provides a similar recipe in *The Art of Pennsylvania Dutch Cooking* (213).

12. Collected by Patricia A. Shaffer from Mrs. Sarah Felmy Shaffer, Mifflinburg, Pennsylvania.

13. Collected by Karen Hart, Shippensburg, Pennsylvania, April 1979.

14. The first recipe was collected by Karen Hart, April 1979, and is identical to one called "Helen's Smierkase" in the *Pennsylvania Dutch Cook Book* (23). The second was collected by Chris L. Hottinger in Muncie, Indiana, October 8, 1977, from his aunt, Mary Bibler (Indiana University Folklore Archives, MC 79/2). This flavorful form of cottage cheese was usually enjoyed wherever Pennsylvania Germans settled; see H. M. Hays, "On the German Dialect Spoken in the Valley of Virginia," *Dialect Notes* 3 (1908): 275: "Schmier-Käs is a common dish in the Valley." In Pennsylvania German homes, Schmierkase and apple butter were nearly always eaten together as a bread spread or as an appetizer. In Texas it was served at women's gatherings along with *Mandelbrot* (almond bread), *Zimsterne* (cinnamon stars), *Lebkuchen* (ginger bread), "and other fattening foods" (Francis Abernethy, *"Deutschtum* in Texas," *German Culture in Texas,* ed. Glen Lich and Dona Reeves [Boston: Twayne, 1980], 220).

15. Collected by Lori Ziegler from Mrs. Erma May Gettle, Franklin County, Pennsylvania. There is a similar recipe in Heller's *Art of Pennsylvania Dutch Cooking* (208–9).

16. Written into Mrs. Annie Stover's copy of *Martha Washington Cook Book,* Cumberland County, Pennsylvania.

17. Collected by Mark Perkins, Lancaster, Pennsylvania, April 1984. In Cumberland County, Pennsylvania, apple dumplings often constituted a complete meal, being served hot with fresh milk (with sugar and vanilla added). Similar recipes appear in the *Pennsylvania Dutch Cook Book* (40), Heller's *Art* (146–47) and the *Pennsylvania State Grange Cookbook* (1972, 282–83).

18. Collected by Renee Strzelecki, April 30, 1981, from her grandmother. Other recipes appear in the *Pennsylvania Dutch Cook Book* (36) and Heller (*Art,* 5–7). In Pennsylvania the traditional fastnacht is rectangular, rather than round, with a slit, not a hole, in the center. Tradition says that these cakes are fried to use up the last of the animal fats on Shrove Tuesday, before the beginning of Lent, hence the name Fastnacht, "eve of the fast."

19. Collected by Chris L. Hottinger, in Muncie, Indiana, October 8, 1977, from his aunt, Mary Bibler.

20. Collected by Patricia A. Shaffer from Mrs. Sarah Felmy Shaffer, Mifflinburg, Pennsylvania, with the notation, "first made in 1839." Weaver notes that "by the mid-nineteenth century, plum pudding was one of the commonest Christmas foods made and sold in Pennsylvania" (108).

21. Collected by Vicki Latsha, in Harrisburg, Pennsylvania, April 19, 1981, from her grandmother, Steena Hepner Latsha, a native of Northumberland County. A similar recipe appears in the *Pennsylvania Dutch Cook Book* (12).

22. Collected by Vicki Latsha from Steena Hepner Latsha, Harrisburg, Pennsylvania, April 19, 1981. Mrs. Heller provides a variety of recipes for chicken potpie, beef potpie, and one called "the slippy kind" (*Art of Pennsylvania Dutch Cooking,* 38–41, 121–23). There is a recipe for chicken potpie (with egg noodles) in Jean Anderson, *Recipes from America's Restored Villages* (Garden City: Doubleday, 1975), 96. Rather than a true pie, this dish is in fact a stew, thickened with large noodles, called in Pennsylvania German *Botboi,* whence the English name.

23. Collected by Chris L. Hottinger, in Muncie, Indiana, October 8, 1977, from his aunt Mary Bibler. The word *Hausfrauenart* means "home-made." The collector has apparently

confused the words *Haus* (home) and *Hase* (hare). This dish would more likely be called *Hase im Topf* (rabbit stew); see Rippley, 242.

24. Collected by Linda J. Adams, from Mrs. Ivo Bauman, Mt. Angel, Oregon, December 9, 1970 (Northwest Folklore Archive, No. 120070138).

25. Collected from J. Russell Barrick, Carlisle, Pennsylvania, June 21, 1963. Some farm homes made an entire meal of boiled or fried mush, to the extent that one hired man at Indiantown Gap, Pennsylvania, invited to say grace, prayed, "Oh Gott! Sei gneedich, ich bin der mush so leedich! Amen" (Oh God, be gracious! I'm so tired of mush!) (Anna Fry Hellman, "Too Much Mush," *Pennsylvania Dutchman* 1.15 [1949]: 3). Lewis Miller has a drawing of "Dr. John Rause and Family, at the dinner table eating nudelsup, and in the Evening meal, mush and milk" (*Sketches and Chronicles* [York: Historical Society of York County, 1966], 57). Don Yoder has made an exhaustive study of the role of mush in German American folk culture ("Pennsylvanians Called It Mush," *Pennsylvania Folklife* 13.2 [1962–63]: 27–49).

26. Collected by Lori Zeigler, April 1979, from Mrs. Erma May Gettle, Franklin County, Pennsylvania. A similar recipe appears in Heller, *Art,* 50. Onion, cabbage, or other vegetables are sometimes added. Politely called Hog Maw, this dish is given the opprobrious epithet "French Goose" in Northumberland County, Pennsylvania.

27. Collected by Renee Strzelecki, April 1981, Shippensburg, Pennsylvania. Heller lists a recipe for pork, sauerkraut, and dumplings in which pork loin is substituted for the ribs (*Art,* 47–48).

28. Collected by Vicki Latsha, April 19, 1981, from Steena Hepner Latsha, Harrisburg, Pennsylvania. Similar recipes appear in the *Pennsylvania Dutch Cook Book* (9) and in Heller's *Art* (46–47). Schnitz are of course dried apple slices. Weaver notes that "apple schnitz have been found among the remains of Stone Age lake dwellings in Switzerland," and that their use is a culinary tradition brought from southern Germany (121–22). This recipe has been carried into most areas settled by the Palatines; see, for example, H. M. Hays, *Dialect Notes* 3 (1908): 275: "Schnitz un' Knöpp is a common Valley dish."

29. Collected by Linda J. Adams, from Mrs. Ivo Bauman, Mt. Angel, Oregon, December 9, 1970 (Northwest Folklore Archive, No. 120070138). Heller lists a recipe like this for "Gschmelzte Nudle" (Buttered Noodles) (*Art,* 131).

30. Collected from Ella Stover Barrick, Carlisle, Pennsylvania, June 4, 1963. There are many variations on this recipe. One in the *Pennsylvania Dutch Cook Book* (45) adds green tomatoes and cauliflower to the vegetables and ground mustard to the spices. Heller collected two similar recipes in Lancaster, Pennsylvania ("Chow-Chow," *Pennsylvania Dutchman* 1.18 [1949]: 4), and more recently she published a "modern" recipe requiring packages of frozen vegetables and jars of pickle slices, gherkins, and cocktail onions ("Traditional Favorites Go Modern," *Pennsylvania Folklife* 16.4 [1967]: 45). Chow-chow, of Oriental origin, was introduced into Pennsylvania as a result of the British trade contacts with the Far East (Weaver, 152).

31. Written by Simon Stover (1870–1942; Cumberland County, Pennsylvania) in his wife's *Martha Washington Cook Book,* this recipe provides only the items used in the liquid. Presumably anyone making pickles would know that the cucumbers would be peeled and sliced, covered with salt, and let stand overnight; after the other ingredients were added, the pickles were placed in airtight jars, as instructed in the *Pennsylvania Dutch Cook Book* (44). Under the traditional division of labor from medieval Germany to the Pennsylvania German farm home, pickling was man's work, from the preservation of meats to the pickling of sauerkraut and other vegetables; see Weaver, 153–54.

32. An Emke family recipe, Gifford, Illinois, 1977, in the Indiana University Folklore archives (No. 77/109).

33. Written on a page of a pocket ledger by Mrs. Bertha Gutshall (1892–1980), Cumberland County, Pennsylvania. The *Pennsylvania State Grange Cookbook,* 409, has a similar recipe requiring 2 cups sugar and 1 cup buttermilk.

34. Collected from Mrs. Ella Stover Barrick, Carlisle, Pennsylvania, May 31, 1963. A more detailed recipe appears in Heller, *Art,* 165. Such pies were often prepared as a salvage operation. When an early frost threatened the remaining tomatoes, they were picked green, some to ripen on a sunny windowsill while others went into pies.

35. Collected from Steena Hepner Latsha by Vicki Latsha, Harrisburg, Pennsylvania, April 19, 1981. This was a much more popular recipe among the Pennsylvania Germans than lemon meringue pie. Variant recipes exist: Heller, *Art,* 170–73; Gerald Lestz, *The Pennsylvania Dutch Cookbook* (New York: Grosset & Dunlap, 1970), 65.

36. Collected from Mrs. Ella Stover Barrick, Carlisle, Pennsylvania, May 20, 1963. Similar recipes (with smaller amounts of molasses and larger amounts of flour) appear in the *Pennsylvania Dutch Cook Book* (31) and Heller's *Art* (155–56).

37. Collected by Renee Strzelecki, Shippensburg, Pennsylvania, April 1981. There are many versions of this recipe; Heller lists two with a greater variety of spices (*Art,* 162–63), and the *Pennsylvania Dutch Cook Book* has one requiring "1 cup whiskey" (31). The German pie pumpkin was the long-neck or crookneck pumpkin; the dark orange, round Halloween pumpkin was considered fit only for animal fodder (Weaver, 129–31).

38. Collected by Vicki Latsha, April 19, 1981, in Harrisburg, Pennsylvania, from her grandmother, Steena Hepner Latsha. In many cookbooks this recipe is titled "Funeral Pie," since raisin pie was the common dessert served at funeral suppers, either because of its mournful color, or more likely because raisins were available year-round. Ken Whisler of Newville, Pennsylvania, once asked me (June 18, 1972), "Do you know why they have raisin pie at funerals?" "No, why?" "To eat."

39. Collected by Vicki Latsha from Steena Hepner Latsha, Harrisburg, Pennsylvania, April 19, 1981. Weaver has a recipe for dried apple pie (*Apfelschnitz Pei*) in *Sauerkraut Yankees* (121–22).

40. Collected by Patricia A. Shaffer from an Amish girl from Swengel, Union County, Pennsylvania, April 1985. Shoofly pie, so often emphasized at folk festivals, has come to be identified as a traditional Pennsylvania German dessert. Its popularity is partly the result of its availability any time of the year, unlike other pies which depend on seasonal fillings. There is a recipe for every taste, from sticky to dry, from sweet to spicy. Heller has published a variety of them in "Displaced Dutchmen Crave Shoo-Flies," *Pennsylvania Dutchman* 8.3 (1957): 32–33, and in *The Art of Pennsylvania Dutch Cooking,* 152–54. Lestz provides four more (59–61). The name, it has been suggested, is a corruption of the French *choufleur* (cauliflower) because of its resemblance to that vegetable. Others attribute the name to the flies attracted by the pie's sweetness.

41. Written in a small account book among the effects of Gertrude Schmoll, Carlisle, Pennsylvania, December 1972. Similar recipes for "Sour Cream Raisin Pie" are in the *Pennsylvania State Grange Cookbook* (431) and Lestz (64).

42. Collected by Lori Ziegler, April 1979, from Mrs. Erma May Gettle, Franklin County, Pennsylvania. There are similar recipes in the *Pennsylvania Dutch Cook Book* (18) and Heller (*Art,* 29).

43. Edna Eby Heller, "Chicken Corn Soup," *Pennsylvania Dutchman* 1.14 (1949): 4. Mrs. Heller suggested adding 2 cups of noodles, though more commonly the noodle dough is rolled into small lumps called *rivvels* (see the "Rivvel Soup" recipe below). Chicken corn soup is a popular dish at public sales and fireman's festivals, and on rare occasions when the amount of chicken is insufficient, someone remarks, "They must have let the chicken walk through the soup."

44. Collected by Linda J. Adams from Mrs. Ivo Bauman, Mt. Angel, Oregon, December 9, 1970 (Northwest Folklore Archive, 120070138).

45. Collected by Vicki Latsha from Steena Hepner Latsha, Harrisburg, Pennsylvania, April 19, 1981. Similar recipes appear in the *Pennsylvania Dutch Cook Book* (20), Heller (*Art,* 26), and Lestz (45).

46. Collected by Chris L. Hottinger, in Muncie, Indiana, October 8, 1977, from his aunt,

Mary Bibler (Indiana University Folklore Archives, MC 79/2).

47. Collected by Cindy Painter from her mother, Mrs. Betty Painter, Birdsboro, Pennsylvania. A recipe for corn pie in Heller's *Art of Pennsylvania Dutch Cooking* (80) eliminates the eggs and substitutes chopped parsley or green pepper for the onion.

48. Collected from Mrs. Harman Huffman, Cumberland County, Pennsylvania, April 1979, by Kathleen Bolger. This is identical to a recipe in Heller (*Art,* 80). A similar recipe appears in the *Pennsylvania Dutch Cook Book,* 23.

49. Collected by Cindy Painter, from her mother, Mrs. Betty Painter, Birdsboro, Pennsylvania, May 1980. There is a similar recipe in the *Pennsylvania Dutch Cook Book* (18) that adds salt pork and soda crackers.

50. Collected from Ella Stover Barrick, Carlisle, Pennsylvania, May 31, 1963. Most versions of the recipe suggest pouring the hot bacon dressing over the leaves, rather than frying them; see the *Pennsylvania Dutch Cook Book,* 22, and Heller, *Art,* 111. Lestz describes a similar dressing to be used with lettuce (47).

51. Collected from Erma May Gettle, Franklin County, Pennsylvania, by Lori Ziegler. Similar recipes appear in the *Pennsylvania Dutch Cook Book* (21) and in Heller (*Art,* 78).

52. Collected by Cindy Painter, May 1980, from her mother, Mrs. Betty Painter, Birdsboro, Pennsylvania. Each cook seems to have had a favorite version of potato filling, since numerous recipes exist: Heller, *Art,* 66–67, Lestz, 42–43, etc.

53. Collected from George Morrison, Landisburg, Pennsylvania, by Mark Carpenter, March 20, 1979.

54. Collected from Mrs. Elsie Stover Snyder, Carlisle, Pennsylvania, September 10, 1969. One informant noted that the oftener sauerkraut is reheated, the better it becomes. The process of making sauerkraut was so well-known that few early recipes exist. Weaver publishes one from Chester County, Pennsylvania, 1838 (174–75), and Heller has a more recent example (*Art,* 86). Yoder wrote a definitive study of "Sauerkraut in the Pennsylvania Folk-Culture" (*Pennsylvania Folklife* 12.2 [1961]: 56–69), examining methods of preparation, social and cultural functions, and the mention of sauerkraut in folk and popular literature. Besides the custom of eating sauerkraut on New Year's Day, there are many superstitions relating to its preparation. If made in the moon-sign of Pisces, the Fish, it will become slimy (George Dunkelberger, *The Story of Snyder County* [Selinsgrove, Pennsylvania: Snyder County Historical Society, 1948], 333; Fogel, *Beliefs,* No. 904). Sauerkraut made during "Bitter Week" [St. Gall, October 16] will be bitter (J. Gruber's *Hagerstown* [Md.] *Almanack,* 1973, 35; Fogel, *Beliefs,* No. 939). "Make your sauerkraut when the sign is up to keep the broth [brine] up over the cabbage" (collected from Mrs. Marilyn Strait, Fulton County, Pennsylvania, February 1979). "Sourkraut will spoil if made by a woman in her periods" (Fogel, *Beliefs,* No. 1862).

55. Collected from Mrs. Ella Barrick, Carlisle, Pennsylvania, May 31, 1963. The relatively small quantities of such wines produced suggest that they were intended primarily for cordials and medicinal purposes. Blackberry wine was particularly good for treating diarrhea.

56. Collected by Patricia Shaffer from her grandmother, Sarah Felmy Shaffer, of Mifflinburg, Pennsylvania.

57. Collected by Patricia Shaffer from Sarah Felmy Shaffer, Mifflinburg, Pennsylvania.

58. Written by Mrs. Annie Stover in the margins of her *Martha Washington Cook Book.* William Woys Weaver provides a recipe for a much larger quantity, noting that, in the nineteenth century, spruce beer was not regarded as intoxicating and was in fact promoted as a temperance drink (183–84).

CHAPTER 10. SUPERSTITIONS AND FOLK BELIEF

[1]Collected by Carol Johansen from Kurt Neustadter, Eugene, Oregon, May 10, 1974 (Northwest Folklore Archive, No. 060074067).

[2]Collected by Alfred Shoemaker from Calvin Stump, Maxatawny, Pennsylvania (Shoemaker, "The Folklore of Bread," *Pennsylvania Dutchman* 1.2 [1949]: 3). Loss of cud, an ailment of cattle similar to indigestion, was treated in various ways, but usually by giving the cow a greasy dishrag to replace the lost cud. The belief that killing toads caused cows to give bloody milk was widespread (Edwin M. Fogel, *Beliefs and Superstitions of the Pennsylvania Germans* [Philadelphia: Americana Germanica, 1915], No. 762).

[3]Collected by Justine Newman from Agate Nesoule, Bloomington, Indiana, in 1957.

[4]One collected in Detroit, Michigan, in 1964, is, "To determine the sex of an unborn child attach a ring to a piece of string and hold the end of the string above the abdomen of the expectant mother while she is lying down. If the ring swings in a circle, the child will be a girl. If it hangs directly down, the child will be a boy" (Wayne State University Archives, 1964 [142]).

[5]Collected by Roberta Wilkens from her grandmother, Emilie Hepperle Renz, of Philadelphia, Pennsylvania, April 1981. Mrs. Renz was born in Holzgerlingen, Germany, in 1908, and died in 1983.

[6]Tacitus, *Germania,* translated by H. Mattingly (New York: Penguin Books, 1948), 108–10.

[7]"Moonology," *The Historical Record* 4 (Wilkes-Barre, Pennsylvania, 1893): 16. See also Mac E. Barrick, "Moon-Signs in Cumberland County," *Pennsylvania Folklife* 15.4 (1966), 41–43. German and English almanacs regularly provide information on the moon's position in the Zodiac and in relation to the ecliptic. The mention of the moon's pointing up or down refers to a small almanac symbol indicating whether the moon is in the ascending or descending mode.

[8]Collected from Eugene Utech, Carlisle, Pennsylvania, January 16, 1969. On the same occasion, Samuel Burkholder, druggist from Newville, Pennsylvania, recalled another old remedy: "Stick your finger in your ear and get some wax and rub on the lips. Be sure the finger is clean."

[9]Collected from Hans D. Meurer, Shippensburg, Pennsylvania, November 16, 1976; April 7, 1977; February 17, 1978.

[10]Collected from Mrs. Miller Schmuck, York, Pennsylvania, April 1982. Similar remedies call for hanging a spider or a woodlouse around the neck.

[11]Collected by Alfred Shoemaker from Carl L. Trexler, Topton, Pennsylvania, March 7, 1950. Similar beliefs are listed by Ezra Grumbine, "Folk-Lore of Lebanon County," *Lebanon County Historical Society Papers* 3 (1905–6), 276; and Fogel, *Beliefs,* Nos. 1788, 1798.

[12]Phebe Gibbons, *Pennsylvania Dutch and Other Essays* (Philadelphia: Lippincott, 1882), 401. The same practice is also recorded in Virginia by Elmer L. Smith and John Stewart, "The Mill as a Preventive and Cure of Whooping Cough," *Journal of American Folklore* 77 (1964): 76–77.

[13]Collected from Tom Weidensaul, Mifflin County, Pennsylvania, July 1, 1976. The same belief is listed by Grumbine ("Folk-Lore," 276), Fogel (*Beliefs,* Nos. 1791 and 1792), and Isaac Shirk Simmons, "Dutch Folk Beliefs," *Pennsylvania Dutchman* 5.14 (1954): 2.

[14]Collected from John Strait, McConnellsburg, Pennsylvania, February 1979. Also reported from Elk County, Pennsylvania, March 1976.

[15]Collected from Fred W. Diehl, Danville, Pennsylvania, May 15, 1976. The same belief is listed by Simmons, "Dutch Folk Beliefs," 2, and Vaughn E. Whisker, *Tales from the Allegheny Foothills,* vol. 1 (Bedford: Bedford Gazette, 1975), 47.

[16]Grumbine, "Folk-Lore," 276. Compare also Thomas R. Brendle and Claude W. Unger, *Folk Medicine of the Pennsylvania Germans* (New York: Augustus M. Kelley, 1970), 132. Fogel indicates that the blue tumbler must be "stolen" (*Beliefs,* No. 1797).

[17]Collected from Mrs. Grace Hamma, Detroit, Michigan, July 12, 1965. (Wayne State University Folklore Archives, 1965 [78]).

[18]Among the earliest extant examples are ninth- and tenth-century manuscript texts

of veterinary charms in Old High German, known as the Merseburg Charms, some of whose phrases are still used in twentieth-century powwowing; see Gerhard Eis, *Altdeutsche Zaubersprüche* (Berlin: Walter de Gruyter, 1964), 7–12, and plate 1.

[19]A collection of remedies and charms written in Bohemia in 1795 was found in Texas by Christine Boot, "Home and Farm Remedies in a German Manuscript from a Texas Ranch," *Paisanos: A Folklore Miscellany,* ed. Francis Abernethy (Austin: Encino Press, 1978), 111–31. Another from West Virginia was described by John Stewart and Elmer Smith, "An Occult Remedy Manuscript from Pendleton County, West Virginia," *Madison College Studies and Research Bulletin* 22.2 (1964): 77–83. A list of eleven cures compiled by Jacob Harshman (1831–1892) of Franklin County, Pennsylvania, was printed in the *Chambersburg* (Pa.) *Public Opinion,* on September 20, 1984. Brendle and Unger list fifty items of this nature, many of them still unpublished (*Folk Medicine,* 291–303).

[20]Yoder has shown that Hohman drew heavily on a German charm book called the *Romanusbüchlein,* published in Silesia in 1788 ("Hohman and Romanus: Origins and Diffusion of the Pennsylvania German Powwow Manual," *American Folk Medicine,* ed. Wayland Hand [Berkeley: University of California Press, 1976], 235–48). Some of Hohman's charms are still in use. His cure for "wheal in the eye" ("Take a dirty plate; if you have none, you can easily dirty one, and the person for whom you are using sympathy shall in a few minutes find the pain much relieved. You must hold the side of the plate or dish, which is used in eating, toward the eye. While you hold the plate before the eye, you must say: Dirty plate, I press thee,/Wheal in the eye, do flee/+ + +") is still reported in Schuylkill County, Pennsylvania (Tom Graves, March 24, 1984) and in Ohio (Ann Hark, *Blue Hills and Shoofly Pie* [Philadelphia: Lippincott, 1952], 186).

[21]Collected by Alfred Shoemaker from H. Wayne Gruber, Reading, Pennsylvania (*Pennsylvania Dutchman* 1.2 [1949]: 2). Variants with the word *Katzedreck* (cat shit) have been collected in Somerset County, Pennsylvania (Buffington, *Ebbes fer Alle-Ebber,* 23) and in Allentown, Pennsylvania (Paul Frazier, "Some Lore of Hexing and Powwowing," *Midwest Folklore* 2 [1952]: 103), and Elmer Smith collected a version with *Kelvers* [calf] *Dreck* (*Pennsylvania Germans of the Shenandoah Valley,* 158). Gilbert Jordan collected a different "pain-easing song" in Texas: "Heile, heile, Segen,/Drei Tage Regen,/Drei Tage Dreck,/Und jetzt ist alles weg" (*German Texana,* 20).

[22]Aunt Sophia Bailer, "How I Learned Powwowing," *Pennsylvania Dutchman* 4.2 (1952): 8. Compare John R. Costello, "Cultural Vestiges and Cultural Blends among the Pennsylvania Germans," *New York Folklore* 3 (1977): 103. This is Motif D1504.1, "Charm stanches blood."

[23]Collected from Lottie M. Krebs, Brodbecks, Pennsylvania, March 7, 1979. The belief was also collected by the Union County (Pa.) Oral Traditions Project (tape 98 R; April 13, 1976). The practice is cited widely: W. B. Raber, *The Devil and Some of His Doings* (Dayton: 1855), 279; Betty Snellenburg, "Four Interviews with Powwowers," *Pennsylvania Folklife* 18.4 (1969): 42; Robert L. Dluge, Jr., "My Interview with a Powwower," *Pennsylvania Folklife* 21.4 (1972): 41.

[24]Cited in the Harshman MS, Franklin County, Pennsylvania, 1860s (see note 19 above). The three + 's apparently mean one should make the sign of the cross three times. Jeanne Coleman collected a similar charm in Somerset County, Pennsylvania, in January 1980, from Mrs. Robert Mostoller: "'Mary passed over the land with fire in her hand;/As she turned about the fire went out.' Begin by passing the hand over the burned area clockwise 3 times until you come to the part, 'as she turned about,' then counterclockwise 3 times, following by blowing over area 3 times."

[25]Collected from Marjorie Shue, Hanover, Pennsylvania, November 19, 1976, and from Ruth Witter, Fulton County, Pennsylvania, November 15, 1976. "Passing through" is a magic process of transference of sickness to the object passed through; see Wayland D. Hand, "'Passing Through': Folk Medical Magic and Symbolism," *Magical Medicine* (Berkeley: University of California Press, 1980), 133–85; and Brendle and Unger, *Folk Medicine,* 192–98.

[26]From the Harshman MS, Franklin County, Pennsylvania, 1860s. Sophia Bailer described a similar process with this verse: "Liver grown heart span/Move out of this body/Like Jesus Christ moved out of the Manger!/God the Father God the Son and God the Holy Ghost/Help to this amen!" (*Pennsylvania Dutchman* 4.2 [1952]: 8).

[27]H. G. Buch, *A Compilation of Valuable Recipes* (Lititz, Pennsylvania, 1886). Ironically, most Pennsylvania Germans believed that corns should be trimmed in the *decrease* of the moon (Fogel, *Beliefs,* Nos. 1254, 1512).

[28]Collected from Mrs. Clarence G. Darkes, Cleona, Pennsylvania, October 1978. For a similar cure for wens, see Brendle and Unger, *Folk Medicine,* 79–80.

[29]Stewart and Smith, "An Occult Remedy Manuscript," 80; Brendle and Unger, *Folk Medicine,* 113–14; Smith, *Pennsylvania Germans of the Shenandoah Valley,* 159–60.

[30]W. J. Hoffman, "Popular Superstitions," *Pennsylvania German Society Proceedings* 5 (1894): 78. Variants are cited by Brendle and Unger (*Folk Medicine,* 202–4); Simmons (*Pennsylvania Dutchman* 5.14, 3) and Alfred Shoemaker ("Some Powwowing Formulas from Juniata County," *Pennsylvania Dutchman* 3.10 [1951]: 4). Most of these are based on Hohman's formula "To Cure the Bite of a Snake" (23).

[31]Collected from Samuel A. Miller, Newville, Pennsylvania, September 10, 1972. The same belief was found in Chester County, Pennsylvania, about 1780 (John Futhey and Gilbert Cope, *History of Chester County* [Philadelphia: L. H. Merts, 1881], 414); in Alabama (Fanny D. Bergen, *Animal and Plant Lore* [Boston: American Folklore Society, 1899], 15); and in Cincinnati, Ohio (collected from Russell D. Steele, July 18, 1978). See also Sener, 240, and Fogel, *Beliefs,* No. 635. Baughman lists this as Motif G271.4.2 (ba).

[32]Collected by Debbie Orlando from her mother, Mrs. Jean Orlando, Claymont, Delaware, October 15, 1973. Brendle and Troxell list five variants of the story (*Folk Tales,* 138–42), in one of which the treatment is ineffective. The story is unusual in that the one disobeying supernatural instructions is not punished for it.

[33]Collected by Duane Buffington, Spring Glen, Pennsylvania, April 1983. The same charm in English and German is recorded by John Joseph Stoudt (*Sunbonnets and Shoofly Pies* [New York: A. S. Barnes, 1973]: 162–64) and by Richard H. Shaner (*Hexerei: A Practice of Witchcraft among the Pennsylvania Dutch* [Macungie, Pennsylvania: Progress Printing House, 1963], 15). Shaner also notes that sacks of mercury or asafetida were sometimes hung in the stables to ward off evil (15–17). One traditional way to outwit the devil or other evil spirit was to set for him an impossible task, such as going in and out of every opening in a sieve. The middle part of this charm does essentially the same thing.

[34]John George Hohman, *Pow-Wows; or, Long Lost Friend* (Harrisburg: Aurand Press, 1929), 35. The identical formula appears in the Pendletown County charm book; see Stewart and Smith, "An Occult Remedy Manuscript," 82. Similar plates were enclosed in the walls at the Ephrata Cloisters as protection from fire; see Julius Sachse, *The German Sectarians of Pennsylvania, 1742–1800* (Philadelphia: 1910), 374–75.

[35]Both charms collected by Jeanne Coleman from Mrs. Robert Mostoller, Somerset County, Pennsylvania, January 1980.

[36]E. M. Fogel connects these letters to the powwow-formula tradition, seeing a relationship between them and the Merseburger *Zaubersprüche* previously mentioned ("The Himmelsbrief," *Pennsylvania-German* 9 [1908]: 217–22). See also Fogel, "The Himmelsbrief," *German American Annals* 10 (1908): 286–301, and John Joseph Stoudt, "Himmelsbrief: The Letter from Heaven," *Historical Review of Berks County* 42 (1977): 102, 115. Elmer Smith describes an example found in Rockingham County, Virginia (*The Pennsylvania Germans of the Shenandoah Valley,* 152–53). Wilbur Oda notes the letters' use as protection in wartime ("The Himmelsbrief," *Pennsylvania Dutchman* 1.21 [1949]: 3). The concept is identified as Motif D1381.24, "Magic letter protects against attack."

[1]Monroe H. Fabian, *The Pennsylvania-German Decorated Chest* (New York: Universe Books, 1978).

[2]Most hex signs in use today are tourist-oriented decorations on food packages, plastic drinking cups, and urban garages, with no awareness of this symmetrical factor; see Tom Graves, "Ethnic Artists, Artifacts, and Authenticity: Pennsylvania German and Ukrainian Folk Crafts Today," *Pioneer America* 15 (1983): 24–26.

[3]Henry C. Mercer first applied the term to this style of writing, in his pioneering study, "The Survival of the Mediaeval Art of Illuminative Writing among Pennsylvania Germans," *Proceedings of the American Philosophical Society* 36 (1897): 424–33.

[4]Recently identified as Joseph Lochbaum, a Dunkard schoolmaster in Franklin County, Pennsylvania, the "Nine Hearts Artist" moved to Canada about 1820, where examples of his work are found in York County, Ontario; see Michael S. Bird, *Ontario Fraktur: A Pennsylvania-German Folk Tradition in Early Canada* (Toronto: M. F. Feheley, 1977), 70–71.

[5]Frederick S. Weiser, "Piety and Protocol in Folk Art: Pennsylvania German Fraktur Birth and Baptismal Certificates," *Winterthur Portfolio* 8 (1973): 20–32.

[6]Frederick S. Weiser, *The Pennsylvania German Fraktur of the Free Library of Philadelphia* (Breinigsville, Pa.: Pennsylvania German Society, 1976), vol. 1, xvi–ix.

[7]Henry S. Borneman, *Pennsylvania German Illuminated Manuscripts* (New York: Dover, 1973), plates 8–10, 29–33.

[8]Elmer L. Smith et al., *The Pennsylvania Germans of the Shenandoah Valley,* 165–79; Klaus Wust, *Virginia Fraktur: Penmanship as Folk Art* (Edinburg, Virginia: Shenandoah History, 1972); Olive G. Zehner, "Ohio Fractur," *Pennsylvania Dutchman* 6.3 (1954–55): 13–15.

[9]Examples of Miller's work appear in Lewis Miller, *Sketches and Chronicles* (York: Historical Society of York County, 1966). Biographical information is drawn from Donald Shelley's introduction to that work and from Preston and Eleanor Barba, "Lewis Miller, Pennsylvania German Folk Artist," *Pennsylvania German Folklore Society* 4 (1939).

[10]Simon Bronner discusses the artist's work in *Grasping Things: Folk Material Culture and Mass Society in America* (Lexington: University Press of Kentucky, 1986), 124–31 and color plates 7–12. "Anna Bock" is a pseudonym used by Bronner at the artist's request.

[11]Alexander Sackton, "Eddie Arning: Texas Folk Artist," *Folk Art in Texas,* ed. Francis Abernethy (Dallas: Southern Methodist University Press, 1985), 191.

[12]See numerous examples in Rachel and Kenneth Pellman, *The World of Amish Quilts* (Intercourse, Pennsylvania: Good Books, 1984).

[13]Milton E. Flower, "Schimmel the Woodcarver," *The Antiques Book,* ed. Alice Winchester (New York: Bonanza Books, 1950), 277–82; Paul Hoch, "Old Schimmel," *Early American Life* 8.1 (1977), 44–47.

[14]Examples of Schimmel's work appear in many museum collections and are illustrated in Clarence P. Hornung, *Treasury of American Design* (New York: Harry N. Abrams, 1976), vol. 2, 680–91, and similar books.

[15]Examples of Mountz's work are shown in Hornung, *Treasury* 2, 686–87; in Robert Bishop, *American Folk Sculpture* (New York: Bonanza, 1985), 209–11; and in Milton Flower, *Three Cumberland County Wood Carvers* (Carlisle: Cumberland County Historical Society, 1986), 12–15.

[16]Walter Gottshall, "Primative [sic] Pennsylvania Dutch Carving," *Pennsylvania Folklife* 35 (1986), 180–81.

[17]Charles van Ravenswaay, *The Arts and Architecture of German Settlements in Missouri* (Columbia and London: University of Missouri Press, 1977), figs. 15–6, 15–7.

[18]Katherine C. Grier, *Celebrations in Wood: The Sculpture of John Scholl* (Harrisburg: William Penn Memorial Museum, 1979), unpaginated.

[19]Simon Bronner discusses the work of several German chain carvers in Indiana in *Chain Carvers: Old Men Crafting Meaning* (Lexington: University Press of Kentucky, 1985), showing how such carvings are a form of reaction against the dehumanizing effect of mechanized factory production.

[20]David G. Lowe, "Wooden Delights," *American Heritage* 20.1 (1968), 18–23; "Wonderful Pennsylvania Dutch Whittling," *Woman's Day* 31.11 (1968), 25–27.

CHAPTER 12. FOLK ARCHITECTURE

[1]Albert J. Petersen, "The German-Russian House in Kansas: A Study in Persistence of Form," *Pioneer America* 8 (1976): 19.

[2]Fred Kniffen and Henry Glassie, "Building in Wood in the Eastern United States," *Geographical Review* 56 (1966): 58–59.

[3]Henry C. Mercer, "The Origin of Log Houses in the United States," *Bucks County Historical Society Papers* 5 (1926): 568–83.

[4]Warren Roberts, "Some Comments on Log Construction in Scandinavia and the United States," *Folklore Today*, ed. Linda Dégh et al. (Bloomington: Indiana University, 1976), 445; Roberts, *Log Buildings of Southern Indiana* (Bloomington: Trickster Press, 1984), 27–35.

[5]Henry Glassie, "The Types of the Southern Mountain Cabin," *The Study of Folklore*, ed. Jan Brunvand (New York: Norton, 1978), 401–2.

[6]"The evidence presented so far would lead any objective scholar to reject the likelihood of significant Alpine-Alemannic influence in Midland American log architecture" (Terry Jordan, "Alpine, Alemannic, and American Log Architecture," *Annals of the Association of American Geographers* 70 [1980]: 165).

[7]Charles van Ravenswaay, *The Arts and Architecture of German Settlements in Missouri* (Columbia: University of Missouri Press, 1977), 113–15; Richard Perrin, "German Timber Farmhouses in Wisconsin," *Wisconsin Magazine of History* 44.3 (1961).

[8]G. Edwin Brumbaugh, *Colonial Architecture of the Pennsylvania Germans* (Lancaster: Pennsylvania German Society, 1933), 21–30, shows the extent to which the Germans used log architecture. For recent log construction, see Mac E. Barrick, "The Log House as Cultural Symbol," *Material Culture* 18 (1986): 9–10.

[9]William J. Murtagh, "Half-Timbering in American Architecture," *Pennsylvania Folklife* 9.1 (1958): 2–11; Brumbaugh, *Colonial Architecture*, 26–28; K. Edward Lay, "European Antecedents of Seventeenth and Eighteenth Century Germanic and Scots-Irish Architecture in America," *Pennsylvania Folklife* 32 (1982): 9–11. Lewis Miller made drawings of several York County examples (*Sketches and Chronicles*, 23, 32).

[10]Brumbaugh, 28.

[11]Information collected by Brian Hess in an interview with the present owner, Mrs. J. Newton Shreiner, April 1985, who also provided a photograph of the old house.

[12]Francis Griffin, *Old Salem* (Winston-Salem: Old Salem, Inc., 1970), 31; Noble, *Wood, Brick, and Stone* vol. 1: *Houses* (Amherst: University of Massachusetts Press, 1984), 119.

[13]Hubert Wilhelm and Michael Miller, "Half-Timber Construction: A Relic Building Method in Ohio," *Pioneer America* 6.2 (1974), 43–51. Compare Kniffen and Glassie, "Building in Wood," 45.

[14]Richard Perrin, *Historic Wisconsin Buildings: A Survey of Pioneer Architecture, 1835–1870* (Milwaukee: Milwaukee Public Museum, 1962), 14–25; van Ravenswaay, 149–51, who notes the similarity between techniques used in Wisconsin and Missouri; Hubert Wilhelm, "German Settlement and Folk Building Practices in the Hill Country of Texas," *Pioneer America* 3.2 (1971): 20–21.

[15]Lay, 6–8; Noble, *Wood, Brick, and Stone* vol. 1, 28. LaVern Rippley describes a typical German *Bauernhaus* that has such a divided function (*Of German Ways*, 185–86).

[16]Alfred L. Shoemaker, *The Pennsylvania Barn* (Lancaster: Pennsylvania Dutch

Folklore Center 1955, 9. Compare Lay, 8.

[17]Don Yoder, frontispiece to *Pennsylvania Folklife* 9.3 (1958).

[18]Lay, 8.

[19]The Pelster Housebarn was the subject of a traveling exhibition, "The German Housebarn in America: Object and Image," organized in 1983 by the Missouri Culture Heritage Center at the University of Missouri–Columbia. Howard Marshall, one of the curators of the exhibit, described the building and its significance in "German-American Architecture on the Missouri Frontier: The Pelster Housebarn" (*Journal of NAL Associates* NS 9 [1984]: 14–30) and "The Pelster Housebarn: Endurance of Germanic Architecture on the Midwestern Frontier" (*Material Culture* 18 [1986]: 65–104).

[20]Such doors provided cross-ventilation and led to the house's being called a *Flürkuchenhaus* (corridor kitchen house); see John Milner, "Germanic Architecture in the New World," *Journal of the Society of Architectural Historians* 34 (1975): 299.

[21]For a detailed description of the Herr House, see Robert A. Barakat, "The Herr and Zeller Houses," *Pennsylvania Folklife* 21.4 (1972): 2–22.

[22]Robert Bucher identified sixteen one-and-a-half-story "cabins" and two-and-a-half-story "houses" with central chimneys, suggesting that log construction is an essential feature of the type ("The Continental Log House," *Pennsylvania Folklife* 12.4 [1962]: 14–19). However, Henry Glassie identified several others, including the Herr house, built of stone and other materials ("A Central Chimney Continental Log House," *Pennsylvania Folklife* 18.2 [1968–69]: 32–39). Restored examples in log and half-timber can still be seen in Winston-Salem, North Carolina; see William J. Murtagh, *Moravian Architecture and Town Planning* (Chapel Hill: University of North Carolina Press, 1967), 122, and Noble, *Wood, Brick and Stone* vol. 1, 42.

[23]Henry and Ottalie Williams, *A Guide to Old American Houses, 1700–1900* (South Brunswick and New York: A. S. Barnes, 1962), 54.

[24]Thomas Waterman, *The Dwellings of Colonial America* (Chapel Hill: University of North Carolina Press, 1950), 44–46.

[25]Edward A. Chappell, "Lighting the *Stube:* Oral Tradition and a Shenandoah County *Flürkuchenhaus,*" *Folklore and Folklife in Virginia* 3 (1984): 37–43.

[26]Henry Glassie, "Eighteenth-Century Cultural Process in Delaware Valley Folk Building," *Winterthur Portfolio* 7 (1972): 41–42. A Georgian style house typically has two rooms on each side of a central hall and stairway to form a four-over-four room arrangement. A two-thirds Georgian house has only two rooms on each level adjacent to the hall and stairway, which is at one end of the house.

[27]Roberts, *Log Buildings of Southern Indiana,* 115–16; Glassie, "Types of the Southern Mountain Cabin," 406; Terry Jordan, *Texas Log Buildings* (Austin: University of Texas Press, 1978), 107–13.

[28]Glassie, "Types," 394–96; Lay, 16; Jordan, *Texas,* 40.

[29]Warren E. Roberts, "Ananias Hensel and His Furniture: Cabinetmaking in Southern Indiana," *Midwestern Journal of Language and Folklore* 9 (1983): 76–77.

[30]Richard Perrin, *The Architecture of Wisconsin* (Madison: State Historical Society of Wisconsin, 1967), 12; Noble, *Wood, Brick and Stone,* vol. 1, 120.

[31]Sunday houses are discussed in detail by Julia Estill ("Customs among the German Descendants of Gillespie County," *Coffee in the Gourd,* ed. J. Frank Dobie [Austin: Texas Folklore Society, 1923], 68–69) and by Allen Noble (*Wood, Brick and Stone,* vol. 1, 120).

[32]Martin Wright, "The Antecedents of the Double-Pen House Type," *Annals of the Association of American Geographers* 48 (1958): 109–17; Henry Glassie, "The Pennsylvania Barn in the South," *Pennsylvania Folklife* 15.2 (1965–66): 16; Robert F. Ensminger, "A Search for the Origin of the Pennsylvania Barn," *Pennsylvania Folklife* 30 (1980–81): 53–54.

[33]Glassie, "The Pennsylvania Barn in the South," 12–16.

[34]Henry Glassie has provided an exhaustive examination of three such barns in northern York and Adams Counties, Pennsylvania ("The Double-Crib Barn in South

Central Pennsylvania," *Pioneer America* 1.1 [1969]: 9–16; 1.2 [1969]: 40–45; 2.1 [1970]: 47–52; 2.2 [1970]: 23–34. The Cumberland County barn figured here is previously undocumented.

[35]"The Pennsylvania Barn in the South, Part 2," *Pennsylvania Folklife* 15.4 (1966): 23. Compare also Henry J. Kauffman, "The Log Barn," *The Pennsylvania Barn,* ed. Alfred L. Shoemaker (Lancaster: Pennsylvania Dutch Folklore Center, 1955), 28–34.

[36]Glassie, "The Pennsylvania Barn in the South, Part 2," 24–25; Robert F. Ensminger, "A Search for the Origin of the Pennsylvania Barn," *Pennsylvania Folklife* 30 (1980–81): 50–71; Lay, 28.

[37]Ensminger, "Search," 68; Terry Jordan, *American Log Buildings* (Chapel Hill and London: University of North Carolina Press, 1985), 101–2.

[38]See Peter M. Ennals, "Nineteenth-century Barns in Southern Ontario," *Canadian Geographer* 16 (1972), 260–63; Eric Arthur and Dudley Witney, *The Barn: A Vanishing Landmark in North America* (Greenwich, Conn.: New York Graphic Society, 1972), 84–113; Glassie, "The Pennsylvania Barn in the South, Part 2," 12–25.

[39]David Cohen, *The Folklore and Folklife of New Jersey* (New Brunswick: Rutgers University Press, 1983), 132–35; Ludwig, "Influence of the Pennsylvania Dutch in the Middle West," 73; Ohio barns have been studied by William I. Schreiber, "The Pennsylvania Dutch Bank Barns of Ohio," *Journal of the Ohio Folklore Society* 2 (1967): 15–28. In Indiana, Pennsylvania-type barns are found along the old National Road and other major travel routes: Robert W. Bastian, "Indiana Folk Architecture," *Pioneer America* 9 (1977), 130–31; Susanne S. Ridlen, "Bank Barns in Cass County, Indiana," *Pioneer America* 4.2 (1972), 25–43. Alan Noble notes, however, that "forebay barns are extremely rare in Iowa and the rest of the German settled prairies" (*Wood, Brick, and Stone,* vol. 2: *Barns and Farm Structures* [Amherst: University of Massachusetts Press, 1984], 60).

[40]Robert W. Bastian, "Southeastern Pennsylvania and Central Wisconsin Barns: Examples of Independent Development," *Professional Geographer* 27 (1975): 200–204; Robert F. Ensminger, "A Comparative Study of Pennsylvania and Wisconsin Forebay Barns," *Pennsylvania Folklife* 32 (1983): 98–114.

[41]Van Ravenswaay, *Art and Architecture,* 268–69.

[42]Terry Jordan, "A Forebay Bank Barn in Texas," *Pennsylvania Folklife* 30 (1980–81): 72–77.

Bibliography

Aarne, Antti, and Stith Thompson. *The Types of the Folktale: A Classification and Bibliography.* Helsinki: Suomalainen Tiedeakatemia, 1964.

Abernethy, Francis Edward. *"Deutschtum* in Texas: A Look at Texas-German Folklore." In *German Culture in Texas,* ed. Glen E. Lich and Dona B. Reeves. Boston: Twayne, 1980.

_____, ed. *Folk Art in Texas.* Dallas: Southern Methodist University Press, 1985.

_____, ed. *Paisanos: A Folklore Miscellany.* Austin: Encino Press, 1978.

Abrahams, Roger D., and Lois Rankin, eds. *Counting-Out Rhymes: A Dictionary.* Austin and London: University of Texas Press, 1980.

Anderson, Harry H., ed. *German-American Pioneers in Wisconsin and Michigan.* Milwaukee: Milwaukee County Historical Society, 1971.

Anderson, Jean. *Recipes from America's Restored Villages.* Garden City: Doubleday, 1975.

Arthur, Eric, and Dudley Witney. *The Barn: A Vanishing Landmark in North America.* Greenwich, Conn.: New York Graphic Society, 1972.

Bailer, Sophia. "How I Learned Powwowing." *Pennsylvania Dutchman* 4.2 (1952): 8.

Barakat, Robert A. "The Herr and Zeller Houses." *Pennsylvania Folklife* 21.4 (1972): 2–22.

Barba, Preston, and Eleanor Barba. "Lewis Miller, Pennsylvania German Folk Artist." *Pennsylvania German Folklore Society* 4 (1939): 1–40.

Barrick, Mac E. "The Competitive Element in the Cante Fable." *Southern Folklore Quarterly* 45 (1981): 123–34.

_____. "Folk Toys." *Pennsylvania Folklife* 29.1 (1979): 27–34.

_____. "The Image of the Jew in South-Central Pennsylvania." *Pennsylvania Folklife* 34 (1985): 133–38.

_____. "The Log House as Cultural Symbol." *Material Culture* 18 (1986): 1–19.

_____. "Moon-Signs in Cumberland County." *Pennsylvania Folklife* 15.4 (1966): 41–43.

_____. "Numskull Tales in Cumberland County." *Pennsylvania Folklife* 16.4 (1967): 50–52.

_____. "Popular Comparisons and Similes." *Keystone Folklore Quarterly* 10 (1965): 3–34.

_____. "Pulpit Humor in Central Pennsylvania." *Pennsylvania Folklife* 19.1 (1969): 28–36.

_____. "Riddles from Cumberland County." *Keystone Folklore Quarterly* 8 (1963): 59–74.

Bastian, Robert W. "Indiana Folk Architecture." *Pioneer America* 9 (1977): 115–36.

_____. "Southeastern Pennsylvania and Central Wisconsin Barns: Examples of Independent Development." *Professional Geographer* 27 (1975): 200–204.

Baughman, Ernest W. *Type and Motif-Index of the Folktales of England and North America.* The Hague: Mouton & Co., 1966.

Beidelman, William. *The Story of the Pennsylvania Germans.* Detroit: Gale Research Co., 1969.

Benson, Evelyn A. "Don't Got None." *Pennsylvania Dutchman* 3.3 (1951): 2.

Bergen, Fanny D. *Animal and Plant Lore.* Boston: American Folklore Society, 1899.

Berkey, Andrew S. "Christmas Customs of the Perkiomen Valley." *Pennsylvania Dutchman* 4.8 (1952): 3.

Bird, Michael S. *Ontario Fraktur: A Pennsylvania-German Folk Tradition in Early Canada.* Toronto: M. F. Feheley, 1977.

Bishop, Robert. *American Folk Sculpture.* 1974. Reprint. New York: Bonanza Books, 1985.

Blasig, Anne. *The Wends of Texas.* San Antonio: Naylor, 1954.

Boatright, Mody C., ed. *The Sky Is My Tipi.* Austin: Texas Folklore Society, 1949.

Boatright, Mody C., et al., eds. *Singers and Storytellers.* Dallas: Southern Methodist University Press, 1961.

Böhme, Franz. *Deutsches Kinderlied und Kinderspiel.* Leipzig: Breitkopf und Härtel, 1897.

A Book of Vulgar Verse. Toronto: Checkerbooks, 1981.

Boot, Christine. "Home and Farm Remedies in a German Manuscript from a Texas Ranch." In *Paisanos: A Folklore Miscellany,* ed. Francis Abernethy. Austin: Encino Press, 1978.

Borneman, Henry S. *Pennsylvania German Illuminated Manuscripts.* 1937. Reprint. New York: Dover, 1973.

Bortner, Arta M. "Shafely, Gay Hame!" *Pennsylvania Dutchman* 3.5 (1951): 1, 3.

Boyer, Walter E. "The New Year Wish of the Pennsylvania Dutch Broadside." *Pennsylvania Folklife* 10.2 (1959): 45–49.

Boyer, Walter, Albert Buffington, and Don Yoder, eds. *Songs along the Mahantongo: Pennsylvania Dutch Folksongs.* Lancaster: Pennsylvania Dutch Folklore Center, 1951.

Brendle, Thomas R., and William S. Troxell, eds. *Pennsylvania German Folk Tales, Legends, Once-Upon-a-Time Stories, Maxims, and Sayings.* Norristown: Pennsylvania German Society, 1944.

———. "Pennsylvania German Songs." In *Pennsylvania German Songs and Legends,* ed. George Korson. Baltimore: Johns Hopkins Press, 1949.

Brendle, Thomas R., and Claude W. Unger. *Folk Medicine of the Pennsylvania Germans: The Non-Occult Cures.* 1935. Reprint. New York: Augustus M. Kelley, 1970.

Bronner, Simon J. *Chain Carvers: Old Men Crafting Meaning.* Lexington: University Press of Kentucky, 1985.

———. *Grasping Things: Folk Material Culture and Mass Society in America.* Lexington: University Press of Kentucky, 1986.

Brown, Frank C., Collection of North Carolina Folklore. Ed. Newman Ivey White. 7 vols. Durham, N.C.: Duke University Press, 1952–1964.

Brumbaugh, G. Edwin. *Colonial Architecture of the Pennsylvania Germans.* Lancaster: Pennsylvania German Society, 1933.

Buch, H. G. *A Compilation of Valuable Recipes.* Lititz, Pa., 1886.

Bucher, Robert. "The Continental Log House." *Pennsylvania Folklife* 12.4 (1962): 14–19.

Buck, William J. "Popular Superstitions." *Collections of the Historical Society of Pennsylvania* 1 (1853): 377–81.

Buffington, Albert F. "Maidel wilscht du heirathen—A Hybrid Poem." *American-German Review* 12 (1946): 30–32.

———. *Pennsylvania German Secular Folksongs.* Breinigsville, Pa.: Pennsylvania German Society, 1974.

———. "Schwoweschtories." *Folkways* 3 (1964): 22–24.

Buffington, Albert F., and others. *Ebbes fer Alle-Ebber—Ebbes fer Dich. Something for Everyone—Something for You.* Breinigsville, Pa.: Pennsylvania German Society, 1980.

Cannon, Anthon S. *Popular Beliefs and Superstitions from Utah.* Ed. Wayland D. Hand and Jeannine E. Talley. Salt Lake City: University of Utah Press, 1984.

Cerf, Bennett. *Good for a Laugh.* Garden City, N.Y.: Doubleday, 1952.

Chandler, Roy F. *Tales of Perry County.* Deer Lake, Pa.: Bacon and Freeman, 1973.

Chappell, Edward A. "Lighting the *Stube:* Oral Tradition and a Shenandoah *Flürkuchenhaus.*" *Folklore and Folklife in Virginia* 3 (1984): 37–43.

Clements, William M. *The Types of the Polack Joke.* Folklore Forum, A Bibliographic and Special Series, vol. 3. Bloomington: Folklore Institute, 1969.

Cobb, Irvin S. *Many Laughs for Many Days.* New York: Garden City, 1925.

Cohen, David Steven. *The Folklore and Folklife of New Jersey.* New Brunswick, N. J.: Rutgers University Press, 1983.

Coffin, Tristram Potter. *The Illustrated Book of Christmas Folklore.* New York: Seabury Press, 1973.

Cornwell, John J. *A Mountain Trail.* Philadelphia: Dorrance, 1939.

Costello, John R. "Cultural Vestiges and Cultural Blends among the Pennsylvania

Germans." *New York Folklore* 3 (1977): 101–13.

Coy, Errol Vincent. *Cracker Barrel Tales.* Shippensburg: News-Chronicle, 1977.

Crawford, Joanna. *Birch Interval.* New York: Dell, 1976.

Cressman, Paul K. "Pennsylvania German Secular Songs." *Pennsylvania Dutchman* 3–9 (1951): 7.

Dahlgren, Madeleine Vinton. *South-Mountain Magic.* Boston: Osgood, 1882.

Dieffenbach, Victor C. "Riddles." *Pennsylvania Dutchman* 5.12 (1954): 15.

Dluge, Robert L. "My Interview with a Powwower." *Pennsylvania Folklife* 21.4 (1972): 39–42.

Dobie, J. Frank, ed. *Coffee in the Gourd.* Austin: Texas Folklore Society, 1973.

Druckenbrod, Richard. "Kie-Schwans." *Pennsylvania Dutchman* 1.6 (1949): 2.

Duden, Gottfried. *Report on a Journey to the Western States of North America and a Stay of Several Years along the Missouri: During the Years 1824, '25, '26 & '27.* Ed. James W. Goodrich and trans. George H. Kellner and others. Columbia: University of Missouri Press, 1980.

Dundes, Alan, ed. *Cinderella, a Casebook.* New York: Wildman Press, 1983.

Dundes, Alan, and Robert A. Georges. "Some Minor Genres of Obscene Folklore." *Journal of American Folklore* 75 (1962): 221–26.

Dundore, M. Walter. "The Saga of the Pennsylvania Germans in Wisconsin." *Pennsylvania German Folklore Society* 19 (1954): 33–166.

Dunkelberger, George. *The Story of Snyder County.* Selinsgrove, Pa.: Snyder County Historical Society, 1948.

Egle, William, ed. *Notes and Queries, Historical, Biographical and Genealogical.* 1894. Reprint, vol. 1. Baltimore: Genealogical Publishing Company, 1970.

Eichhoff, Jürgen. "The German Language in America." In *America and the Germans,* ed. Frank Trommler and Joseph McVeigh. 2 vols. Philadelphia: University of Pennsylvania Press, 1985.

Eis, Gerhard. *Altdeutsche Zaubersprüche.* Berlin: Walter de Gruyter, 1964.

Engerrand, George C. *The So-Called Wends of Germany and Their Colonies in Texas and Australia.* Austin: University of Texas, 1934.

Ennals, Peter M. "Nineteenth-Century Barns in Southern Ontario." *Canadian Geographer* 16 (1972): 256–70.

Ensminger, Robert F. "A Comparative Study of Pennsylvania and Wisconsin Forebay Barns." *Pennsylvania Folklife* 32 (1983): 98–114.

――――. "A Search for the Origin of the Pennsylvania Barn." *Pennsylvania Folklife* 30 (1980–81): 50–71.

Estill, Julia. "Children's Games." In *The Sky Is My Tipi,* ed. Mody C. Boatright. Dallas: Southern Methodist University Press, 1966.

――――. "Customs among the German Descendents of Gillespie County." In *Coffee in the Gourd,* ed. J. Frank Dobie. Austin: Texas Folklore Society, 1923.

Fabian, Monroe H. *The Pennsylvania-German Decorated Chest.* New York: Universe Books, 1978.

Faust, Albert Bernhardt. *The German Element in the United States.* 2 vols. New York: Arno Press, 1969.

Ferris, William R., Jr. "More of Ray Lum's Horse Sense." *Mid-South Folklore* 6 (1978): 43–50.

Fisher, H. L. *Olden Times: or, Pennsylvania Rural Life, Some Fifty Years Ago, and Other Poems.* York: Fisher Bros., 1888.

Flower, Milton E. "Schimmel the Woodcarver." In *The Antiques Book,* ed. Alice Winchester. New York: Bonanza Books, 1950.

――――. *Three Cumberland County Wood Carvers: Schimmel, Mountz, Barrett.* Carlisle, Pa.: Cumberland County Historical Society, 1986.

Fogel, Edwin Miller. *Beliefs and Superstitions of the Pennsylvania Germans.* Philadelphia: Americana Germanica, 1915.

———. "Himmelsbrief." *Pennsylvania-German* 9 (1908): 217–22.

———. "The Himmelsbrief." *German American Annals* 10 (1908): 286–301.

———. *Proverbs of the Pennsylvania Germans.* Fogelsville: Americana Germanica Press, 1929.

Forbes, Thomas R. *The Midwife and the Witch.* New Haven and London: Yale University Press, 1966.

Frazier, Paul. "Some Lore of Hexing and Powwowing." *Midwest Folklore* 2 (1952): 101–7.

Freud, Sigmund. *Jokes and Their Relation to the Unconscious.* Trans., ed. James Strachey. New York: W. W. Norton, 1963.

Frey, J. William. "The Dutch in Word and Song." *Pennsylvania Dutchman* 2.9 (1950): 8; 3.5 (1951): 8.

———. "Let's Play Fickmiel!" *Pennsylvania Dutchman* 1.15 (1949): 2.

Friedrich, Carl J. "The European Background." In *The Forty-Eighters,* ed. A. E. Zucker. New York: Russell & Russell, 1967.

Futhey, John, and Gilbert Cope. *History of Chester County, Pennsylvania, with Genealogical and Biogaphical Sketches.* Philadelphia: L. H. Everts, 1881.

Gabel, Marie. "Proverbs of Volga German Settlers in Ellis County." *Heritage of Kansas* 9.2–3 (1976): 55–58.

Gardner, Emelyn Elizabeth. *Folklore from the Schoharie Hills, New York.* Ann Arbor: University of Michigan Press, 1937.

Gehman, Henry Snyder. "An Octogenarian's Reminiscences of Ghost Stories in Lancaster County." *Historic Schaefferstown Record* 9.1 (1975): 38–43.

"German Proverbs Collected in Los Angeles." *California Folklore Quarterly* 4 (1945): 433.

Gibbons, Phebe. *Pennsylvania Dutch and Other Essays.* Philadelphia: Lippincott, 1882.

Gillette, Robert. "Poles Seeking Solace in Humor and Drink." *Philadelphia Inquirer* (4 May 1986): 8.

Glassie, Henry. *All Silver and No Brass: An Irish Christmas Mumming.* Bloomington & London: Indiana University Press, 1975.

———. "A Central Chimney Continental Log House." *Pennsylvania Folklife* 18.2 (1968–69): 32–39.

———. "The Double-Crib Barn in South Central Pennsylvania." *Pioneer America* 1.1 (1969): 9–16; 1.2 (1969): 40–45; 2.1 (1970): 47–52; 2.2 (1970): 23–34.

———. "Eighteenth-Century Cultural Process in Delaware Valley Folk Building." *Winterthur Portfolio* 7 (1972): 29–57.

———. "The Pennsylvania Barn in the South." *Pennsylvania Folklife* 15.2, 4 (1965–66): 8–19, 12–25.

———. "The Types of the Southern Mountain Cabin." In *The Study of American Folklore: An Introduction,* Jan Harold Brunvand. 2nd ed. New York: W. W. Norton, 1978.

Glimm, James. *Flatlanders and Ridgerunners.* Pittsburgh: University of Pittsburgh Press, 1983.

Goldstein, Kenneth S. "Riddling Traditions in Northeastern Scotland." *Journal of American Folklore* 76 (1963): 330–36.

Goldstein, Kenneth S., and Robert H. Byington, eds. *Two Penny Ballads and Four Dollar Whiskey: A Pennsylvania Folklore Miscellany.* Hatboro, Pa.: Folklore Associates, 1966.

Gordon, Edmund I. *Sumerian Proverbs.* Philadelphia: University of Pennsylvania Press, 1959.

Gottshall, Walter. "Primative [sic] Pennsylvania Dutch Carving." *Pennsylvania Folklife* 35 (1986): 180–81.

Graeff, Arthur. "The Colonial Melting Pot." In *The Pennsylvania Germans,* ed. Ralph Wood. Princeton: Princeton University Press, 1942.

———. *The Pennsylvania Germans in Ontario, Canada.* Allentown: Pennsylvania German Folklore Society, 1946.

———. *Selections from Arthur D. Graeff's Scholla.* Breinigsville, Pa.: Pennsylvania German Society, 1971.

Graves, Tom. "Ethnic Artists, Artifacts, and Authenticity: Pennsylvania German and Ukrainian Folk Crafts Today." *Pioneer America* 15 (1983): 21–33.

Grier, Katherine C. *Celebrations in Wood: The Sculpture of John Scholl.* Harrisburg: William Penn Memorial Museum, 1979.

Griffin, Francis. *Old Salem.* Winston-Salem: Old Salem, Inc., 1970.

Gruber, H. Wayne. "Dialect Jests." *Pennsylvania Dutchman* 1.23 (1950): 2.

Grumbine, Ezra. "Folk-Lore of Lebanon County." *Lebanon County Historical Society Papers* 3 (1905–06): 254–94.

Haan, Marina, and Richard Hammerstrom. *Graffiti in the Pac Ten.* New York: Warner, 1981.

Hain, Mathilde. *Rätsel.* Stuttgart: Metzlersche, 1966.

Halpert, Herbert. "The Humorous Grace Cante Fable." *Mid-South Folklore* 3 (1975): 71–82.

Hammond, Olive. "Social Life and Customs in Early Armstrong County, Pennsylvania." M.A. thesis, University of Pittsburgh, 1930.

Hand, Wayland D., ed. *American Folk Medicine: A Symposium.* Berkeley and Los Angeles: University of California Press, 1976.

———. " 'Passing Through': Folk Medical Magic and Symbolism." *Magical Medicine.* Berkeley, Los Angeles, London: University of California Press, 1980.

Hark, Ann. *Blue Hills and Shoofly Pie.* Philadelphia: Lippincott, 1952.

Harrod, Hazel. "A Tale of Two Thieves." In *The Sky Is My Tipi,* ed. Mody C. Boatright. Austin: Texas Folklore Society, 1949.

Harshman, Jacob. Manuscript list of powwow cures.

Hart, Donn V. *Riddles in Filipino Folklore: An Anthrogological Analysis.* Syracuse: Syracuse University Press, 1964.

Hartman, Harvey H. "Jests and Legends from Upper Bucks." *Pennsylvania Dutchman* 2.7 (1950): 2.

Hausman, Ruth L. *Sing and Dance with the Pennsylvania Dutch.* New York: Edward B. Marks Music Co., 1953.

Hays, H. M. "On the German Dialect Spoken in the Valley of Virginia." *Dialect Notes* 3 (1908): 263–78.

Heller, Edna Eby. *The Art of Pennsylvania Dutch Cooking.* Garden City: Doubleday, 1968.

———. "Chicken Corn Soup." *Pennsylvania Dutchman* 1.14 (1949): 4.

———. "Chow-Chow." *Pennsylvania Dutchman* 1.18 (1944): 4.

———. "Displaced Dutchmen Crave Shoo-Flies." *Pennsylvania Dutchman* 8.3 (1957): 32–33.

———. "Traditional Favorites Go Modern." *Pennsylvania Dutchman* 16.4 (1967): 44–45.

Hellman, Anna Fry. "Too Much Mush." *Pennsylvania Dutchman* 1.15 (1949): 3.

Hertzog, Phares H. "Pennsylvania German Snakelore." *Pennsylvania Folklife* 17.4 (1968): 16–19.

———. *Songs, Sayings and Stories of a Pennsylvania Dutchman.* Lebanon, Pa.: Applied Arts Publishers, 1966.

Hoch, Paul. "Old Schimmel." *Early American Life* 8.1 (1977): 44–47.

Hoffman, W. J. "Folk-lore of the Pennsylvania Germans." *Journal of American Folklore* 1 (1888): 125–35; 2 (1889): 23–35, 191–202.

———. "Popular Superstitions." *Pennsylvania German Society Proceedings* 5 (1894): 70–81.

Hohman, John George. *Pow-Wows; or, Long Lost Friend.* Harrisburg: Aurand Press, 1929.

Hommel, Rudolf. "On the Trail of the First Christmas Tree." *Pennsylvania Dutchman* 1.21 (1949): 1.

Horne, Abraham. "Proverbs and Sayings of the Pennsylvania-Germans." *Pennsylvania German Society Proceedings* 2 (1892): 47–54.

Hornung, Clarence P. *Treasury of American Design.* 2 vols. New York: Harry N. Abrams, 1976.

"Hunting 'Elbetritches.' " *Pennsylvania-German* 7 (1906): 35–37.

Jente, Richard. "Der Apfel fällt nicht weit vom Stamm." *PMLA* 48 (1933): 26–30.

_____. *Proverbia Communia: A Fifteenth Century Collection of Dutch Proverbs.* Bloomington: Indiana University, 1947.

Johns, J. R. "Outdoor Sports around 1800." *Pennsylvania Dutchman* 1.18 (1949): 3.

Johnson, Elmer E. S. "More about 'Elbetritches.'" *Pennsylvania-German* 7 (1906): 122–23.

Johnson, F. Roy. *Oral Folk Humor from the Carolina and Virginia Flatlands.* Murfreesboro, N.C.: Johnson Publishing Co., 1980.

Jordan, Gilbert. "German Cultural Heritage in the Hill Country of Texas." In *German Culture in Texas,* ed. Glen E. Lich and Dona B. Reeves. Boston: Twayne, 1980.

_____. *German Texana.* Austin: Eakin Press, 1980.

_____. *Yesterday in the Texas Hill Country.* College Station and London: Texas A&M University Press, 1979.

Jordan, Mildred. *The Distelfink Country of the Pennsylvania Dutch.* New York: Crown, 1978.

Jordan, Terry G. "Alpine, Alemannic, and American Log Architecture." *Annals of the Association of American Geographers* 70 (1980): 154–80.

_____. *American Log Buildings.* Chapel Hill and London: University of North Carolina Press, 1985.

_____. "A Forebay Bank Barn in Texas." *Pennsylvania Folklife* 30 (1980–81): 72–77.

_____. *German Seed in Texas Soil: Immigrant Farmers in Nineteenth-Century Texas.* 1966. Austin: University of Texas Press, 1985.

_____. *Texas Log Buildings: A Folk Architecture.* Austin: University of Texas Press, 1978.

Kaiser, Leo. "German Verse in American Cemeteries." *German American Review* 26 (1960): 25–28.

Kalm, Peter. *Travels in North America: The English Version of 1770.* 2 vols. New York: Wilson-Erickson, 1937.

Kauffman, Henry J. "The Log Barn." In *The Pennsylvania Barn,* ed. Alfred L. Shoemaker and others. Lancaster: Pennsylvania Dutch Folklore Center, 1955.

Keller, Daniel C. "Dialect Jests." *Pennsylvania Dutchman* 1.12 (1949): 2.

Kettelkamp, Gilbert C. "Country School Games of the Past." *MidAmerica Folklore* 8 (1981): 113–23.

Kliewer, Warren. "Collecting Folklore among Mennonites." *Mennonite Life* 16 (1961): 109–12.

Knapp, Mary, and Herbert Knapp. *One Potato, Two Potato: The Folklore of American Children.* New York: W. W. Norton, 1976.

Kniffen, Fred, and Henry Glassie. "Building in Wood in the Eastern United States." *Geographical Review* 56 (1966): 40–66.

Knohr, E. L. "Customs and Beliefs in South-Eastern Pennsylvania Concerning the Holidays of the Year." *Pennsylvania Dutchman* 2.20 (1951): 5–7.

Korson, George. *Black Rock: Mining Folklore of the Pennsylvania Dutch.* Baltimore: Johns Hopkins Press, 1960.

_____. *Minstrels of the Mine Patch: Songs and Stories of the Anthracite Industry.* 1938. Reprint. Hatboro, Pa.: Folklore Associates, 1964.

_____. "'My Sweetheart's the Mule in the Mines': Memories of Tom and Maggie Hill." In *Two Penny Ballads and Four Dollar Whiskey,* ed. Kenneth S. Goldstein and Robert H. Byington. Hatboro, Pa.: Folklore Associates, 1966.

_____, ed. *Pennsylvania Songs and Legends.* Baltimore: Johns Hopkins Press, 1949.

Krappe, Alexander H. *The Science of Folklore.* 1930. New York: W. W. Norton, 1964.

Kuhns, Oscar. *The German and Swiss Settlements of Colonial America.* New York: Holt, 1901.

Laatz, A. Eugene. "German Games and Plays." *Bucks County Historical Society Papers* 4 (1917): 30–34.

Lawson, Sarah. "'Where Was Moses When the Lights Went Out?'" *Journal of American Folklore* 85 (1972): 183–84.

Lay, K. Edward. "European Antecedents of Seventeenth and Eighteenth Century

Germanic and Scots-Irish Architecture in America." *Pennsylvania Folklife* 32 (1982): 1–43.

Legman, Gershon. *The Limerick: 1700 Examples, with Notes Variants and Index.* New York: Brandywine Press, 1970.

———. *Rationale of the Dirty Joke: An Analysis of Sexual Humor.* First Series, New York: Grove Press, 1968. Second Series, New York: Breaking Point, 1975.

Lehmann-Nitsche, Robert. "Zur Volkskunde argentiniens." *Zeitschrift des Vereins für Volkskunde* 24 (1914): 240–55.

Lestz, Gerald. *The Pennsylvania Dutch Cookbook.* New York: Grosset & Dunlap, 1970.

Lévi-Strauss, Claude. *The Raw and the Cooked: Introduction to a Science of Mythology*, vol. 1. Trans. John and Doreen Weightman. New York: Harper & Row, 1970.

Lich, Glen E., and Dona B. Reeves, eds. *German Culture in Texas: A Free Earth, Essays from the 1978 Southwest Symposium.* Boston: Twayne, 1980.

Lick, David E., and Thomas R. Brendle. *Plant Names and Plant Lore among the Pennsylvania Germans.* Lancaster: Pennsylvania German Society, 1923.

Long, Theodore K. *Forty Letters to Carson Long.* New Bloomfield, Pa.: Carson Long Institute, 1931.

Lowe, David G. "Wooden Delights." *American Heritage* 20.1 (1968): 18–23.

Ludwig, G. M. "The Influence of the Pennsylvania Dutch in the Middle West." *Pennsylvania German Folklore Society* 10 (1945): 31–36, 55.

Luebke, Frederick C. *Immigrants and Politics: The Germans of Nebraska, 1880–1900.* Lincoln: University of Nebraska Press, 1969.

Marshall, Howard Wight. "German-American Architecture on the Missouri Frontier: The Pelster Housebarn." *Journal of the NAL Associates* NS 9 (1984): 14–30.

———. "Meat Preservation on the Farm in Missouri's 'Little Dixie.'" *Journal of American Folklore* 92 (1979): 400–17.

———. "The Pelster Housebarn: Endurance of Germanic Architecture on the Midwestern Frontier." *Material Culture* 18 (1986): 65–104.

Martha Washington Cook Book. New York: F. Tennyson Neely, 1897.

Mehl, Ervin. "Baseball in the Stone Age." *Western Folklore* 7 (1948): 145–61.

Mencken, Henry L. *Happy Days, 1880–1892.* New York: Knopf, 1940.

Mercer, Henry C. "Folk Lore, Notes Taken at Random." *Bucks County Historical Society Papers* 2 (1909): 406–16.

———. "The Origin of Log Houses in the United States." *Bucks County Historical Society Papers* 5 (1926): 568–83.

———. "The Survival of the Mediaeval Art of Illuminative Writing among Pennsylvania Germans." *Proceedings of the American Philosophical Society* 36 (1897): 424–33.

Mercier, Denis, and others. "'Nipsy': The Ethnography of a Traditional Game of Pennsylvania's Anthracite Region." *Pennsylvania Folklife* 23.4 (1974): 12–21.

Meuser, Mary Jo. *German Rhymes and Songs.* [Jasper, Ind.,] 1978.

Mieder, Wolfgang. *International Bibliography of Explanatory Essays on Individual Proverbs and Proverbial Expressions.* Bern: Herbert Lang, 1977.

"Mike Moyer's Mush Mehl." *Pennsylvania-German* 10 (1909): 358.

Miller, Lewis. *Sketches and Chronicles: The Reflections of a Nineteenth Century Pennsylvania German Folk Artist.* York: Historical Society of York County, 1966.

Milner, John. "Germanic Architecture in the New World." *Journal of the Society of Architectural Historians* 34 (1975): 299.

Montell, William Lynwood. *Ghosts along the Cumberland: Deathlore in the Kentucky Foothills.* Knoxville: University of Tennessee Press, 1975.

Montgomery, Morton L. "Boyhood Sports in Reading in the Fifties." *Historical Review of Berks County* 9 (1943): 17–21.

———. "Games a Century Ago." *Pennsylvania Dutchman* 5.12 (1954): 12–13.

———. "Games of Reading in Last Century." *Pennsylvania Dutchman* 1.17 (1949): 2.

"Moonology." *Historical Record* 4 (1893): 16.

Moore, George L. "My Childhood Games." *Pennsylvania Folklife* 13.4 (1964): 42–57.

Morley, Christopher. *Thorofare.* New York: Harcourt, Brace, 1942.

Moyer, Nevin. "Moyerettes." Unpublished typescript. Linglestown, Pa., 1915–40.

Murtaugh, William J. "Half-Timbering in American Architecture." *Pennsylvania Folklife* 9.1 (1958): 2–11.

——— . *Moravian Architecture and Town Planning: Bethlehem, Pennsylvania, and Other Eighteenth-Century American Settlements.* Chapel Hill: University of North Carolina Press, 1967.

Nead, Daniel. *The Pennsylvania-German in the Settlement of Maryland.* Lancaster: Pennsylvania-German Society, 1914.

Nettl, Bruno. "The Hymns of the Amish." *Journal of American Folklore* 70 (1957): 323–28.

"New Year's Eve in the Olden Time." *Pennsylvania Dutchman* 2.15 (1951): 1.

Newell, William W. *Games and Songs of American Children.* New York: Harper, 1883.

Nielson, George R. "Folklore of the German-Wends in Texas." In *Singers and Storytellers,* ed. Mody C. Boatright and others. Dallas: Southern Methodist University Press, 1961.

Nitzsche, George E. "The Christmas Putz of the Pennsylvania Germans." *Pennsylvania German Folklore Society* 6 (1941): 3–28.

Noble, Allen G. *Wood, Brick, and Stone: The North American Settlement Landscape.* Vol. 1, *Houses.* Vol. 2, *Barns and Farm Structures.* Amherst: University of Massachusetts Press, 1984.

Norton, F. J. "Prisoner Who Saved His Neck with a Riddle." *Folk-Lore* 53 (1942): 27–57.

O'Conner, Richard. *The German-Americans.* Boston: Little, Brown, 1968.

Oda, Wilbur. "The Himmelsbrief." *Pennsylvania Dutchman* 1.21 (1949): 3.

Ohrn, Stephen. *Passing Time and Tradition: Contemporary Iowa Folk Artists.* Des Moines: Iowa Arts Council, 1984.

Opie, Iona, and Peter Opie. *The Lore and Language of Schoolchildren.* Oxford: Oxford University Press, 1959.

Owens, William. *Texas Folk Songs.* Austin: Texas Folklore Society, 1950.

P.C.C. "Quaint and Humorous Epitaphs." *Pennsylvania-German* 1.4 (1900): 33.

Partridge, Eric. *A Dictionary of Catch Phrases: British and American from the Sixteenth Century to the Present Day.* New York: Stein and Day, 1977.

Pellman, Rachel, and Kenneth Pellman. *The World of Amish Quilts.* Intercourse, Pa.: Good Books, 1984.

Pennsylvania Dutch Cook Book. Reading, Pa.: Culinary Arts Press, 1936.

"Pennsylvania-German Proverbs." *Penn Germania* 7 (1906): 265.

"Pennsylvania Legislators in 1774 Oppose Shooting in the New Year." *Pennsylvania Dutchman* 3.15 (1952): 1, 3.

Pennsylvania State Grange Cookbook. [Harrisburg?]: 1972.

Perrin, Richard W. E. *The Architecture of Wisconsin.* Madison: State Historical Society of Wisconsin, 1967.

——— . "German Timber Farmhouses in Wisconsin: Terminal Examples of a Thousand-year Building Tradition." *Wisconsin Magazine of History* 44 (1961): 199–202.

——— . *Historic Wisconsin Buildings: A Survey of Pioneer Architecture, 1835–1870.* Milwaukee: Milwaukee Public Museum Press, 1962.

Petersen, Albert J. "The German-Russian House in Kansas: A Study in Persistence of Form." *Pioneer America* 8 (1976): 19–27.

Puckett, Newbell Niles. *Popular Beliefs and Superstitions: A Compendium of American Folklore from the Ohio Collection of Newbell Niles Puckett,* ed. Wayland D. Hand and others. 3 vols. Boston: G. K. Hall, 1981.

Raber, W. B. *The Devil and Some of his Doings.* Dayton: Printed for the author, 1855.

Ranke, Kurt. *Folktales of Germany.* Chicago: University of Chicago Press, 1966.

Reber, B. Franklin. "Boona-Sack." *Pennsylvania Dutchman* 1.13 (1949): 2.

_____. "Dutch Game." *Pennsylvania Dutchman* 5.12 (1954): 15.

Richter, Conrad. *The Grandfathers.* New York: Knopf, 1964.

_____. *The Fields.* New York: Knopf, 1946.

_____. *A Simple Honorable Man.* New York: Knopf, 1962.

_____. *The Town.* New York: Knopf, 1950.

Ridlen, Susanne S. "Bank Barns in Cass County, Indiana." *Pioneer America* 4.2 (1972): 25–43.

Rippley, LaVern. *Of German Ways.* 1970. New York: Gramercy Publishing Co., 1986.

Robbins, Walter L. "Wishing in and Shooting in the New Year among the Germans in the Carolinas." In *American Folklife,* ed. Don Yoder. Austin and London: University of Texas Press, 1976.

Roberts, Warren E. "Ananias Hensel and his Furniture: Cabinetmaking in Southern Indiana." *Midwestern Journal of Language and Folklore* 9 (1983): 69–122.

_____. *Log Buildings of Southern Indiana.* Bloomington: Trickster Press, 1984.

_____. "Some Comments on Log Construction in Scandinavia and the United States." In *Folklore Today: A Festschrift for Richard M. Dorson,* ed. Linda Dégh and others. Bloomington: Indiana University, 1976.

[Roth, Samuel.] *Anecdota Americana.* New York: Nesor, 1934.

Rowan, Steven. *Germans for a Free Missouri.* Columbia: University of Missouri Press, 1983.

Rush, Benjamin. *Account of the Manners of the German Inhabitants of Pennsylvania.* Ed. I. D. Rupp. Philadelphia: S. P. Town, 1875.

Ryman, William. *The Early Settlement of Dallas Township, Luzerne County, Pennsylvania.* Wilkes-Barre, 1901.

Sachse, Julius. *The German Sectarians of Pennsylvania, 1742–1800.* 2 vols. Philadelphia: 1899–1900.

Sackton, Alexander. "Eddie Arning: Texas Folk Artist." In *Folk Art in Texas,* ed. Francis Abernethy. Dallas: Southern Methodist University Press, 1985.

Schanbacher, J. Lewis. *Boys of Appalachia.* Elmira, N.Y., 1973.

Schreiber, William I. "The Pennsylvania Dutch Bank Barns of Ohio." *Journal of the Ohio Folklore Society* 2 (1967): 15–28.

Schroeder, Adolf E. "The Contexts of Continuity: Germanic Folklore in Missouri." *Kansas Quarterly* 13 (1981): 89–102.

_____. "Traditional Song Current in the Midwest." *Proceedings of the International Centenary Conference of the Folklore Society* (July 1978), ed. Venetia Newall. London, 1981.

Schwartz, Alvin. *A Twister of Twists, a Tangler of Tongues.* Philadelphia: J. B. Lippincott, 1972.

Schwieder, Dorothy. "A Cultural Mosaic: The Settling of Iowa." In *Passing Time and Tradition,* ed. Steven Ohrn. Des Moines: Iowa Arts Council, 1984.

Shaner, Richard H. *Hexerei: A Practice of Witchcraft among the Pennsylvania Dutch.* Macungie, Pa.: Progress Printing House, 1963.

Shively, Jacob G. "Tales of Old Pastor Fries." *Pennsylvania Dutchman* 2.13 (1951): 6.

Shoemaker, Alfred L. *Christmas in Pennsylvania: A Folk-Cultural Study.* Kutztown: Pennsylvania Folklore [sic] Society, 1959.

_____. "Dialect Rhymes and Jingles." *Pennsylvania Dutchman* 1.1 (1949): 2; through 2.10 (1950): 2.

_____. *Eastertide in Pennsylvania: A Folk Cultural Study.* Kutztown: Pennsylvania Folklife Society, 1960.

_____. "Epitaph Hunting—A Good Sport." *Pennsylvania Dutchman* 1.2 (1949): 2; 1.5 (1949): 2.

_____. "February Lore." *Pennsylvania Dutchman* 5.11 (1954): 11.

_____. "The First Week of Lent in Pennsylvania Dutch Lore." *Pennsylvania Dutchman* 1.23 (1950): 3.

————. "The Folklore of Bread." *Pennsylvania Dutchman* 1.2 (1949): 3.

————. "German Epitaphs in the Dutch Country." *Pennsylvania Dutchman* 2.1 (1950): 2.

————. "Guessing Riddles." *Pennsylvania Dutchman* 1.1 (1949): 2; 1.2 (1949): 2.

————. "Let's All Play Nipsi." *Pennsylvania Dutchman* 1.3 (1949): 2.

————. "Let's Play 'Katzakoop.' " *Pennsylvnia Dutchman* 1.16 (1949): 2.

————. "Let's Play Scheefli." *Pennsylvania Dutchman* 1.20 (1949): 2.

————. "Let's Play Sei Balla." *Pennsylvania Dutchman* 1.1 (1949): 2.

————. "Old Berks Folklore, Legends and History." *Reading Eagle* (21 February 1949): 20; (11 March 1949): 9.

————, ed. *The Pennsylvania Barn.* Lancaster: Pennsylvania Dutch Folklore Center, 1955.

————. "Proverbs." *Pennsylvania Dutchman* 1.7 (1949): 2 through 2.5 (1950): 2.

————. "Riddles." *Pennsylvania Dutchman* 1.3 (1949): 2 through 1.24 (1950): 2.

————. "Some Powwow Formulas from Juniata County." *Pennsylvania Dutchman* 3.10 (1951): 1, 4.

————. "Strick-Noodla." *Pennsylvania Dutchman* 1.5 (1949): 2.

————. "The Strongest Man That Ever Lived on Earth." *Pennsylvania Dutchman* 2.2 (1950): 2.

————. "Tongue Twisters." *Pennsylvania Dutchman* 5.9 (1954): 4.

————. *Traditional Rhymes and Jingles of the Pennsylvania Dutch.* Lancaster: Pennsylvania Dutch Folklore Center, 1951.

Shoemaker, William P. "Der Babbegoi." *Pennsylvania Dutchman* 1.2 (1949): 2.

————. "Two Folktales." *Pennsylvania Dutchman* 1.19 (1949): 2.

Showalter, Henry A. "Blummsack." *Pennsylvania Dutchman* 1.9 (1949): 2.

Shuman, George A. "Apple Kretchers." *Pennsylvania Dutchman* 2.20 (1951): 1.

Simmons, Isaac Shirk. "Dutch Folk-Beliefs." *Pennsylvania Dutchman* 5.14 (1954): 2–3, 15.

————. "Haunted Places and Tales of Black Magic." *Pennsylvania Dutchman* 2.11 (1950): 2.

Singer, Samuel. *Sprichwörter des Mittelalters.* 3 vols. Bern: Herbert Lang, 1944–47.

Smith, Elmer, and John Stewart. "The Mill as a Preventive and Cure of Whooping Cough." *Journal of American Folklore* 77 (1964): 76–77.

Smith, Elmer, John Stewart, and M. Ellsworth Kyger. *The Pennsylvania Germans in the Shenandoah Valley.* Allentown, Pa.: Pennsylvania German Folklore Society, 1964.

Smith, Ely J. "Games and Plays of Children." *Bucks County Historical Society Papers* 4 (1917): 1–6.

Smith, Ray F. "Pennsylvania German Folklore—Introducing a Few Snyder County Ghosts." *Snyder County Historical Society Bulletin* 2 (1972): 909–16.

Snellenburg, Betty. "Four Interviews with Powwowers." *Pennsylvania Folklife* 18.4 (1969): 40–45.

Stephens, Wendell. "Hog-Killing Time in Middle Tennessee." *Tennessee Folklore Society Bulletin* 36.3 (1970): 83–91.

Stewart, John, and Elmer L. Smith. "An Occult Remedy Manuscript from Pendleton County, West Virginia." *Madison College Studies and Research Bulletin* 22.2 (1964): 77–83.

Stoudt, John Baer. *The Folklore of the Pennsylvania Germans.* Philadelphia: William J. Campbell, 1916.

————. "Some Palatine Riddles." *Olde Ulster* 9 (1913): 285–86.

————. "Weather-Prognostications and Superstitions among the Pennsylvania Germans." *Pennsylvania-German* 6 (1905): 328–35; 7 (1906): 242–43.

Stoudt, John Joseph. "Himmelsbrief: The Letter from Heaven." *Historical Review of Berks County* 42 (1977): 102, 115.

————. "Pennsylvania German Folklore—An Interpretation." *Pennsylvania German Folklore Society* 16 (1951): 157–70.

————. *Sunbonnets and Shoofly Pies: A Pennsylvania Dutch Cultural History.* New York: A. S. Barnes, 1973.

Tacitus. *Germania.* Trans. H. Mattingly. New York: Penguin Books, 1948.

Taylor, Archer. *English Riddles from Oral Tradition.* Berkeley and Los Angeles: University of California Press, 1951.

————. "In the Evening Praise the Day." *Modern Language Notes* 36 (1921): 115–18.

————. *An Index to 'The Proverb.'* Helsinki: Suomalainen Tiedeakatemia, 1934.

————. "The Riddle." *California Folklore Quarterly* 2 (1943): 129–47.

————. "Riddles." In *Frank C. Brown Collection of North Carolina Folklore,* vol. 1. Durham: Duke University Press, 1952.

Thompson, Stith. *Motif-Index of Folk Literature.* 6 vols. Bloomington: Indiana University Press, 1955–58.

Trommler, Frank, and Joseph McVeigh, eds. *America and the Germans.* 2 vols. Philadelphia: University of Pennsylvania Press, 1985.

Trumbore, Mark S. *A Superficial Collection of Penna. German Erotic Folklore.* Pennsburg, Pa.: 1978.

Twain, Mark. *The Adventures of Huckleberry Finn.* New York: P. F. Collier.

Updike, John. *Rabbit Is Rich.* New York: Knopf, 1981.

van Ravenswaay, Charles. *The Arts and Architecture of German Settlements in Missouri.* Columbia: University of Missouri Press, 1977.

Vinton, Iris. *The Folkways Omnibus of Children's Games.* Harrisburg: Stackpole, 1970.

Vonnegut, Kurt. *Deadeye Dick.* New York: Delacorte, 1982.

Walker, Mack. *Germany and the Emigration, 1816–1885.* Cambridge: Harvard University Press, 1964.

Wander, K. *Deutsches Sprichwörter-lexikon.* 5 vols. 1867–80. Darmstadt: Wissenschaftliche Buchgesellschaft, 1964.

Waterman, Thomas Tileston. *The Dwellings of Colonial America.* Chapel Hill: University of North Carolina Press, 1950.

Weaver, William Woys. *Sauerkraut Yankees: Pennsylvania German Foods and Foodways.* Philadelphia: University of Pennsylvania Press, 1983.

Weigel, Lawrence A. "German Proverbs from around Fort Hays, Kansas." *Western Folklore* 18 (1959): 98.

Weiser, Frederick S. *The Pennsylvania German Fraktur of the Free Library of Philadelphia.* 2 vols. Breinigsville, Pa.: Pennsylvania German Society, 1976.

————. "Piety and Protocol in Folk Art Pennsylvania German Fraktur Birth and Baptismal Certificates." *Winterthur Portfolio* 8 (1973): 19–43.

Wells, F. L. "Frau Wirtin and Associates: A Note on Alien Corn." *American Imago* 8 (1951): 93–97.

Welsch, Roger. "Molbo Tales." *Folkways* 3 (1964): 20–22.

Whisker, Vaughn E. *Tales from the Allegheny Foothills.* 5 vols. Bedford, Pa.: Bedford Gazette, 1975–76.

White, Max E. "Sernatin : A Traditional Christmas Custom in Northeast Georgia." *Southern Folklore Quarterly* 45 (1981): 89–99.

Whitney, Annie, and Caroline Bullock. *Folk-Lore from Maryland.* New York: American Folklore Society, 1925.

Wieand, Paul R. "Broot Backa." *Pennsylvania Dutchman* 1.2 (1949): 2.

————. *Outdoor Games of the Pennsylvania Germans.* Home Craft Course 28. Plymouth Meeting, Pa.: Mrs. C. Naaman Keyser, 1950.

Wilde, Larry. *The Last Official Italian Joke Book.* Los Angeles: Pinnacle, 1978.

Wilhelm, Hubert G. H. "German Settlement and Folk Building Practices in the Hill Country of Texas." *Pioneer America* 3.2 (1971): 15–24.

Wilhelm, Hubert G. H., and Michael Miller. "Half-Timber Construction: A Relic Building Method in Ohio." *Pioneer America* 6.2 (1974): 43–51.

Williams, Henry Lionel, and Ottalie K. Williams. *A Guide to Old American Houses, 1700–1900.* South Brunswick–New York: A. S. Barnes, 1962.

"Wonderful Pennsylvania Dutch Whittling." *Woman's Day* 31.11 (1968): 25–27.

Wood, Ralph. "Das bucklige Männlein." *American-German Review* 8 (1942): 27–30.

———, ed. *The Pennsylvania Germans.* Princeton: Princeton University Press, 1942.

Wright, Martin. "The Antecedents of the Double-Pen House Type." *Annals of the Association of American Geographers* 48 (1958): 109–17.

Wust, Klaus. *Virginia Fraktur: Penmanship as Folk Art.* Edinburg, Va.: Shenandoah History, 1972.

Yoder, Don, ed. *American Folklife.* Austin and London: University of Texas Press, 1976.

———. "Hohman and Romanus: Origins and Diffusion of the Pennsylvania German Powwow Manual." In *American Folk Medicine: A Symposium,* ed. Wayland D. Hand. Berkeley and Los Angeles: University of California Press, 1976.

———. "Let's Play 'Gluck un Awdler.'" *Pennsylvania Dutchman* 1.14 (1949): 2.

———. *Pennsylvania Spirituals.* Lancaster: Pennsylvania Folklife Society, 1961.

———. "Pennsylvanians Called It Mush." *Pennsylvania Folklife* 13.2 (1962–63): 27–49.

———. "Sheep, Sheep, Come Home!" *Pennsylvania Dutchman* 2.6 (1950): 5.

Yoder, Jacob H. "Proverbial Lore from Hegins Valley." *Pennsylvania Dutchman* 3.16 (1952): 3.

Yoder, Joseph W. *Rosanna of the Amish.* Huntingdon, Pa.: Yoder Publishing Co., 1940.

Zehner, Olive G. "The Egg Tree Recognized as Pa. Dutch Custom as Far as Seattle, Washington." *Pennsylvania Dutchman* 3.21 (1952): 3.

———. "Ohio Fractur." *Pennsylvania Dutchman* 6.3 (1954–55): 13–15.

Zucker, A. E., ed. *The Forty-Eighters: Political Refugees of the German Revolution of 1848.* 1950. Reprint. New York: Russell & Russell, 1967.

WITHDRAWAL